August 11. 177[

which your Country is engaged

tract your Attention, more

time, and as the future Cir

untry, may require other wars,

nd Negotiations, similar to

e Agitations, I wish to turn

Such Studies, as will afford

struction and Improvement

ay be allotted you to act

The Founding Fathers

The Founding Fathers

The Founding Fathers

JOHN ADAMS

A Biography in His Own Words

VOLUME 2

Edited by

JAMES BISHOP PEABODY

JOAN PATERSON KERR
Picture Editor

NEWSWEEK
New York

ISBN: Clothbound Edition 0-88225-041-8; ISBN: Deluxe Edition 0-88225-042-6
Library of Congress Catalog Card Number 72-92141
Copyright © 1973 by Newsweek, Inc.
All rights reserved. Printed and bound in the United States of America
Endpapers: John Adams to John Quincy Adams, August 11, 1777; THE ADAMS PAPERS

Hamilton delin. *Noble sculp.*

The Manner *in which the* American Colonies *Declared themselves*

INDEPENDANT *of the* King *of* ENGLAND,

throughout the different Provinces, on July 4, 1776.

English engraving depicting the reading of the Declaration of Independence, July 4, 1776

Chapter 7

An American in Paris

Reelected to the Continental Congress in November, 1776, John Adams once again took up his duties in Philadelphia. Among numerous other tasks, he presided over the Board of War and Ordnance, the committee that bore the burden of Congress's routine communications with the Commander in Chief of the armies and dealt with innumerable other matters relating to the conduct of the war. Washington's defeat at Brandywine Creek in September, 1777, and the British occupation of Philadelphia were severe setbacks soon to be compensated for by the surrender of General John Burgoyne in October at Saratoga. It was the victory at Saratoga that convinced the French government it could take the risk of striking at Great Britain by recognizing the independence of the United States, by openly supplying them with military aid and financial and diplomatic support, and finally by engaging in warfare against the British on land and sea.

As early as March, 1776, Congress had dispatched its secret agent, Silas Deane, to France to obtain military and financial assistance. The mission was an initial success, for even before formal recognition of the United States, France sent at least eight cargoes of arms to America in time to make a decisive contribution to the victory at Saratoga. At the end of October, 1777, Congress sent Benjamin Franklin and Arthur Lee to join Deane in Paris as joint commissioners to press for recognition and to sign treaties of alliance and commerce with France. These goals were achieved on February 6, 1778, though word of the commissioners' success did not reach Congress until May.

The auspicious entry of the United States onto the stage of world diplomacy, however, was soon clouded by a dreadful row in Congress, precipitated by charges of peculation brought by Arthur Lee against his colleague Silas Deane. Although the charges were not proved in his lifetime, it became clear to all that Deane had been imprudent and self-serving. To the great embarrassment of Congress, he had promised too many commissions to French officers in Washington's army. He had also been on close terms with unreliable persons like Dr. Edward Bancroft, an arch-traitor and master spy whom the British had skillfully planted in Benjamin Franklin's household. Furthermore, Deane had been duped by John Vardill, Vicar of Trinity Church and Regius Professor of Divinity at King's College in New York, who, on behalf of the British government, arranged the theft from Deane's own hands of the confidential correspondence and dispatches of the American commissioners. These and other suspicious involvements with the French sullied Deane's reputation. Recalled by Congress to face charges of embezzlement, Deane was ruined. Benjamin Franklin, the senior member of the American mission, barely survived the scandal, eventually to become sole American Minister to the Court of Louis XVI.

In November, 1777, John Adams was appointed by Congress to replace Deane as one of the joint commissioners in Paris. Neither Adams's personality, qualifications, nor experience marked him for the Talleyrand school of diplomacy; but his native shrewdness, his trained intelligence, and above all his unswerving integrity protected him in at least some degree from the snares and pitfalls that were soon to threaten him. It is abundantly clear today that he performed successfully during this period the most indispensible services for his country under the most difficult conditions. Adams sailed from Braintree in February, 1778, with his ten-year-old son, John Quincy, aboard the Continental frigate *Boston,* thereby beginning a period of ten years of foreign service, half of them without Abigail, who remained at home with the younger children. Later, he incorporated his original *Diary* notes of the hazardous voyage into his *Autobiography*.

Autobiography, 1802–7

I was almost out of Patience, in Waiting for the Frigate till the Thirteenth day of February 1778, when Captain Samuel Tucker, Commander of the Frigate Boston, met me at the House of Norton Quincy Esquire, in Braintree, where We dined.

After dinner I bid Adieu to my Friend and Unkle Quincy, sent my Baggage, and walked myself with Captain Tucker, Mr. Griffin a Midshipman, and my eldest Son, John Quincy Adams between ten and eleven years of Age, down to the Moon Head where lay the Bostons Barge. In our Way We made an halt of a few minutes at the House of Mr. Seth Spear on Hoffs neck, where some Sailors belonging to our barge had been waiting for Us. The good Lady, who was an Adams, came out very civilly to invite Us in. We had no time to spare and excused ourselves. She was an amiable Woman, with very delicate health, much afflicted with hysterical complaints, often a little disarranged in her imagination. At

Silas Deane (above), accused of peculation by Arthur Lee (below), his fellow joint commissioner in Paris, was recalled by Congress.

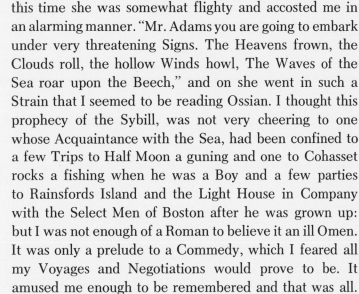

this time she was somewhat flighty and accosted me in an alarming manner. "Mr. Adams you are going to embark under very threatening Signs. The Heavens frown, the Clouds roll, the hollow Winds howl, The Waves of the Sea roar upon the Beech," and on she went in such a Strain that I seemed to be reading Ossian. I thought this prophecy of the Sybill, was not very cheering to one whose Acquaintance with the Sea, had been confined to a few Trips to Half Moon a guning and one to Cohasset rocks a fishing when he was a Boy and a few parties to Rainsfords Island and the Light House in Company with the Select Men of Boston after he was grown up: but I was not enough of a Roman to believe it an ill Omen. It was only a prelude to a Commedy, which I feared all my Voyages and Negotiations would prove to be. It amused me enough to be remembered and that was all.

The Wind was high and the Sea, very rough, but by means of a quantity of Hay in the bottom of the boat, and good Watch Coats with which We were covered, We arrived on board the Boston, about five O Clock, tolerably warm and dry....

[Owing to a bad storm, almost a week passed before the frigate *Boston* was able to sail, only to come upon British warships blockading the American coast.]

February 19. Thursday. 1778. Arose at four O Clock. The Wind and Weather still fair. The Ship rolled less than the day before, and I neither felt nor heard any thing of Sea Sickness last night nor this morning. Monsieur Parison, one of General Du Coudrai's Captains of Artillery, dined with Us Yesterday, and behaved like [a] civil and sensible Man. We learned from him, that the roads from Nantes to Paris are very good; no mountains, no rocks, no Hills, all as smooth as the Ships deck, and a very fine Country: But that the roads from Bourdeaux to Paris are bad and mountainous.

The Mal de mer, seems to be the Effect of Agitation. The vapours and exhalations from the Sea; the Smoke of Seacoal, the Smell of stagnant, putrid Water, the Odour of the Ship where the Sailors sleep, or any other offensive Odour will increase the Qualminess, but of themselves, without the violent Agitation they will not produce it.

211

February 19. 1778. In the morning We discovered three Vessells a head of Us. They appeared to be large Ships, and Captain Tucker observing them with his Glasses, gave it as his Opinion that they were British Frigates and was preparing to give order to avoid them. But a murmur arising among the Men which was countenanced by some of the petty Officers, if not by some of the three Lieutenants, who were eager for Prizes; "They would not run from an Enemy before they saw him; they would not fly from danger before they knew they were in it. They were only three fine rich English Merchantmen, or perhaps transports, and would make fat Prizes" &c. To humour his Men Captain Tucker gave orders to make all sail towards them. It was not long before We were near enough to see they were Frigates and count their Guns, to the full Satisfaction of every Man on board. No man had an Appetite for fighting three Frigates at once in our feeble State. Orders were given to put away, and our Officers had discovered that our Frigate sailed uncommonly fast near the Wind. This Course was therefore taken, and We soon lost Sight of two of the Ships, but the third chased Us the whole day. Sometimes she gained up[on] Us, and sometimes We gained in our distance from her.

February the 20th. Fryday. In the morning nothing to be seen: but soon after a Sail discovered a head: supposed to be the same Frigate. She pursued Us the whole day. When the night approached, the Wind died away and We were left rolling and pitching in a Calm, with our Guns all out, our Courses or Coursers, I know not which is the right Word, all drawn up and every Way prepared for battle, the Officers and Men appeared in good Spirits and Captain Tucker said his orders were to carry me to France and to take any Prizes that might fall in his Way; he thought it his duty therefore to avoid fighting especially with an unequal force if he could, but if he could not avoid an Engagement he would give them something that should make them remember him. I said and did all in my power to encourage the Officers and Men, to fight them to the last Extremity. My Motives were more urgent than theirs, for it will easily be believed that it would have been more eligible for me to be killed on board the *Boston* or sunk to the bottom in her, than to

Detail from a painting by Francis Holman of the frigate Boston, *which carried Adams and his son to France*

be taken Prisoner. I sat in the Cabin at the Windows in the Stern and saw the Ennemy gaining upon Us very fast, she appearing to have a Breeze of Wind, while We had none. Our Officers were of Opinion she had Oars out or some other machinery to accellerate her Course. Our Powder, Catridges and Balls were placed by the Guns and every thing ready to begin the Action. Although it was calm on the Surface of the Sea where we lay, the heavens had been gradually overspred with very thick black clouds and the Wind began to spring up, our Ship began to move, the night came on and it was soon dark. We lost Sight of our Enemy who did not appear to me to be very ardent to overtake Us. But the Wind increased to a Hurricane. The Ship laboured under the Weight of her Guns which were all out ready for Use, she shuddered and shivered like a Man in an Ague, she darted from Side to Side and pitched forward with such Velocity, that it was a very dangerous Operation to get the Guns into their places. If by any Accident or want of Skill or care, one of those heavy cannon had got loose, it would have rolled with the Vessel and infallibly have gone through the Side. All hands were called, and with much difficulty the Guns were all got in and secured. As it was impossible to sleep upon deck or in the Cabin one of the Lieutenants came to me and begged me to go down to his Birth below. But such was the Agitation of the Vessell that instead of sleeping it was with the Utmost difficulty that my little Son and I could hold ourselves in bed with both our hands, and bracing our selves against the boards, planks and timbers with our feet. In this Situation, all of a sudden, We heard a tremendous Report. Whether the British Frigate had overtaken Us, and fired upon Us, or whether our own Guns had been discharged We could not conjecture, but immediately an Officer came down to Us and told Us that the Ship had been struck with lightening and the Noise we had heard, was a Crash of Thunder: that four Men had been struck down by it upon deck, one of them wounded by a Scortch upon his Shoulder as large as a Crown. This Man languished and died in a few Weeks. That the Mainmast was struck and it was feared, damaged, but to what degree could not yet be ascertained. In the midst of all this terror and confusion, I heard a Cry that the Powder room was open. Cartridges, Powder horns, if not some small casks of Powder had been left rather carelessly in various parts of the Ship, near the Guns. If a Spark of the lightening had touched any of these, the Consequences might have been disagreable enough, but if it had reached the Powder room, it would have made an End of the Business. The Men were allarmed at the danger of the Powder room, and Sailors and Marines scampered away with their Lanthorns in such a hurry, that I apprehended more danger to the Powder room from their candles than from the Lightening, but instantly I heard the Voice of an Officer. "Be cool! No Confusion! come back with all your lanthorns. I will go with mine and secure the Powder room." I was as much pleased to perceive the immediate Obedience of the Men, as to hear the Voice of the Officer. He soon returned and proclaimed that he had secured the Powder room and all was Safe.

February 21. Saturday. 22 Sunday. and 23. Monday exhibited such Scænes as were new to me, except in the Histories of Voyages, and the descriptions of the Poets. We lost sight of our Ennemy it is true, but We found Ourselves in the Gulph Stream, in one of the most furious Storms, that ever Ship survived, the Wind North East, then North and then North West. It would be fruitless to attempt a description of what I saw, heard and felt, during these three days and nights. Every School Boy can turn to more than one description of a Storm in his Virgil, but no description in P[r]ose or Verse of a hurricane in the Gulph Stream, the Wind always crossing the rapid current in various Angles, has ever yet been Attempted, as far as I know. To describe the Ocean, the Waves, the Winds, The Ship, her motions, rollings, pitches, Wringings and Agonies, The Sailors, their countenances, language and behaviour, is impossible. No man could stand upon his legs; nothing could be kept in its place; an universal Wreck of every thing in all parts of the Ship, Chests, casks, chairs, Bottles &c.; no place or person was dry. The Wind blowing against the current, not directly, but in various Angles, produced a tumbling Sea, vast mountains of Water above Us, and as deep caverns below Us, the mountains sometimes dashing against each other, and sometimes piling up on one another like Pelion on Ossa, and not unfrequently breaking on the Ship threatened to bury Us all at once in the deep.

*The "Gulph Stream" was observed
on an earlier transatlantic
crossing by Benjamin Franklin, who
then published this chart of it.*

The Sails were all hauled down but a foresail under which We hoped to scudd, but a sudden Gust of Wind rent it in an instant from the bottom to the top, and We were left with bare poles entirely at the Mercy of Wind and Water. The Noises were such that We could not hear each other speak at any distance. The Shrouds and every other rope in the Ship exposed to the Wind became a Cord of a very harsh musick. Their Vibrations produced a constant and an hideous howl, of itself enough to deafen Us, added to this the howl and Whistle of the Winds, and incessant roar of the Ocean all in boiling rage and fury, white as Snow with foam through the whole Extent of the horrison; and to compleat the whole, a Sound more allarming I found to our Officers than all the rest, a constant Cracking night and day, from a thousand places in all parts of the Ship, excited very serious Apprehensions of the Starting of the Butts.

Tuesday. 24. Wednesday 25. and Thursday 26 of February. 1778. Our Mainmast and Maintopmast had been hurt by the Lightening. On Tuesday We espyed a Sail and gave her chase. We gained upon her, and upon firing a Gun to leward and hoisting American Colours, she fired a friendly Gun and hoisted the French Colours of the Province of Normandy. She lay to, for Us, and we were coming about to speak to her, when the Wind sprung up fresh of a sudden, and carried away our Maintopmast. We lost the Opportunity which I greatly regretted of speak[ing] to our Friend the Norman, and were sufficiently employed for the remainder of the three days, in getting in a new Maintopmast, repairing the Sails and rigging, which were much damaged in the late Storm and in cleaning the Ship and putting her in order. From the thirty sixth to the thirty ninth degree are called the Squally Latitudes and We found them fully to answer their Character. It was reported among the Seamen that two Sailors who happened to be aloft, had no way to save themselves but by wrapping themselves in the Sail and going over with it. Whether it was true or not, and for what purpose it was propagated if it was not true, I know not: but the report itself was a sufficient illustration of a great Truth of which I have had abundant Experience both before and since that Event, that He who builds on Popularity is like a Sailor on a topmast

whether drunk or sober, ready at the first blast to plunge
into the briny deep....

It was a vast Satisfaction to me to recollect, that I had
been perfectly calm and collected during the whole of
the late Chases and Tempests. I found by the Opinion of
all the People on board, as well as that of the Captain
and all the Officers that We had been in great danger,
and of this I had all along been very certain by my own
Observation, but I thought myself in the Way of my duty,
and I did not for one moment repent of my Voyage. I
often regretted however that I had brought my Son with
me. I was not so clear that it had been my duty to expose
him as well as myself: but I had been led to it, by his
Inclination and by the Advice of all his Friends. The
Childs Behaviour gave me a Satisfaction, that I cannot
express. Fully sensible of our Danger, he was constantly
endeavouring to bear up under it with a manly courage
and patience, very attentive to me, and his thoughts
always running in a serious Strain. In this he was not
singular, for I found that Seamen have their religion as
well as Landsmen, and that Sailors, as Corporal Trim
said of Soldiers, have sometimes more pressing motives
to Prayer than the Clergy. I believe there was not a Soul
on board, who was wholly thoughtless of a Divinity. I
more than once heard our Captain, who was no Fanatic,
on stepping into his Cott, towards morning, offering up
his Prayers to his God, when he had no Suspicion that
any one heard him, and in a very low but audible Voice,
devoutly imploring the Protection of Heaven for the Ship,
and the preservation of himself, his officers, Passengers
and Men.

February 27. Fryday. 1778. A calm. As soft and
warm as Summer....

I was constantly giving hints to the Captain concerning
Order, Œconomy and regularity. He seemed to be sensible of the necessity of them, and exerted himself to introduce them. He cleared out the 'Tween decks, ordered up
the Hammocks to be aired, and ordered up the Sick, such
at least as could bear it, upon Deck for sweet Air. That
Ship would have bred the Plague or the Goal fever, if
there had not been great exertions after the Storm to
wash, sweep, Air, and purify Cloaths, Cotts, Cabins,
Hammocks, and all other things, places, and Persons. In

the Morning I very seriously advised the Captain to reform his Cockpit. I said to him "if you intend to have any reputation for Œconomy, Discipline or any thing that is good, look into that Scæne." He went down, accordingly and ordered up every body from that Sink of Devastation, Putrefaction and Ruin. He ordered up the Hammocks and every thing else that could be removed, and that required to be aired and cleansed.

March 7. Saturday. 1778.   The same prosperous Wind and the same beautifull Weather continued. We proceeded on our course about two hundred miles in twenty four hours. We had passed all the dangers of the American Coast; those of the Bay of Biscay and those of the Coast of France, and as it happened those of the English Channel remained to be encountered.

Yesterday the Ship had been all in an Uproar, with laughter. The Boatswains Mate asked one of the Officers if they might have a little Sport. The Answer was Yes. Jere accordingly, with the Old Sailors, proposed to build a Galley, and all the green hands to the Number of twenty or thirty were taken in, and suffered themselves to be tied together by their Legs. When, all on a sudden, Jere, and his knowing ones, were found, handing bucketts of Water over the Sides, and pouring them upon the poor Dupes till they were wet to the Skin. The Behaviour of the Gullies, their passions, Speeches and countenances, were diverting enough. So much for Jere's fun. This frolick I suppose, according to the Sailors reasoning was to conjure up a Prize.

This morning the Captain ordered all hands upon Deck, and took an Account of the Number of Souls on board, who amounted to one hundred and seventy two. Then the Articles of War were read to them. Then he ordered all hands upon the Forecastle, and then upon the Quarter Deck, to determine by Experiments whether any difference was made in the Sailing of the Ship, by the Weight of the Men when forward, or Aft. Then all hands were ordered to their Quarters to exercise them at the Guns. Mr. Barron gave the Words of command and they spent an hour at their exercise in which they appeared to be tolerably expert. After this a dance was ordered by the Captain upon the main Deck, and all hands, Negroes, Boys and Men were obliged to join in

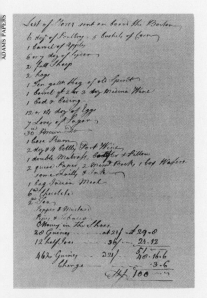

List of stores Adams sent on board the Boston *included "2 fatt Sheep."*

List of supplies for John Adams's use during the long voyage to France

it.... When this was over the Old Sailors sett on foot another game, which they called The Miller. I will not spend time to describe this odd Scæne: but it ended in a very wild Vagary, in which all the Men were powdered over with flour, and wet again to the Skin. Whether these whimsical Diversions are indulged in order to compell the Men to wash themselves, shift their Cloaths and wash away Vermin, or whether it is to awaken the Spirits of the Men which are very apt to sink in a long Voyage, I know not: but there is not in them the least Appearance of Elegance, very little Wit, and a humour of the coarsest kind. It is not superiour to the dances of Indians.

Tuesday March 10. 1778.   We espied a Sail and gave her chace. We soon came up with her, but as we had borne directly down upon her, she had not seen our Broadside and knew not our force. She was a Letter of Mark, with fourteen Guns, Eight nines and Six Sixes. She suddenly turned and fired a broadside into Us, but did Us no other damage, than by cutting some of our rigging, piercing some of our Sails, and sending one of her Shot through our Mizzen Yard. I happened to be standing in the gang Way between the Quarter Deck and the Main Deck, and in the direction from the Ship to the Yard, so that the Balls flew directly over my head. We upon this Salutation, turned our broadside towards her. As soon as she saw this she struck her colours. Our Sailors were all in a rage to sink her for daring to fire. But Captain Tucker very promptly and prudently ordered his Officers not to fire, for he wanted the Egg, without breaking the Shell. I suspected however that the Captain of the Prize knew our force better than he pretended, and that he discharged his Broadside, that he might have it to say that he had not surrendered his Ship, without firing a Gun.

The Prize was the Ship *Martha*, Captain McIntosh from London to New York, loaded with a Cargo of great Value. The Captain told me that seventy thousand Guineas had been insured upon her at Lloyds and that she was worth Eighty thousand. The Behaviour of the Captain was that of a Gentleman, and he bore his misfortune with fortitude but his Mate cryed like a Child in despair. The Sailors seemed to me to felicitate themselves that it was not a British Man of War, and that they were not impressed. There were two Gentlemen on board as Passengers. Mr. R. Gault was One, and Mr. Wallace of New York the other. There were two young Jews, on board. That and the next day were spent in dispatching the Prize, under the command of the third Lieutenant, Mr. Wells, to Boston.

Many years later Captain Samuel Tucker reported in a letter to James Hovey his version of the part John Adams took in the action.

August 22, 1826

About the 20th of March I fell in with a very large Ship—armed but not a cruiser, but however she soon appeared in a posture of engageing, my Ship in readiness and men at their quarters, it became my duty to give Mr. Adams such information as was necessary. He followed me on deck where we expostulated a few minutes on the subject of taking the Ship, finally after listening a minute or two, to my entreaties he took me by the hand, with a god bless you, and descended the gangway ladder into the cockpit. I stept aft and came alongside the Ship I hailed, his answer was a broadside and immediately struck his colours, before I could, to a good advantage discharge a broadside into him, being very near and in such a position the smoke blew over my ship, and looking round on the Quarter deck and observing the Damage I had received from his fire, I discovered Mr. Adams Among my marines accoutred as one of them, and in the act of defence. I then went unto him and Said my dear Sir, how came you here, and with a smile he replied; I ought to do my Share of fighting. This was Sufficient for me to judge of the bravery of my venerable and patriotic Adams and the foregoing is all that ever I related on that Subject to anyone and quite enough to convince them of the bravery of Such a Man.

One sad loss occurred before the *Boston* reached France.

Autobiography, 1802–7

Tuesday March 10. 1778.... We soon fell in chace of another Vessell, and overtaking her, found her to be a French Snow, from Bourdeaux to Miquelon. We then saw another Vessell, chaced and came up with her. She proved to be a French Brig from Marseilles to Nantes. This last cost Us very dear.... Mr. Barrons our first Lieutenant, attempting to fire a Gun as a Signal to the Brigg, the Cannon burst, and tore in pieces the right leg of this worthy officer so that the Surgeon was obliged to amputate it, a little below the Knee.

I was present at this afflicting Scæne, and, together with Captain Tucker, held Mr. Barron in our Arms, while the Doctor put on the Turnequett and cutt off the Limb. Mr. Barron bore it with fortitude, but thought he should die, and his principal concern seemed to be for his family.

I could not but think the fall of this officer, a great loss to the United States. His Prudence, moderation, Attention and Zeal were qualities much wanted in our Infant Navy. He was by Birth a Virginian.

He said he had a Mother, a Wife and Children who were dependant on him and in indigent Circumstances, and intreated me to take care of his Family. I promised him, that as soon as I could write to America I would recommend his Family to the Care of the Public as well as of Individuals.

March 21. Saturday 1778. Five Weeks had elapsed Yesterday, since my Embarkation. We went East South East.

March 27. Fryday.   On Wednesday Evening Mr. Barrons died, and Yesterday was committed to the Deep, from the Quarter Deck. He was laid in a Chest made for the purpose by the Carpenter; about a Dozen twelve pound Shot were put in with him and then nailed up. The Fragment of the Gun which destroyed him, was lashed on the Chest, and the whole launched overboard, through one of the Ports, in presence of all the Ships company after the funeral Service had been read by Mr. Cooper.

March 28. Saturday. 1778.... All day Yesterday, and all the forenoon of this day We had been looking out for Land, with no light Apprehensions on our Approach to the dangerous and unexperienced Coast of France, where a sandy Shore generally extends a great Way into the Sea, and very shoal Water is often at a great distance from Land. The Country also is very flatt and low so that a Vessell gets into very shallow Water before the Land is discerned. About four O Clock, We cryed France! France! We saw the Isles of Rhee and Oleron, between which two, is the Entrance into the Harbour of Rochelle, which is about half way between Nantes and Bourdeaux. The land was extreamly level and low, scarcely visible. We saw a Tower. The Water was but twenty or thirty fathoms deep. The Bottom all Sand: in all respects the reverse of the Spanish Coast on the other Side of the Bay of Biscay. In the Afternoon We had an entire calm and Mr. Goss played upon his Violin and the Sailors danced, which seemed to have a happy effect on their Spirits and put them all in good humour. Numbers of small Birds from the Shore, came along to day, some of which alighted on our Rigging, Yards, &c. One of them a little Lark We caught. These Birds venture from the Shore till they loose sight of it, and then they fly till they are so fatigued, that the instant they alight upon a Ship, they drop to sleep.

Eighteenth-century view of Bordeaux

The *Boston* sailed up the Garonne River to Bordeaux, where John Adams and his party were politely received and quickly introduced to the customs and manners of France.

Autobiography, 1802–7

April 1. Wednesday. 1778.... This Morning I took Leave of the Frigate *Boston*, and excepting a short Visit or two on board, before I satt out on my Journey to Paris never saw her afterwards. She was injudiciously ordered to Charleston to defend that City, which a dozen such Ships would not have been able to effect, and was taken by the English. I went up to the City of Bourdeaux with my Son and Servant, Mr. Vernon, Mr. Jesse Deane [Silas Deane's eleven-year-old son] who were all my Suite, and Dr. Noel as an Interpreter, in the Pinnace. When We came up to the Town We had the good Luck to see Mr. McCreery and Major Fraser, on the Wharf. McCrery I had known in America. It had happened that I had ridden a long Journey with him. He came on board our Boat and conducted Us up to his Lodgings, where We dined, in the fashion of the Country. Among many other Things We had fish, and Salad, and Claret, Champaign and Mountain Wines. After Dinner Mr. Bondfield, whom I had known also in America, and who was agent at this place, invited me to a Walk. We went first to his Lodgings where We drank Tea, and then walked around the Town and went to see the new Comedy, a most splendid Building erecting for the Amusement of the Town. After this We went to the Opera, where the Scenery, dancing and Music aforded to my Curiosity a chearful and sprightly entertainment, having never seen any Thing of the kind before. Our American Theatres had not then existed even in Contemplation.

April 2 Thursday.   Walked round the Town to see the Parliament which was sitting, where We heard but understood not the Counsel, then to see the Council and chamber of Commerce. Then We went round to the Ship Yards, made many Visits, dined at the Hotel D'Angleterre, visited the Custom house, the Post Office, the Chatteau Trompette a famous Fortification of Vaubans and its Commandant. Then visited the Premier President of the Parliament of Bourdeaux. Here I met a reception that was not only polite and respectfull but really tender and seemingly affectionate. He asked Permission to embrace me A la francaise. He said he had long felt for me an Affection resembling that of a Brother. He had pitied me and trembled for me, and was cordially rejoiced to see me. He could not avoid sympathizing with every sincere friend of Liberty in the World. . . . We supped with Messieurs Reuilles [Reculès] De Basmarein and Raimbeaux [of Bordeaux, the "outstanding shipowners of France"]. Here I expected nothing but a common Supper and a small Company; but found myself much disappointed. Among many others in a large Company of both Sexes, were the Count de Viralade, the eldest Son of the first President whom I had just visited. . . . One of the most elegant Ladies at Table, young and handsome, tho married to a Gentleman in the Company, was pleased to Address her discourse to me. Mr. Bondfield must interpret the Speech which he did in these Words "Mr. Adams, by your Name I conclude you are descended from the first Man and Woman, and probably in your family may be preserved the tradition which may resolve a difficulty which I could never explain. I never could understand how the first Couple found out the Art of lying together?" Whether her phrase was L'Art de se coucher ensemble,

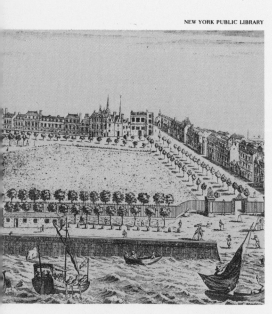

Adams walked around Bordeaux along these tree-lined promenades near the Château Trompette.

or any other more energetic, I know not, but Mr. Bondfield rendered it by that I have mentioned. To me, whose
Acquaintance with Women had been confined to America, where the manners of the Ladies were universally
characterised at that time by Modesty, Delicacy and
Dignity, this question was surprizing and shocking: but
although I believe at first I blushed, I was determined
not to be disconcerted. I thought it would be as well for
once to set a brazen face against a brazen face and
answer a fool according to her folly, and accordingly
composing my countenance into an Ironical Gravity I
answered her "Madame My Family resembles the first
Couple both in the name and in their frailties so much
that I have no doubt We are descended from that in
Paradise. But the Subject was perfectly understood by
Us, whether by tradition I could not tell: I rather thought
it was by Instinct, for there was a Physical quality in Us
resembling the Power of Electricity or of the Magnet,
by which when a Pair approached within a striking
distance they flew together like the Needle to the Pole
or like two Objects in electric Experiments." When this
Answer was explained to her, she replied "Well I know
not how it was, but this I know it is a very happy Shock."
I should have added "in a lawfull Way" after "a striking
distance," but if I had her Ladyship and all the Company
would only have thought it Pedantry and Bigottry.

April 4. Saturday. 1778. About ten O Clock We
commenced our journey to Paris and went about fifty
miles.

April 8th. Wednesday 1778. We rode through Orleans,
and arrived at Paris about nine O Clock. For thirty
miles from Paris the Road was paved and the Scænes
were delightfull.

On our Arrival at a certain Barrier We were stopped
and searched and paid the Duties for about twenty five
Bottles, of Wine which were left, of the generous present
of Mr. Delap at Bourdeaux. We passed the Bridge over
the River Seine, and went through the Louvre. The
Streets crouded with Carriages with a multitude of
Servants in Liveries.

At Paris We went to several Hotells which were full;
particularly the Hotel D'Artois, and the Hotel Bayonne.

We were then advised to the Hotel de Valois, Rue de Richelieu, where We found Entertainment, but We could not have it, without taking all Chambers upon the Floor, which were four in number, very elegant and richly furnished, at the small price of two Crowns and an half a day without any thing to eat or drink. I took the Apartments only for two or three days, and sent for Provisions to the Cooks. Immediately on our Arrival We were called upon for our Names, as We had been at Mrs. Rives's at Bourdeaux. My little Son had sustained this long Journey of nearly five hundred miles, at the rate of an hundred miles a day, with the utmost firmness, as he did our fatiguing and dangerous voyage.

Eighteenth-century map showing the suburbs of Paris, including Auteuil and Passy near the Bois de Boulogne

April 9. Thursday. 1778. Though the City was very silent and still in the latter part of the night, the Bells, Carriages and Cries in the Street, were noisy enough in the morning.

Went in a Coach to Passy with Dr. Noel and my Son. [We visited] Dr. Franklin with whom I had served the best part of two Years in Congress in great Harmony and Civility, and there had grown up between Us that kind of Friendship, which is commonly felt between two members of the same public Assembly, who meet each other every day not only in public deliberations, but at private Breakfasts, dinners and Suppers, and especially in secret confidential Consultations, and who always agreed in their Opinions and Sentiments of public affairs. This had been the History of my Acquaintance with Franklin and he received me accordingly with great apparent Cordiality. Mr. Deane was gone to Marseilles to embark with D'Estaing for America. Franklin undertook the care of Jesse Deane, as I suppose had been agreed between him and the Childs Father before his departure. And he was soon sent, with my Son and Dr. Franklins Grandson Benjamin Franklin Bache, whom as well as William Franklin whom he called his Grandson, the Dr. had brought with him from America, to the Pension of Mr. Le Coeur at Passy.

John Adams soon became acquainted with the difficulties that had divided the American commissioners. His account of Benjamin Franklin's approach to the problems besetting the American mission suggests the difference in temperament between these two great Americans. The coolness and self-control of Franklin contrasted sharply with the warmth and occasional unrestrained bursts of intensity on the part of Adams. These opposing qualities of character were destined to make their own particular contributions to the success of the American cause by complementing each other in a remarkable way during the next five years.

Autobiography, 1802–7

SIR CHARLES CLORE, LONDON

A Franklin miniature

April 10. Fryday. 1778.   The first moment Dr. Franklin and I happened to be alone, he began to complain to me of the Coolness as he very coolly called it, between the American Ministers. He said there had been disputes between Mr. Deane and Mr. Lee....

I heard all this with inward Grief and external patience and Composure. I only answered, that I was personally much a Stranger to Mr. Izard and both the Lees. That I was extreamly sorry to hear of any misunderstanding among the Americans and especially among the public Ministers, that it would not become me to take any part in them. That I ought to think of nothing in such a Case, but Truth and Justice, and the means of harmonizing and composing all Parties: But that I foresaw I should have a difficult, dangerous and disagreable part to Act, but I must do my duty as well as I could.

While John Adams performed the routine duties of his post, he worked hard at studying the French language, met the celebrities of the day, including the king, and reflected upon the differences between monarchical and republican institutions.

Autobiography, 1802–7

April 15. Wednesday. 1778. Dined with Madam Helvetius. One Gentleman and one Lady, besides Dr. Franklin, his Grandson and myself, made the Company. An elegant Dinner. This was a Lady of established Reputation also: The Widow of the famous Helvetius, who, as Count Sarsefield once said to me, if he had made a few millions of Livres the more as one of the Farmers General, and written a few Books the less as a Philosopher it might have been better for France and the World. She has erected a Monument to her Husband, a Model of which She has in her House. It is a Statue of herself, weeping over his Tomb... That She might not be, however, entirely without the Society of Gentlemen, there were three or four, handsome Abby's who

225

*The family of Madame Helvetius
before the death of her husband*

daily visited the House and one at least resided there. These Ecclesiasticks, one or more of whom reside in allmost every Family of Distinction, I suppose have as much power to Pardon a Sin as they have to commit one, or to assist in committing one. Oh Mores! said I to myself. What Absurdities, Inconsistencies, Distractions and Horrors would these Manners introduce into our Republican Governments in America: No kind of Republican Government can ever exist with such national manners as these. Cavete Americani [Take care Americans].

Here I saw a little Book of Fenelons, which I had never met before, "Directions for the Conscience of a King, composed for the Instruction of Louis of France, Duke of Burgundy."

We had here Grapes at this Season of the Year as fresh as if taken off the Vines. I asked how they were preserved. She said, "Sans Air." That is, the Air was exhausted by an Air Pump, from the Vessells in which they were kept, and excluded till they were wanted for Use. Apples, Pears and other fruits are preserved here in great perfection in the same Way.

April 16. Thursday 1778. From my first Arrival in France I had employed every moment of my time, when Business and Company would permit, in the Study of the French Language. I had not engaged any Master and determined to engage none. I thought he would break in upon my hours in the necessary division of my time, between Business, and Study and Visits, and might often embarrass me. I had other reasons too, but none were sufficient to justify me. It was an egregious Error and I have seen cause enough to regret it.

April 20. Monday 1778. My Son had been with me since Saturday. This was delicious repast for me: but I was somewhat mortified to find that this Child among the Pupills at the Pension and my American Servant among the Domesticks of the Hotel, learned more french in a day than I could learn in a Week with all my Books.

Dined with the Dutchess D'Anville, at the Hotel de Rochefaucault, with the Duke de la Rochefoucault her Son, her Daughter and Grand Daughter whom the Duke afterwards married, with a dispensation from the Pope, with a large Company of Dukes, Abbes and Men of

Science and Learning among whom was Mr. Condorcet, a Philosopher with a face as pale or rather as white as a Sheet of paper, I suppose from hard Study....

Recollecting as I did the Expedition of the Duke D'Anville against America, and the great Commotion in the Massachusetts, and the Marches of the Militia to defend Boston, when his Squadron and Army were expected to attack that Town, it appeared a very singular Thing that I should be very happy in his House at Paris at a splendid Dinner with his family. But greater Vicissitudes than this have become more familiar to me, since that time. The Lady appeared to me to possess a great Understanding and great Information.

April 21. Tuesday. 1778.... I may have said before, that Public Business had never been methodically conducted. There never was before I came, a minute Book, a Letter Book or an Account Book, or if there had been Mr. Deane and Dr. Franklin had concealed them from Mr. Lee, and they were now no where to be found. It was utterly impossible to acquire any clear Idea of our Affairs. I was now determined to procure some blank books, and to apply myself with Diligence to Business, in which Mr. Lee cordially joined me. To this End it was necessary to alter the Course of my Life. Invitations were sent to Dr. Franklin and me, every day in the Week to dine in some great or small Company. I determined on my part to decline as many as I could of these Invitations, and attend to my Studies of french and the Examination and execution of that public Business which suffered for want of our Attention Every day. An Invitation came from the Duke of Brancard to dine with him at his Seat. I determined to send an Apology....

April 22. Wednesday 1778 Dined at home and spent the day on Business with Mr. Lee.

April 23 Thursday. 1778. Dined at home with Company.

April 24 Fryday 1778. Dined at Mr. Buffauts with much Company.

April 25. Saturday. Dined at Mr. Chaumonts with Company.

April 26. Sunday 1778. Dined at home.

Monday April 27. 1778. Dined with Mr. Boulainvilliers, at his house in Passi, with Generals and Bishops and Ladies. In the Evening I went to the French Comedy, and happened to be placed in the Front Box very near to Voltaire, who was then upon his last Visit to Paris, and now attended the representation of his own Alzire. The Audience between the several Acts, called Out, Voltaire! Voltaire! Voltaire! and clapped and applauded him during all the intervals. The Aged Poet on Occasion of some extraordinary Applause arose and bowed respectfully to the Spectators. Although he was very far advanced in Age, had the Paleness of death and deep lines and Wrinkles in his face, he had at some times an eager piercing Stare, and at others a sparkling vivacity in his Eyes. They were still the Poets Eyes with a fine frenzy rolling. And there was yet much vigour in his Countenance.

April 29. Wednesday. 1778.... After dinner We went to the Accademy of Sciences, and heard Mr. D'Alembert as Secretary perpetual, pronounce Eulogies on several of their Members lately deceased. Voltaire and Franklin were both present, and there presently arose a general Cry that Monsieur Voltaire and Monsieur Franklin should be introduced to each other. This was done and they bowed and spoke to each other. This was no Satisfaction. There must be something more. Neither of our Philosophers seemed to divine what was wished or expected. They however took each other by the hand.... But this was not enough. The Clamour continued, untill the explanation came out "Il faut s'embrasser, a la francoise." The two Aged Actors upon this great Theatre of Philosophy and frivolity then embraced each other by hugging one another in their Arms and kissing each others cheeks, and then the tumult subsided. And the Cry immediately spread through the whole Kingdom and I suppose over all Europe Qu'il etoit charmant. Oh! il etoit enchantant, de voir Solon et Sophocle embrassans. How charming it was! Oh! it was enchanting to see Solon and Sophocles embracing!

May 8. Fryday. 1778. Dr. Franklin and Mr. Lee went with me to Versailles to attend my Presentation to the

After the first meeting between Voltaire and Franklin, the latter brought his grandson to meet the renowned French philosopher.

Louis XVI

King. We visited the Count de Vergennes at his Office, and at the hour of eleven, the Count conducted Us, into the Kings Bed Chamber, where his Majesty was dressing. One Officer putting on his Coat, another his Sword &c. The Count went up to the King and informed him that Mr. Adams was present to be presented to his Majesty, the King turned round and looked upon me and smiled. "Is that Mr. Adams," said his Majesty? Being answered in the affirmative by the Count, he began to talk to me, and with such rapidity that I could not distinguish one Syllable nor understand one Word. But it was observed by others as well as by me that he discovered a great inclination to have a dialogue with me, whether from mere curiosity, or a desire to impress upon his Courtiers, an unusual number of whom were collected upon that occasion, an idea of his Attention and Attachment to the American cause. It was agreed on all hands that the King was the best friend We had in France. The Count de Vergennes observing his Majestys Zeal went up to him and very respectfully, said, Mr. Adams will not answer your Majesty, for he neither speaks nor understands our Language as yet.... "Pas un mot" said the King.... In what he had said to me before, I thought he said among other things Y a-t-il long tems que vous avez ete dans ce pays ci? or Il n'y a pas long tems que vous avez été dans ce pays ci. But that was all that I even suspected that I understood.... The Count de Vergennes then conducted me to the Door of another Room, and desired me to stand there, which I did untill the King passed. After the usual Compliments of the King to the Ambassadors, his Majesty was preparing to retire when the Count de Vergennes again repeated to the King that I did not take upon me to speak french and the King repeated his question does he not speak it att all? and passing by all the others in the Row made a full Stop before me, and evidently intended to observe and remember my Countenance and Person as I certainly meant to remark those of his Majesty. I was deeply impressed with a Character of Mildness, Goodness and Innocence in his face. It seemed to me impossible that an ill design could be harboured in that breast.... This Monarch was then in the twenty fourth year of his Age, having been born the 23d of August 1754. He had the Appearance of a strong constitution capable of enduring to a great Age.

Madame de Pompadour BY EDMOND AND JULES DE CONCOURT, 1888

Bellevue, built by Louis XV for his mistress Madame de Pompadour

His Reign had already been distinguished by two great Events. The first was the restoration of Harmony in his dominions, by the extinction of those Parties which had rent the Nation under his Predecessor, and the other was the Treaty with the United States of America an Epocha in the History of France which would have reflected Glory upon that Country in all future Ages, if she had known how to improve it. But for Want of Wisdom, it has proved fatal to the Monarch and many of his Family, torn France in Pieces by factions, and swelled her to an enormous and unnatural Power, dangerous to herself, destructive to Europe, and precarious in its duration.

June 2. Tuesday. 1778.... On the Road from Paris and from Passi to Versailles, beyond the River Seine and not far from St. Cleod [Cloud] but on the opposite side of the Way, stood a pallace of uncommon beauty in its Architecture, situated on one of the finest Elevations in the neighbourhood of the River, commanding a Prospect as rich and variegated as it was vast and sublime. For a few of the first times that I went to Versailles I had other Things to occupy my Attention: but after I had passed through my Ceremonies and began to feel myself more at Ease, I asked some Questions about this place and was informed that it was called Bellevue and was the Residence of the Kings Aunts Adelaide and [Victoire,] two of the surviving Daughters of Louis the fifteenth. That this palace had been built and this Establishment made by that Monarch for Madame Pompadour, whom he visited here, almost every night for twenty Years, leaving a worthy Woman his virtuous Queen alone at Versailles, with whom he had sworn never to sleep again. I cannot describe the feelings, nor relate half the reflexions which this object and history excited. Here were made Judges and Councillors, Magistrates of all Sorts, Nobles and Knights of every order, Generals and Admirals, Ambassadors and other foreign Ministers, Bishops, Archbishops, Cardinals and Popes, in the Arms of a Strumpet. Here were directed all Eyes that wished and sought for Employment, Promotion and every Species of Court favour. Here Voltaire and Richelieu and a thousand others of their Stamp, obtained Royal favour and Commissions. Travellers of all Ranks and Characters from all Parts of Europe, were continually passing from Paris to Versailles and spreading the Fame of this House, its Inhabitants and Visitors and their Commerce, infamous in every point of view, civil, political, moral and religious, all over the World. The Eyes of all France had been turned to Bellevue, more than to Paris or Versailles. Here Letters de Cachet, the highest Trust and most dangerous Instrument of arbitrary Power in France were publickly sold, to any Persons who would pay for them, for any the vilest Purposes of private Malice, Envy, Jealousy or Revenge or Cruelty. Here Licences were sold to private Smugglers to contravene the Kings own Laws, and defraud the public Revennue. Here were sold Dukedoms and Peerages, and even the Cordon blue of the Knights of the Holy Ghost. Here still lived the Daughters of the last King and the Aunts of the present. Instead of wondering that the Licentiousness of Women was so common and so public in France, I was astonished that there should be any Modesty or Purity remaining in the Kingdom, as there certainly was, though it was rare. Could there be any Morality left among such a People where such Examples were set up to the View of the whole Nation? Yes there was a Sort of Morality, there was a great deal of humanity, and what appeared to me real benevolence. Even their politeness was benevolence. There was a great deal of Charity and tenderness for the poor. There were many other qualities that I could not distinguish from Virtues.... This very Monarck had in him the Milk of human Kindness, and with all his open undisguised Vices was very superstitious. Whenever he met the Host, he would descend from his Coach and [fall?] down upon his Knees in the Dust or even in the Mud and compell all his Courtiers to follow his Example. Such are the Inconsistencies in the human Character.

From all that I had read of History and Government, of human Life and manners, I had drawn this Conclusion, that the manners of Women were the most infallible Barometer, to ascertain the degree of Morality and Virtue in a Nation. All that I have since read and all the observations I have made in different Nations, have confirmed me in this opinion. The Manners of Women, are the surest Criterion by which to determine whether a Republican Government is practicable, in a Nation or not. The Jews, the Greeks, the Romans, the Swiss, the Dutch, all lost their public Spirit, their Republican Principles and habits,

231

and their Republican Forms of Government, when they lost the Modesty and Domestic Virtues of their Women.

At the end of May, 1778, having had time to size up the situation of the American mission, John Adams wrote a confidential letter to Samuel Adams urging that the Continental Congress appoint a single minister to France.

> Passi May 21. 1778
>
> My Idea is this, seperate the Offices of Public Ministers from those of commercial Agents.... Recall, or send to some other Court, all the Public Ministers but one, at this Court. Determine with Precision, the Sum that shall be allowed to the remaining one, for his Expences and for his Salary, i.e. for his Time, Risque, Trouble &c., and when this is done see that he receives no more than his allowance.
>
> The Inconveniences arising from the Multiplicity of Ministers and the Complications of Businesses are infinite.

Congress adopted Adams's plan in September, 1778, appointing Benjamin Franklin sole American representative to the French Court. Adams, meantime, had been addressing himself to the routine affairs of the mission as best he could. He had set up account books covering the expenses of the commissioners and had tried to pour oil on troubled waters.

> *Autobiography, 1802–7*
>
> May 27th. Wednesday.... I found that the Business of our Commission would never be done, unless I did it. My two Colleagues would agree in nothing. The Life of Dr. Franklin was a Scene of continual discipation. I could never obtain the favour of his Company in a Morning before Breakfast which would have been the most convenient time to read over the Letters and papers, deliberate on their contents, and decide upon the Substance of the Answers. It was late when he breakfasted, and as soon as Breakfast was over, a crowd of Carriges came to his Levee or if you like the term better to his Lodgings, with all Sorts of People; some Phylosophers, Accademicians and Economists; some of his small tribe of humble friends in the litterary Way whom he employed to translate some of his ancient Compositions, such as his Bonhomme Richard and for what I know his Polly Baker &c.; but by far the greater part were Women and Children,

come to have the honour to see the great Franklin, and to have the pleasure of telling Stories about his Simplicity, his bald head and scattering strait hairs, among their Acquaintances. These Visitors occupied all the time, commonly, till it was time to dress to go to Dinner. He was invited to dine abroad every day and never declined unless when We had invited Company to dine with Us. I was always invited with him, till I found it necessary to send Apologies, that I might have some time to study the french Language and do the Business of the mission. Mr. Franklin kept a horn book always in his Pockett in which he minuted all his invitations to dinner, and Mr. Lee said it was the only thing in which he was punctual. It was the Custom in France to dine between one and two O Clock: so that when the time came to dress, it was time for the Voiture to be ready to carry him to dinner. Mr. Lee came daily to my Appartment to attend to Business, but we could rarely obtain the Company of Dr. Franklin for a few minutes, and often when I had drawn the Papers and had them fairly copied for Signature, and Mr. Lee and I had signed them, I was frequently obliged to wait several days, before I could procure the Signature of Dr. Franklin to them. He went according to his Invitation to his Dinner and after that went sometimes to the Play, sometimes to the Philosophers but most commonly to visit those Ladies who were complaisant enough to depart from the custom of France so far as to procure Setts of Tea Geer as it is called and make Tea for him. Some of these Ladies I knew as Madam Hellvetius, Madam Brillon, Madam Chaumont, Madam Le Roy &c. and others whom I never knew and never enquired for. After Tea the Evening was spent, in hearing the Ladies sing and play upon their Piano Fortes and other instruments of Musick, and in various Games as Cards, Chess, Backgammon, &c. &c. Mr. Franklin I believe however never play'd at any Thing but Chess or Checquers. In these Agreable and important Occupations and Amusements, The Afternoon and Evening was spent, and he came home at all hours from Nine to twelve O Clock at night. This Course of Life contributed to his Pleasure and I believe to his health and Longevity. He was now between Seventy and Eighty and I had so much respect and compassion for his Age, that I should have been happy to have done all the Business or rather all the

The Hôtel de Valentinois, where John Adams joined Franklin in 1778

MUSÉE DE BLÉRANCOURT

Drudgery, if I could have been favoured with a few moments in a day to receive his Advice concerning the manner in which it ought to be done. But this condescention was not attainable. All that could be had was his Signature, after it was done, and this it is true he very rarely refused though he sometimes delayed.

The work of the American commissioners proceeded well enough under the circumstances, until news reached Paris early in February, 1779, of Silas Deane's disastrous attempt to vindicate himself by publishing his defense in the *Pennsylvania Packet*. This public display of dirty laundry greatly embarrassed the American mission. It caused particularly acute distress to John Adams, who tended to regard the unpleasant situation as a personal crisis, a fact clearly revealed in his *Diary* entries of the time.

1779. Feb. 8.

In Conversation with Dr. Franklin, in the Morning I gave him my Opinion, of Mr. Deanes Address to the People of America, with great Freedom and perhaps with too much Warmth. I told him that it was one of the most wicked and abominable Productions that ever sprung from an human Heart. That there was no safety in Integrity against such a Man. That I should wait upon The Comte de Vergennes, and the other Ministers, and see in what light they considered this Conduct of Mr. Deane. That if they, and their Representatives in America, were determined to countenance and support by their Influence such Men and Measures in America, it was no matter how soon the Alliance was broke. That no Evil could be greater, nor any Government worse, than the Toleration of such Conduct. No one was present, but the Doctor and his Grandson.

In the Evening, I told Dr. Bancroft, to the same Effect, that the Address appeared to me in a very attrocious Light, that however difficult Mr. Lees Temper might be, in my Opinion he was an Honest Man, and had the utmost fidelity towards the united States. That such a Contempt of Congress committed in the City where they set, and the Publication of such Accusations in the Face of the Universe, so false and groundless as the most heinous of them appeared to me, these Accusations attempted to be coloured by such frivolous Tittle Tattle, such Accusations made too by a Man who had been in high Trust,

BRITISH MUSEUM

Dr. Edward Bancroft

against two others, who were still so, appeared to me, Evidence of such a Complication of vile Passions, of Vanity, Arrogance and Presumption, of Malice, Envy and Revenge, and at the same Time of such Weakness, Indiscretion and Folly, as ought to unite every honest and wise Man against him. That there appeared to me no Alternative left but the Ruin of Mr. Deane, or the Ruin of his Country. That he appeared to me in the Light of a wild boar, that ought to be hunted down for the Benefit of Mankind. That I would start fair with him, Dr. Bancroft, and give him Notice that I had hitherto been loath to give up Mr. Deane. But that this Measure of his appeared to Me to be so decisive against him that I had given him up to Satan to be buffeted.

1779 Feb. 9.

The Uncandor, the Prejudices, the Rage, among several Persons here, make me Sick as Death....

There is no Man here that I dare Trust, at present. They are all too much heated with Passions and Prejudices and party disputes. Some are too violent, others too jealous—others too cool, and too reserved at all Times, and at the same time, every day betraying Symptoms of Rancour quite as deep.

The Wisdom of Solomon, the Meekness of Moses, and the Patience of Job, all united in one Character, would not be sufficient, to qualify a Man to act in the Situation in which I am at present—and I have scarcely a Spice of either of these Virtues.

On Dr. F. the Eyes of all Europe are fixed, as the most important Character, in American Affairs in Europe. Neither L. nor myself, are looked upon of much Consequence. The Attention of the Court seems most to F. and no Wonder. His long and great Rep[utation] to which L's and mine are in their infancy, are enough to Account for this. His Age, and real Character render it impossible for him to search every Thing to the Bottom, and L. with his privy Council, are evermore, contriving. The Results of their Contrivances, render many Measures more difficult.

1779. Feb. 11.

When I arrived in France, the French Nation had a great many Questions to settle.

The first was—Whether I was the famous Adams, Le fameux Adams?—Ah, le fameux Adams?—In order to

235

speculate a little upon this Subject, the Pamphlet entitled Common sense, had been printed in the Affaires de L'Angleterre et De L'Amerique, and expressly ascribed to M. Adams the celebrated Member of Congress, le celebre Membre du Congress. It must be further known, that altho the Pamphlet Common sense, was received in France and in all Europe with Rapture: yet there were certain Parts of it, that they did not choose to publish in France. The Reasons of this, any Man may guess. Common sense undertakes to prove, that Monarchy is unlawful by the old Testament. They therefore gave the Substance of it, as they said, and paying many Compliments to Mr. Adams, his sense and rich Imagination, they were obliged to ascribe some Parts to Republican Zeal. When I arrived at Bordeaux, All that I could say or do, would not convince any Body, but that I was the fameux Adams. — Cette un homme celebre. Votre nom est bien connu ici. — My Answer was — it is another Gentlemen, whose Name of Adams you have heard. It is Mr. Samuel Adams, who was excepted from Pardon by Gen. Gage's Proclamation. — Oh No Monsieur, cette votre Modestie.

But when I arrived at Paris, I found a very different Style. I found great Pains taken, much more than the Question was worth to settle the Point that I was not the famous Adams. There was a dread of a sensation — Sensations at Paris are important Things. I soon found too, that it was effectually settled in the English News Papers that I was not the famous Addams. No body went so far in France or England, as to say I was the infamous Adams. I make no scruple to say, that I believe, that both Parties for Parties there were, joined in declaring that I was not the famous Adams. I certainly joined both sides in this, in declaring that I was not the famous Adams, because this was the Truth.

It being settled that he was not the famous Adams, the Consequence was plain — he was some Man that nobody had ever heard of before — and therefore a Man of no Consequence — a Cypher. And I am inclined to think that all Parties both in France and England — Whiggs and Tories in England — the Friends of Franklin, Deane and Lee, differing in many other Things agreed in this — that I was not the fameux Adams.

Seeing all this, and saying nothing, for what could a

Man say?—seeing also, that there were two Parties formed, among the Americans, as fixed in their Aversion to each other, as both were to G. B. if I had affected the Character of a Fool in order to find out the Truth and to do good by and by, I should have had the Example of a Brutus for my Justification. But I did not affect this Character. I behaved with as much Prudence, and Civility, and Industry as I could. But still it was a settled Point at Paris and in the English News Papers that I was not the famous Adams, and therefore the Consequence was settled absolutely and unalterably that I was a Man of whom Nobody had ever heard before, a perfect Cypher, a Man who did not understand a Word of French—awkward in his Figure—awkward in his Dress—No Abilities—a perfect Bigot—and fanatic.

Abigail Adams was managing the farm and taking care of the family in Braintree during these trying times. Lack of cash, discouraging news of the war, and above all, the scanty and thoroughly unreliable means of communication between the members of the family added to the strains under which they all had to live—as "Portia" wrote to "My Dearest Friend."

Febry. 13. 1779

This is the Anniversary of a very melancholy Day to me, it rose upon me this morning with the recollection of Scenes too tender to Name.—Your own Sensibility will supply your Memory and dictate to your pen a kind remembrance of those dear connections to whom you waved an adeiu, whilst the full Heart and weeping Eye followed your foot steps till intervening objects obstructed the Sight.

This Anniversary shall ever be more particularly Devoted to my Friend till the happy Day arrives that shall give him back to me again. Heaven grant that it may not be far distant, and that the blessings which he has so unweariedly and constantly sought after may crown his Labours and bless his country....

And does my Friend think that there are no hopes of peace? Must we still endure the Desolations of war with all the direfull consequences attending it.—I fear we must and that America is less and less worthy of the blessings of peace.

Luxery that bainfull poison has unstrung and enfeabled

237

her sons. The soft penetrating plague has insinuated itself into the freeborn mind, blasting that noble ardor, that impatient Scorn of base subjection which formerly distinguished your Native Land, and the Benevolent wish of general good is swallowed up by a Narrow selfish Spirit, by a spirit of oppression and extortion.

Nourished and supported by the flood of paper which has nearly overwhelmed us, and which depreciates in proportion to the exertions to save it, and tho so necessary to us is of less value than any commodity whatever, yet the demand for it is beyond conception, and those to whom great sums of it have fallen, or been acquired, vest it in Luxurys, dissapate it in Extravagance, realize it at any rate. But I hope the time is not far distant when we shall in some measure be extricated from our present difficulties and a more virtuous spirit succeed the unfealing dissapation which at present prevails, And America shine with virtuous citizens as much as she now deplores her degenerate sons....

You chide me for my complaints, when in reality I had so little occasion for them. I must intreat you to attribute it to the real cause—an over anxious Solicitude to hear of your welfare, and an ill grounded fear least multiplicity of publick cares, and avocations might render you less attentive to your pen than I could wish. But bury my dear Sir, in oblivion every expression of complaint— erase them from the Letters which contain them, as I have from my mind every Idea so contrary to that regard and affection you have ever manifested towards me.

A locket, given by John to Abigail on his departure for France, shows a lonely woman watching a ship sail off.

Abigail's letter crossed with one from her husband that revealed the tension, bordering on despair, under which he was laboring in France.

Feb. 20. 1779

In the Margin are the Dates of all the Letters I have received from you [ten between March 25, 1778, and January 4, 1779]. I have written you, several Times that Number—they are allmost all lost, I suppose by yours.

But you should consider, it is a different Thing to have five hundred Correspondents and but one. It is a different Thing to be under an Absolute Restraint and under none. It would be an easy Thing for me to ruin you and your Children by an indiscreet Letter—and what is more it would be easy, to throw our Country into Convulsions. —For Gods sake never reproach me again with not writing or with Writing Scrips. Your Wounds are too deep.

You know not—you feel not—the dangers that surround me, nor those that may be brought upon our Country.

Millions would not tempt me to write to you as I used. I have no security that every Letter I write you will not be broken open and copied and transmitted to Congress and to English News Papers. They would find no Treason nor Deceipt in them it is true, but they would find Weakness and Indiscretion, which they would make as ill an Use of.

There are Spies upon every Word I utter, and every Syllable I write—Spies planted by the English—Spies planted by Stockjobbers—Spies planted by selfish Merchants—and Spies planted by envious and malicious Politicians.

I have been all along aware of this, more or less, but more so now than ever.

My Life has been often in danger, but I never considered my Reputation and Character so much in danger as now.

I can pass for a Fool, but I will not pass for a dishonest or a mercenary Man.

Be upon your Guard therefore—I must be upon mine—And I will.

Young John Quincy Adams wrote home that same day.

Passy Feby. 20th. 1779

Hond. Mamma

I last night had the honour of reading a letter from you to my Pappa dated Jany. 4th. in which you complain much of my Pappa's not writing. He cannot write but very little because he has so many other things to think of, but he can not let slip one opportunity without writing a few lines and when you receive them you complain as bad or worse than if he had not wrote at all and it really hurts him to receive such letters. But I will write upon another subject. A Charming prospect opens [before] me. I now begin to see a probability of returning to America. Pappa is now at liberty to return home and proposes to do it by the first safe opportunity unless he

Franklin signed this document so
Adams could take his books home.

HISTORICAL SOCIETY OF PENNSYLVANIA

should receive counter orders which I heard him say he did not expect; it is a feast to my thoughts to go home, to run about to my Grandpappa's and grandmamma's, my uncles &c. The joy of meeting my Mamma, sister and brothers will be greater than all the pain I suffer'd when I took my leave of them severe as that was and the pleasure of telling the tale of my travels and adventures will be some compensation for the toils and dangers I have gone through in the course of them but possibly this pleasing dream may be all disapointed by a battle at sea, by captivity or by shipwreck. All that I can say is gods will be done. I am my ever honoured and ever revered Mamma your dutiful son,

JOHN Q. ADAMS

On February 12, 1779, John Adams learned that Congress had dissolved the joint commission, naming Franklin Minister Plenipotentiary to the French Court. Although Congress did not recall him and, indeed, advised him to devote his talents to financial matters, John Adams decided to return home. After some delay, he sailed on June 17, 1779, on the French frigate *La Sensible*, with his son and with the newly appointed French Minister, the Chevalier de La Luzerne, and the minister's secretary, François Barbé-Marbois. During the voyage John Adams prattled too freely with these amiable and clever Frenchmen, who, directed by Vergennes, were soon to make things difficult for Adams and for the joint commission. Years later, looking back on this experience, the more mature American diplomat was convinced that "the most amiable passions in human nature are the most dangerous guides in politics." The *Diary* entries of the time, however, are entirely guileless.

1779. June 17. Thursday. At 6 O Clock this Morning, Monsieur Chavan, Capitain of the *Sensible*, sent his Canot, on Shore for me, and mine, and here I am, in full possession of my Apartment....

The Chevalier is a large, and a strong Man, has a singular Look with his Eyes. Shutts his Eye Lids, &c.

M. Marbois the Secretary, is a tall, genteel Man and has a Countenance extreamly pleasant. He has the Appearance of Delicacy, in his Constitution....

1779. June 18. Fryday. Mr. Marbois discovered an Inclination to day to slide into Conversation with me, to day. I fell down the Stream with him, as easily as possible. He Thought the

240

The Chevalier de La Luzerne

François Barbé-Marbois

Alliance beneficial, to both Countries, and hoped it would last forever. I agreed that the Alliance was usefull to both, and hoped it would last. I could not foresee any Thing that should interrupt the Friendship. Yes, recollecting myself, I could foresee several Things that might interrupt it.—Ay what were they?—I said it was possible, a King of France might arise, who being a wicked Man might make Attempts to corrupt the Americans. A King of France hereafter might have a Mistress, that might mislead him, or a bad Minister. I said I could foresee another Thing that might endanger our Confederation.—What was that?—The Court of France, I said, might, or their Ambassadors or Consuls might, attach themselves to Individuals or Parties, in America, so as to endanger our Union.—He caught at this, with great Avidity, and said it was a great Principle, not to join with any Party. It was the K's Determination and the Chevaliers, not to throw the Weight of the French Court into the Scale of any Individual or Party.

20. Sunday. [1779]

The Chevalier de la Luzerne, and M. Marbois are in raptures with my Son. They get him to teach them the Language. I found this Morning the Ambassador, Seating on the Cushing in our State Room, Mr. Marbois in his Cot at his left Hand and my Son stretched out in his at his Right—The Ambassador reading out loud, in Blackstones Discourse, at his Entrance on his Professorship of the Common Law at the University, and my Son correcting the Pronunciation of every Word and Syllable and Letter. The Ambassador said he was astonished, at my Sons Knowledge. That he was a Master of his own Language like a Professor. Mr. Marbois said your Son teaches Us more than you. He has Point de Grace—Point d'Eloges. He shews us no Mercy, and makes Us no Compliments. We must have Mr. John.

1779 July 17th. Saturday.

Three Days past We have sounded for the Grand banc but have not found it. By the Reckonings of all the officers, We ought to be now Ten Leagues upon the Banch.

Early in August, 1779, John Adams was rowed to Braintree from Nantasket Roads, where he had left *La Sensible*. Destined to return to Europe three months later, he accomplished two important

241

matters during this short reunion with his family: he drafted the Constitution of the Commonwealth of Massachusetts, and he initiated the founding of the American Academy of Arts and Sciences. The Massachusetts Constitution is one of John Adams's greatest legacies to his countrymen. A few sentences from its Preamble and incorporated Declaration of Rights illustrate the clear style and elevated thought of its author.

Massachusetts Constitution, 1780

The end of the institution, maintenance, and administration of government is to secure the existence of the body politic; to protect it, and to furnish the individuals who compose it with the power of enjoying, in safety and tranquillity, their natural rights and the blessings of life; and whenever these great objects are not obtained, the people have a right to alter the government, and to take measures necessary for their safety, happiness, and prosperity.

The body politic is formed by a voluntary association of individuals. It is a social compact, by which the whole people covenants with each citizen, and each citizen with the whole people, that all shall be governed by certain laws for the common good. It is the duty of the people, therefore, in framing a Constitution of Government, to provide for an equitable mode of making laws, as well as for an impartial interpretation and a faithful execution of them, that every man may, at all times, find his security in them.

CHAPTER I ... [ARTICLE] II

It is the right as well as the duty of all men in society, publicly, and at stated seasons, to worship the SUPREME

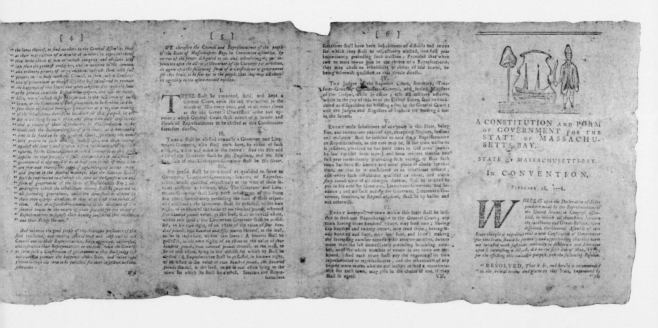

BEING, the great Creator and Preserver of the universe. And no subject shall be hurt, molested, or restrained, in his person, liberty, or estate, for worshipping GOD in the manner and season most agreeable to the dictates of his own conscience; or, for his religious profession or sentiments; provided he doth not disturb the public peace, or obstruct others in their religious worship.

The natural sciences had exerted their fascination upon John Adams from the days of his studies under Professor Winthrop at Harvard College. In a letter written many years later to the *Boston Patriot,* Adams described the genesis of the American Academy of Arts and Sciences, whose president he was to become. The Reverend Dr. Samuel Cooper, who figures in the letter, was John Adams's minister in Boston, had baptized his children, and was the grandfather of Samuel Cooper Johonnot, who was to be under Adams's care on his return voyage to France. Dr. Cooper from about this time was a paid agent of the French Minister La Luzerne.

Quincy, July 31, 1809

In 1779, I returned to Boston in the French frigate *La Sensible,* with the Chevalier de la Luzerne and Mr. Marbois. The corporation of Harvard College gave a public dinner, in honor of the French ambassador and his suite, and did me the honor of an invitation to dine with them. At table, in the Philosophy Chamber, I chanced to sit next to Dr. Cooper. I entertained him during the whole of the time we were together, with an account of Arnold's collections, the collections I had seen in Europe, the compliment I had heard in France upon the Philosophical Society at Philadelphia, and concluded with proposing that the future legislature of Massachusetts should institute an academy of arts and sciences.

The Doctor at first hesitated—thought it would be difficult to find members who would attend to it; but his principal objection was, that it would injure Harvard College by setting up a rival to it, that might draw the attention and affections of the public in some degree from it. To this I answered, first, that there were certainly men of learning enough that might compose a society sufficiently numerous; and secondly, that instead of being a rival to the University, it would be an honor and advantage to it. That the president and principal professors would no doubt be always members of it; and

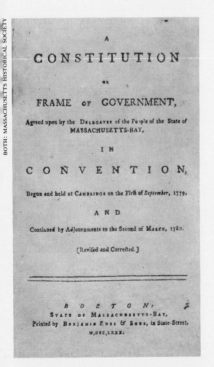

A broadside, outlining "A Constitution and Form of Government" for State of Massachusetts in 1778 (left), was a forerunner of the one that Adams drafted the following year (above).

An ACT

To incorporate and establish a Society for the Cultivation and Promotion of Arts and Sciences.

As the Arts and Sciences are the Foundation and support of Agriculture, Manufactures, and Commerce, as they are necessary to the Wealth, Peace Independence and Happiness of a People; as they essentially promote the Honor and Dignity of the Government which Patronises them; and as they are most effectually cultivated, and diffused through a State, by the forming and incorporating of Men of Genius and Learning into Public Societies: For these beneficial Purposes,

Adams initiated the founding of the American Academy of Arts and Sciences, incorporated by the act (above); its seal is below.

the meetings might be ordered, wholly or in part at the College, and in that room. The Doctor at length appeared better satisfied, and I entreated him to propagate the idea and the plan, as far and as soon as his discretion would justify. The Doctor accordingly did diffuse the project so judiciously and effectually, that the first legislature under the new constitution adopted and established it by law.

Afterwards when attending the convention for forming the constitution, I mentioned the subject to several of the members, and when I was appointed by the subcommittee to make a draught of a project of a constitution to be laid before the convention, my mind and heart was so full of this subject that I inserted the chapter fifth, section second,

"The encouragement of Literature.

"Wisdom and knowledge, as well as virtue, diffused generally among the body of the people, being necessary for the preservation of their rights and liberties: and as these depend on spreading the opportunities and advantages of education, in the various parts of the country, and among the different orders of the people, it shall be the duty of Legislators and Magistrates, in all future periods of this Commonwealth, to cherish the interests of literature, and the sciences, and all seminaries of them; especially the University at Cambridge, public schools and grammar schools in the towns; to encourage private societies and public institutions by rewards and immunities, for the promotion of agriculture, arts, sciences, commerce, trades, manufactures, and a natural history of the country; to countenance and inculcate the principles of humanity and general benevolence, public and private charity, industry, frugality, honesty and punctuality in their dealings: sincerity, good humor, and all social affections and generous sentiments among the people."

I was somewhat apprehensive that criticism and objections would be made to the sections, and particularly that the "natural history" and the "good humor" would be stricken out; but the whole was received very kindly, and passed the Convention unanimously, without amendment. This gave me great encouragement to hope that a natural history of the country would soon be commenced under public authority: But it has been only within four or five years, that any thing has been undertaken in earnest, and that by private subscription, aided however, with a generous grant, by the legislature, of a township of land, which it is to be hoped will be followed by other and more efficacious assistance—for the public property is never more honorably or profitably employed, than in promoting establishments of such extensive and permenant benefits to the present age and to posterity.

On November 4, 1779, John Adams accepted the double congressional commission to be sole American peace commissioner and to negotiate a treaty of commerce with Great Britain. On November 13, he sailed for France on *La Sensible,* which had been refitting in Boston Harbor, taking with him his two sons, John Quincy and Charles, Francis Dana, his diplomatic secretary, John Thaxter, his private secretary and tutor to the boys, and his servant, Joseph Stephens. The French frigate was crowded with three hundred and fifty sailors and other passengers, two of whom, Jeremiah Allen and Samuel Cooper Johonnot, were participants with the Adams party in its trek across northern Spain. The voyage was uneventful, save that the vessel leaked so badly the captain was obliged to put in at Ferrol on the northwestern tip of Spain for repairs. To avoid further delays, John Adams hired mules and carriages and set out in the middle of winter for Paris. He later elaborated on his *Diary* record of this trip.

Autobiography, 1802–7

ADAMS PAPERS

In September, 1779, this commission was issued to John Adams to treat of peace with Great Britain.

December 9. 1779. Thursday. Went on Shore with all my Family, and took Lodgings. Dined with the Spanish Lieutenant General of the Marine with twenty four French and Spanish Officers. Don Joseph, though an old Officer had a great deal of Vivacity and good humour as well as Hospitality. The difference between the Faces and Airs of the French and Spanish Officers was more obvious and striking than that of their Uniforms. Gravity and Silence distinguish the latter: Gaiety, Vivacity and Loquacity the former. The Spanish Uniforms were ornamented with a very broad and even Gold Lace, the French with a narrow and scolloped one. The French Wiggs and Hair had several Rows of curls over the Ears: The Spanish only one. The French Bags were small, the Spanish large: Many of the Spaniards had very long hair quieued, reaching down to their hams almost. All the Officers of both Nations had new Cockades, made up of two, a red and a white one in token of the Union of the two Nations.

In the Evening We went to the Comedy or rather the Italian Opera; where We saw many Officers, and very few Ladies. The Musick and dancing were tolerable; but the Actors and Actresses very indifferent, at least it was a dull Entertainment to me. Perhaps it might have been more pleasing, if I had Understood the Italian Language: but all the Knowledge I ever had of this, which was not much, was acquired after that time.

At La Coruña, Spain, where he hired mules and carriages for the journey to France, John Adams was introduced to other customs, as well as to Spanish wines and pork.

Autobiography, 1802–7

December 16. 1779. Thursday. . . . There are in this Little Town Three Convents of Monks and two of Nuns. One of the Nunneries is of Capuchins, a very austere order. The Girls eat no meat, wear no linnen, sleep on the floor, never on a bed, their faces are always covered with a Veil and they never speak to any body.

1779 December 19. Sunday. Dined with Monsieur De Tournelle, with all my Family. The Regent, or President of the Souvereign Court of the Kingdom of Gallicia, The Attorney General, the Administrator of the Kings Revenue of Tobacco, the Commandant of the Artillery, Mr. Lagoanere and others were there.

The Entertainment was very sumptuous in all respects, but there was the greatest Profusion and Variety of Wines I ever saw brought to any Table. In Addition to the Wines of France, Bourdeaux, Champaigne, Burgundy, We had Constantin and all the best Wines of Spain red and white. The names and qualities of all of them were given Us, but I remember only the Sherry, Alicanté and Navarre. . . .

We found the Pork and Bacon, this day, as We had often found them before, most excellent and delicious, which surprized me the more, as I had always thought the Pork in France very indifferent. . . .

Once on the road John Adams found the sights memorable. The hard-put traveler did not gloss over the hardships of this journey, which must have detracted from the enjoyment of the surroundings.

Receipt for Adams's bill at Hôtel
du Grand Amiral, La Coruña, Spain

Autobiography, 1802–7

1779 December 24. Fryday.... We had now been about sixteen days in Spain at Ferrol and Corunna and had received Every Politeness We could desire from all the Officers civil and military both of the Army and Navy, and from the French Officers as well as the Spanish; the Climate was warm and salubrious, and the Provisions were plentifull, wholesome and agreable. But the Circumstance which destroyed all my Comfort and materially injured my health was the Want of rest. For the first Eight nights I know not that I slept at all and for the other eight very little. The Universal Sloth and Lazyness of the Inhabitants suffered not only all their Beds but all their Appartments to be infested with innumerable Swarms of Ennemies of all repose. And this torment did not cease at Corunna but persecuted me through the whole Kingdom of Spain to such a degree that I sometimes apprehended I should never live to see France.

We were now provided with a Guide and Horses and Mules and Mulateers and such miserable Carriages as the Country afforded, but at an Expence that in any other Country would have procured Us the best accommodations of every kind.

1779 December 27. Monday. We travelled from Betanzos to Castillano. The roads still mountainous and rocky. Neither the Horses nor the Mules could be trusted, in ascending or descending the rocky Steeps of the Mountains in the Carriages without two Men on foot to hold them by their bridles and their heads, and with all our precautions, We broke one of our Axle Trees, early in the day which prevented Us from going more than four Leagues in the whole. The House in Castillano where We lodged was of Stone, two Stories in height....

The Chamber in which We lodged, had a large quantity, perhaps an hundred Bushells of Indian Corn in Ears, very small however, not half so large as our Corn in America. These Ears were hanging over head upon Poles and pieces of Joist. In one Corner was a large Binn, full of Rape Seed, on the other Side, another full of Oats. In another part of the Chamber lay a few Bushells of Chestnuts. There were two frames for Beds with Straw beds upon them, and a Table in the middle. The Floor I believe had never been washed or swept for

247

The American agent at La Coruña gave Adams this Spanish guidebook.

an hundred Years. Smoke, Soot and dirt, every where, and in every Thing. There were in the Chamber two Windows or rather Port holes without any glass. There were wooden dors to open and shut before the Windows. If these were shut there was no light and no Ventilator to draw off the unwholesome Air of the Chamber or let in any pure Air from abroad; if they were open We were exposed to all the cold and Vapours, from the external Air. My Inclination and Advice was to keep the Ports open, choosing to encounter the worst Air from abroad rather than be suffocated or poisoned with the Smoke and contaminated Air within. In addition to all these Comforts in such a Tavern it was not to be expected that We should escape the Bosom Companions and nocturnal Ennemies, which We had found every where else. Nevertheless, amidst all these horrors I slept better, than I had done before since my Arrival in Spain.

1780 January 11. Tuesday....For more than twenty Years I had been almost continually engaged in Journeys and Voyages and had often undergone severe Tryals, as I thought; great hardships, cold, rain, Snow, heat, fatigue, bad rest, indifferent nourishment, want of Sleep &c. &c. &c. But I had never experienced any Thing like this Journey. If it were now left to my Choice to perform my first Voyage to Europe with all its horrors, or this Journey through Spain, I should prefer the former. Every Individual Person in Company had a violent Cold, and were all of Us in danger of fevers. We went along the Road, sneezing and coughing, in all that uncomfortable Weather, and with our uncomfor[t]able Cavalry and Carriages, in very bad roads, and indeed were all of Us fitter for an Hospital than for Travellers with the best Accommodations on the most pleasant Roads. All the Servants in Company, were dull, discouraged and inactive, besides the total Ignorance of any Language in which they could converse with the People. The Children were sick. Mr. Thaxter was not much better, and as he understood neither Spanish nor French, he had enough to do to take care of himself. In short I was in a deplorable Situation. I knew not what to do nor where to go. In my whole Life my Patience was never so near being totally exhausted.

1780 January 20th Thursday. Although We endeavored

The Comte de Vergennes

in Bilbao to take as much Exercise as possible and to amuse ourselves as well as We could, and although the Attention and Hospitality of the House of Gardoqui had done every Thing in their Power to oblige Us, Our Residence in this place was nevertheless very far from being comfortable. We were all sick with violent Colds and Coughs, some of the Servants and Children were so ill that We lived under gloomy Apprehensions, of being detained a long time and perhaps loosing some of our Company. The Houses here as well as every where else were without Chimneys, fires or Windows, and We could find none of those Comforts and Conveniences to which We had been all accustomed from the Cradle, nor any of that sweet and quiet repose in Sleep upon which health and happiness so much depend. On the twentieth, however We summoned Resolution enough to take our departure from Bilbao, and passing over a mountainous Country and very bad roads arrived at the River or rather the Brook that divides Spain from France. The Houses in Biscay and Guipuscua appeared to be larger and more convenient than those in Gallicia, Castile or Leon, but the public Houses were much the same. In the last house in Spain We found one Chimney which was the only one We saw since We left that in the House of Mr. Detournelle the French Consul in Corunna. In our Course We saw a few Villages and particularly Fontarabbia at a distance. We reached St. John De Luz, the first Village in France, and there We dined. And never was a Captive escaped from Prison more delighted than I was, for every Thing here was clean, sweet and comfortable in Comparison of any Thing We had found in any part of Spain.

On reaching Paris in February, 1780, John Adams immediately communicated the purpose of his new mission to French Foreign Minister Vergennes. This cautious and devious diplomat wished to keep control of the peace negotiations in his own hands, and was alarmed lest John Adams obtain undue commercial advantages from Great Britain at the expense of France. He counseled Adams to reveal only his character as peace commissioner and to continue to conceal his authorization to negotiate a treaty of commerce with Great Britain. Although John Adams rightly suspected Vergennes's dissembling policy, he felt constrained to comply for the sake of preserving unity.

In June, complying with Vergennes's request to keep him informed directly of American developments, Adams passed on the news that Congress had recommended the redemption of its depreciated currency at the rate of forty paper dollars to one silver dollar. Vergennes, concerned about the position of French creditors, volunteered a critical reply, addressing himself to Adams instead of to Franklin, who was the properly accredited minister at the Court of Versailles. When Adams answered with a justification of Congress's decision, Vergennes realized he could not control Adams's thinking or behavior and wrote him angrily that he could only discuss the matter with Franklin. Adams later commented on Franklin's role in this imbroglio, prefacing his remarks to the *Boston Patriot* with the amiable doctor's famous judgment on his character: "Mr. Adams is always an honest man, and often a wise one, but he is sometimes completely out of his senses."

Quincy, 15 May 1811

After the arrival of the news from America of the resolution of congress of the 18th of March, 1780, for the redemption of the paper money at forty for one, which perhaps would have been more justly redeemed at seventy for one, M. Leray de Chaumont, Dr. Franklin's landlord and intimate friend and companion, and M. Monthieu, another of his intimate friends, came to visit me in my apartments at the Hotel de Valois, Rue de Richelieu, in Paris, and informed me that they came to me at the request of the Count de Vergennes, who wished to see me and consult with me concerning that resolution of congress which they said had excited a sensation in France, and an alarm at court. These gentlemen were personally, and, as they said, deeply interested in this question of paper money, and entered into a great deal of conversation with me upon the subject. I endeavored to show them the equity, the policy, and the necessity of the measure, and the difficulty, if not impossibility, of making any distinction between natives and foreigners, as well as between Frenchmen and other foreigners. All this conversation passed with the utmost coolness, civility, and good-humor on all sides, and concluded with a message from the Count de Vergennes, requesting me to go to Versailles, and confer with him on the subject. The next morning I went. The Count received me politely, as usual, and informed me that he had written to the Chevalier de la Luzerne, to apply to congress for a repeal of their resolution of the 18th of March, relative to paper money; or at least as far as it respected foreigners, and especially Frenchmen.

M. Leray de Chaumont

NOUVEAU

VOYAGE

DE FRANCE;

A V E C

UN ITINÉRAIRE, ET DES CARTES
faites exprès, qui marquent exactement les
routes qu'il faut suivre pour voyager dans
toutes les Provinces de ce Royaume.

*Ouvrage également utile aux François & aux
Etrangers.*

Nouvelle Edition, revue, corrigée & augmentée.

PAR M. PIGANIOL DE LA FORCE.

TOME PREMIER.

A PARIS,
Chez BAILLY, Libraire, Quai des Augustins.

M. DCC. LXXX.
Avec Approbation, & Privilege du Roi.

John Adams's French guidebook

I answered his Excellency very respectfully and very calmly, endeavoring to explain to him as well as I was able the nature of the subject, the necessity of the measure, and the difficulty and the danger of making any distinctions in favor of foreigners. The conversation was long, and though the Count was very earnest and zealous for a distinction in favor of his nation, it was very decent and civil on both sides. Upon my saying that I knew not whether I had been able to explain myself to his Excellency in French, so as to be perfectly understood, he said he would write to me, for he said he wanted me to join him in his representations to congress. Accordingly, in a few days, I received his letter, proposing and recommending all the things which he mentioned to me in conversation. I might easily have been as wise upon this occasion as Dr. Franklin, and transmitted the Count's letter to congress, and recommended it to their serious consideration, and, in my answer to the Count, have informed him that I had done so, without expressing any opinion of my own in writing either to congress or his Excellency. But such duplicity was not in my character. I thought it my indispensable duty to my country and to congress, to France and the Count himself, to be explicit. I answered his letter with entire respect and decency, but with perspicuity and precision, expressing my own judgment upon the subject, with the reasons on which it was founded. As I could see no practicability of any distinction of all I mentioned now, but I thought, if any was equitable, it would be in favor of American soldiers and early creditors, who had lent gold to the United States, and not in favor of foreigners who had sold nothing in America till the currency had depreciated, and who had sold, perhaps, most of their merchandises after it had undergone its lowest depreciation. However, upon the receipt of my letter the Count fell into a passion, and wrote me a passionate and ungentlemanly reply. I was piqued a little, and wrote him, as I thought, a decent, though, in a few expressions, a gently tingling rejoinder. This was insufferable; and now, both the Count and the Doctor, I suppose, thought they had got enough to demolish me, and get my commission. And I doubt not the Count was sanguine enough to hope that he had got our fisheries, our limits, and a truce secured to his mind, though the Doctor, I believe, did not extend his views and wishes so far. He aimed, I presume, only at the commission....

Franklin had a great genius, original, sagacious, and inventive, capable of discoveries in science no less than of improvements in the fine arts and the mechanic arts. He had a vast imagination, equal to the comprehension of the greatest objects, and capable of a steady and cool comprehension of them. He had wit at will. He had humor that, when he pleased, was delicate and delightful. He had a satire that was good-natured or caustic, Horace or Juvenal, Swift or Rabelais, at his pleasure. He had talents for irony, allegory, and fable, that he could adapt with great skill to the promotion of moral and political truth. He was master of that infantine simplicity which the French call *naïveté*, which never fails to charm, in Phædrus and La Fontaine, from the cradle to the grave. Had he been blessed with the same advantages of scholastic education in his early youth, and pursued a course of studies as unembarrassed with occupations of public and private life, as Sir Isaac Newton, he might have emulated the first philosopher. Although I am not ignorant that most of his positions and hypotheses have been controverted, I cannot but think he has added much to the mass of natural knowledge, and contributed largely to the progress of the human mind, both by his own writings and by the controversies and experiments he has excited in all parts of Europe. He had abilities for investigating statistical questions, and in some parts of his life has written pamphlets and essays upon public topics with great ingenuity and success; but after my acquaintance with him, which commenced in congress in 1775, his excellence as a legislator, a politician, or a negotiator most certainly never appeared....

I must acknowledge, after all, that nothing in life has mortified or grieved me more than the necessity which compelled me to oppose him so often as I have. He was a man with whom I always wished to live in friendship, and for that purpose omitted no demonstration of respect, esteem, and veneration in my power, until I had unequivocal proofs of his hatred, for no other reason under the sun, but because I gave my judgment in opposition to his, in many points which materially affected the interests of our country, and in many more which essentially concerned our happiness, safety, and well-being.

French print glorifying Franklin

I could not and would not sacrifice the clearest dictates of my understanding and the purest principles of morals and policy in compliance to Dr. Franklin....

What shall we do with these gentlemen of great souls and vast views, who, without the least tincture of vanity, *bonâ fide* believe themselves the greatest men in the world, fully qualified and clearly entitled to govern their governors and command their commanders as well as their equals and inferiors, purely for their good and without the smallest interest for themselves? Though it may be true, as Dr. Young says, proud as this world is, there is more superiority in it given than assumed, yet it is certain there is sometimes more assumed than the world is willing to give. Such, unfortunately for Dr. Franklin, was his destiny on this occasion.

The luxury, opulence, and splendor that the observant John Adams saw all around him in prerevolutionary France caused him to reflect upon the role of the arts and sciences in his own country. Characteristically he came to the moral conclusion that the creative impulses behind these accomplishments should be subordinated to the principles of usefulness and duty in his own case as well as that of his sons. He recorded his thoughts in a now famous letter to his wife.

[Paris, May ?, 1780]

The rural Scenes around this Town are charming. The public Walks, Gardens, &c. are extreamly beautifull. The Gardens of the Palais Royal, the Gardens of the Tuilleries, are very fine. The Place de Louis 15, the Place Vendome or Place de Louis 14, the Place victoire, the Place royal, are fine Squares, ornamented with very magnificent statues. I wish I had time to describe these objects to you in a manner, that I should have done, 25 Years ago, but my Head is too full of Schemes and my Heart of Anxiety to use Expressions borrowed from you know whom.

To take a Walk in the Gardens of the Palace of the Tuilleries, and describe the Statues there, all in marble, in which the ancient Divinities and Heroes are represented with exquisite Art, would be a very pleasant Amusement, and instructive Entertainment, improving in History, Mythology, Poetry, as well as in Statuary. Another Walk in the Gardens of Versailles, would be usefull and agreable. — But to observe these Objects with

Trade card of the stationer used by Adams during the years in Paris

Taste and describe them so as to be understood, would require more time and thought than I can possibly Spare. It is not indeed the fine Arts, which our Country requires. The Usefull, the mechanic Arts, are those which We have occasion for in a young Country, as yet simple and not far advanced in Luxury, altho perhaps much too far for her Age and Character.

I could fill Volumes with Descriptions of Temples and Palaces, Paintings, Sculptures, Tapestry, Porcelaine, &c. &c. &c.—if I could have time. But I could not do this without neglecting my duty.—The Science of Government it is my Duty to study, more than all other Sciences: the Art of Legislation and Administration and Negotiation, ought to take Place, indeed to exclude in a manner all other Arts.—I must study Politicks and War that my sons may have liberty to study Mathematicks and Philosophy—my Sons ought to study Mathematicks and Philosophy, Geography, natural History, Naval Architecture, navigation, Commerce and Agriculture, in order to give their Children a right to study Painting, Poetry, Musick, Architecture, Statuary, Tapestry and Porcelaine.

Unable to pursue any part of his double commission in France, John Adams left Paris for Amsterdam on July 27, 1780, as he recalled years later in the *Boston Patriot*. He did not know that Congress had already commissioned him on June 20, 1780, to obtain a loan from the Dutch.

Quincy, June 23, 1809

As I was not limited by my commission or instructions to a residence in any particular place or country, all Europe was open to me, and my intention was to go immediately to Holland, and see if something might not be done there, to render my country somewhat less dependent on France, both for political consideration, for loans of money and supplies for our army. I applied to court for passports, without which I could not travel in France. The Compte de Vergennes advised me to postpone my journey till May, when the country would be in all its beauty and glory. Upon one pretext or another, he evaded my application till midsummer.

A Picture Portfolio

Peppery Minister Plenipotentiary

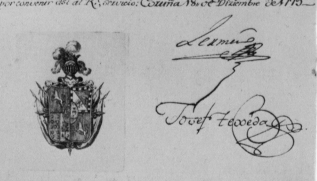

D. Pedro Martin Cermeño

GARCIA DE PAREDES, CAVALLERO DE LA ORDEN
de Alcantara, Administrador de Villafamès en la de
Montesa, Teniente General de los Reales Exercitos,
del Consejo de S. M. en el Supremo de Guerra, Go-
vernador, y Comandante General del Reyno de Ga-
licia, y Presidente de su Real Audiencia.

TRAVELING DIPLOMAT

With the war still raging in America at the end of 1777, John Adams was appointed joint commissioner to France, with Benjamin Franklin and Arthur Lee, to obtain military and financial assistance. For the next ten years he served his country brilliantly in France, Holland, and England. On his second trip to Europe, Adams landed in Spain and was issued the Spanish passport above for his overland journey to Paris. During a harried period in 1781, he described his multiple chores. "I was minister plenipotentiary for making peace...[and] for making a treaty of commerce with Great Britain: minister plenipotentiary to...the States General...the Prince of Orange...[and] commissioner for negotiating a loan of money to the amount of ten millions of dollars.... While I was ardently engaged...to discharge all these duties, I was suddenly summoned to Versailles, to consult with the Comte de Vergennes, upon something relative to peace...." And to peace he did bend his considerable talents. The definitive treaty of peace with Great Britain was signed in 1783, the year Copley painted the striking portrait at right. Peppery, plain-spoken Adams, wearing velvet court dress and holding what is perhaps a copy of the treaty, is shown pointing to a map of America.

258

"THE GREATEST TRIUMPH OF MY LIFE"

Adams's home in Amsterdam was on the lovely Keizersgracht (above). Here he "endeavored to form acquaintances... among such respectable people as were not entirely devoted to the English," in order to obtain loans and later official recognition for his country. But Sir Joseph Yorke (left), the British Ambassador, unexpectedly threatened the Dutch with war and English attacks on Dutch ships increased. Adams wrote to Congress that "War is, to a Dutchman, the greatest of evils.... Yorke is so sensible of this, that he keeps alive a continual fear of it.... while this panic continues, I shall certainly have no success at all." Yorke's recall to England and the British surrender at Yorktown on October 19, 1781, relieved Dutch fears, and Adams's shrewd diplomatic ploys and tireless propaganda began to bring concrete results. In 1782 Prince William V of Orange (left, above) officially received him in the small but richly furnished Huis ten Bosch (far left). A contract for four Dutch loans and a treaty of amity and commerce with the Netherlands followed. Holland understandably became to John Adams the scene of "the greatest triumph of my life."

259

"LE FAMEUX ADAMS?"

On Adams's earliest mission to France in 1778, he found the first question was "whether I was the famous Adams, le fameux Adams?" His success in Holland settled that query, and upon his return to Paris in 1782, he was invited to dine with Foreign Minister Vergennes (left), who had not been noticeably cordial to him. "I was never treated with half the Respect at Versailles in my Life," Adams exulted after dining at the palace (below). "A few of these Compliments would kill Franklin...."Despite their very different approaches to diplomacy, Adams and Franklin, together with John Jay (right, below), drew up what is possibly the most advantageous treaty America has ever signed, the Treaty of Paris of 1783. Adams's own copy is reproduced, in part, at right.

Signature of the present Treaty.

In witness whereof we the undersigned their Ministers Plenipotentiary leave in their Name & in Virtue of our full Powers, signed with our Hands the present *Definitive Treaty*, and caused the Seals of our Arms to be affixed thereto. ———

Done at *Paris*, this third Day of September, In the Year of our Lord, one thousand seven hundred & Eighty three.

D Hartley

John Adams

B Franklin

John Jay

ROYAL APPROVAL

Before Adams left France for England, he called on Vergennes, who said it was a great thing to be the first American representative "to the country you sprung from. It is a mark!" As Adams entered St. James's Palace in London (below), for his first reception with King George III (right, with Queen Charlotte), both he and the King were deeply moved by just that thought. Adams spoke first. ". . . I think myself more fortunate than all my fellow-citizens, in having the distinguished honor to be the first to stand in your Majesty's royal presence in a diplomatic character. . . ." The King, "much affected," responded. "Sir, the circumstances of this audience are so extraordinary, the language you have now held is so extremely Proper, and the feelings you have discovered so justly adapted to the occasion, that I must say that . . . I am very glad the choice has fallen upon you to be their minister. . . ."

264

END OF A LONG JOURNEY

Adams's often frustrating tour of duty in London was made more pleasant by the presence of his wife and his daughter Abigail (below, left), who had joined him in Paris after five long years of separation. They established the first American legation in London in a house on Grosvenor Square (left). "It is a decent house," young Abigail wrote to her brother John Quincy, "... one as you would not blush to see our Foreign Minister in." Abigail, in the throes of getting over an unhappy engagement, fell in love with the dashing Colonel William Stephens Smith (below, far left) and they were married in a quiet ceremony in June, 1786. Two years later, John Adams finally came to the end of his long sojourn abroad. He and his wife left London and the diplomatic scene, arriving in Boston on June 17, 1788, where they were given a well-earned welcome. The official document below greeted them back to their native state: "To the patriot citizen of a free Commonwealth, the affection of an enlightened people will appear the most illustrious reward."

Chapter 8

On the Offensive
in Holland

The brush with Vergennes in the spring of 1780 left no permanent scars on either side. It helped Adams realize that the war in America was being fought by his countrymen for reasons essentially different from those motivating the courts of Europe. What had begun as a local colonial war within the British Empire in 1775 had become a global conflict by the end of 1780, with Great Britain warring not only with the United States but also with France, Spain, and the Dutch for control over their vast colonial empires. Whereas the Americans were fighting a revolutionary, ideological war, the European powers were fighting for essentially limited political and commercial advantages in accordance with their ancient and consecrated system of the balance of power.

During this time it was also becoming more and more apparent that John Adams, a resourceful and tenacious negotiator, did not conform to the style of diplomacy familiar to the age. He was not the polished negotiator moving his pieces on the chessboard of dynastic rivalries and limited, conflicting national interests. Although his direct and peppery personality fitted him to perform great services for his country abroad, it clearly restricted his usefulness at the Court of Louis XVI, where the guile of Franklin matched the dissimulation of Vergennes. Yet the combination of native shrewdness and practicality that was part of his character was soon to bring him a diplomatic triumph in the Netherlands: the recognition of the independence of the United States by a second European power, and financial aid sufficient to support the credit of the United States from the conclusion of the peace to its reorganization in 1789 under the new Constitution. The experience would also enable him to make major contributions to what is possibly the most advantageous treaty the United States has ever signed, the Treaty of Paris of 1783, which ended the war and laid a solid foundation for peace.

But all this was still in the future when Adams set off for Amsterdam with his two sons, John Quincy and Charles, at the end of July, 1780, stopping along the way to see the sights of Brussels and Antwerp. Keeping a record of the journey in his *Diary*, Adams also took the opportunity to observe, moralize, and reflect on how best to make his contribution to the welfare of his own country.

1780 July 27. Thursday.

Setting off on a Journey, with my two Sons to Amsterdam.—Lodged at Compiegne. Fryday night, lodged at Valenciennes. Saturday arrived at Brussells.—This Road is through the finest Country, I have any where seen. The Wheat, Rye, Barley, Oats, Peas, Beans and several other Grains, the Hemp, Flax, Grass, Clover, Lucerne, St. Foin, &c., the Pavements and Roads are good. The Rows of Trees, on each side the Road, and around many Squares of Land.—The Vines, the Cattle, the Sheep, in short every Thing upon this Road is beautiful and plentifull. Such immense fields and heavy Crops of Wheat I never saw any where. The Soil is stronger and richer, than in other Parts.

I lodged in Brussells at L'hotel de L'Imperatrice. The Cathedral Church, the Park, the Ramparts and Canals of this Town, are very well worth seeing.

1780. July 30. Sunday.

Went to the Cathedral Church. A great Feast. An infinite Crowd. The Church more splendidly ornamented than any that I had seen. Hung with Tapestrie. The Church Music here is in the Italian style.

A Picture in Tapestry was hung up, of a No. of Jews stabbing the Wafer, the bon Dieu, and blood gushing in streams, from the B[read?]. This insufferable Piece of pious Villany, shocked me beyond measure. But thousands were before it, on their Knees adoring. I could not help cursing the Knavery of the Priesthood and the brutal Ignorance of the People—yet perhaps, I was rash and unreasonable, and that it is as much Virtue and Wisdom in them to adore, as in me to detest and despise. . . .

In this Town is a great Plenty of stone, which I think is the same with our Braintree North Common stone. It is equally hard, equally fine grain—capable of a fine Polish. I think the Colour is a little darker, than the Braintree stone. There is a new Building here, before which is the Statue of the late Prince Charles, in Front of which are six Pillars, wholly of this stone. Indeed the Steps, and the whole Front is of the same stone.

The town hall of Brussels, a city Adams found "well worth seeing"

Aug. 5. [1780] [Rotterdam] Lodged at the Mareschall De Turenne. Dined with Mr. Dubblemets. Went to see the Statue of Erasmus, the Exchange, the Churches &c. Mr. Dubblemets sent his Coach in the Evening and one of his Clerks. We rode, round the Environs of the Town, then to his Country Seat, where We supped. — The Meadows are very fine, the Horses and Cattle large. The Intermixture of Houses, Trees, Ships, and Canals throughout this Town is very striking. The Neatness here is remarkable.

1780 Aug. 28th. Monday. [Amsterdam] Dined with M. Jacob Van staphorst. A dutch minister from St. Eustatia there. A Lawyer, Mr. Calcoon, Mr. Cromellin, Mr. Le Roi, Gillon, Joiner and a Merchant from Hamborough. The Parson is a warm American. The Lawyer made one observation which [I once?] made to Dr. Franklin, that English would be the general Language in the next Century, and that America would make it so. Latin was in the last Century, French has been so in this, and English will be so, the next.

It will be the Honour of Congress to form an Accademy for improving and ascertaining the English Language.

The statue of Erasmus (far right) that Adams went to see in Rotterdam

Immediately upon arriving in Holland, Adams adopted his usual practice of studying the institutions and customs of the people he had to work with. He applied himself first of all to the difficult task of mastering the intricate system of Dutch republican government, composed of unassimilated monarchic, aristocratic, and democratic elements. He also promptly set himself up as an unofficial American press agency to the Dutch nation, communicating to influential Dutch publicists all sorts of information useful to the American cause. Many years later, in a series of articles published in the *Boston Patriot*, Adams recalled the letter he had written, less than a week after his arrival in Amsterdam, to an eminent writer and professor at the University of Leyden.

Boston Patriot, 1809
August 22, [1780] wrote to Mr. Luzac. "At a time when the British emissaries are filling all Europe with their confident assertions of the distress of the Americans, the enclosed papers shew that both at Philadelphia and at Boston, the people are so much at their ease, as to be busily employed in pursuits of the arts of peace; and in laying foundations for future improvements in science and literature. If you think it worth while to publish

these proceedings they are at your service. I have also received the new constitution of Massachusetts. If you think it of any use to translate it and publish it, it is at your command." Mr. Luzac accordingly translated and published in the *Leyden Gazette,* the law of Massachusetts, establishing the academy of arts and sciences: The proceedings of the Philosophical Society at Philadelphia; with a sensible and elegant introduction.

In early September, 1780, John Adams wrote a letter to the president of Congress in which he developed his ideas concerning the relationship between language and republican institutions. The specific suggestions made in this paper still await congressional action.

Amsterdam, September 5, 1780

As eloquence is cultivated with more care in free republics than in other governments, it has been found by constant experience that such republics have produced the greatest purity, copiousness, and perfection of language. It is not to be disputed that the form of government has an influence upon language, and language, in its turn, influences not only the form of government, but the temper, the sentiments, and manners of the people. The admirable models which have been transmitted through the world and continued down to these days, so as to form an essential part of the education of mankind from generation to generation by those two ancient towns Athens and Rome would be sufficient, without any other argument, to show the United States the importance to their liberty, prosperity, and glory of an early attention to the subject of eloquence and language.

Most of the nations of Europe have thought it necessary to establish by public authority institutions for fixing and improving their proper languages. I need not mention the academies in France, Spain, and Italy, their learned labors, nor their great success. But it is very remarkable, that although many learned and ingenious men in England have from age to age projected similar institutions for correcting and improving the English tongue, yet the government have never found time to interpose in any manner; so that to this day there is no grammer or dictionary extant of the English language which has the least public authority, and it is only very lately that a tolerable dictionary [Samuel Johnson's?] has been

A view of Rotterdam in wintertime

published even by a private person, and there is not yet a passable grammar enterprised by any individual.

The honor of forming the first public institution for refining, correcting, improving, and ascertaining the English language I hope is reserved for Congress; they have every motive that can possibly influence a public assembly to undertake it. It will have a happy effect upon the union of the States to have a public standard for all persons in every part of the continent to appeal to, both for the signification and pronunciation of the language. The constitutions of all the States in the Union are so democratical, that eloquence will become the instrument for recommending men to their fellow-citizens and the principal means of advancement through the various ranks and offices of society.

In the last century Latin was the universal language of Europe. Correspondence among the learned, and indeed among merchants and men of business, and the conversation of strangers and travelers, was generally carried on in that dead language. In the present century Latin has been generally laid aside, and French has been substituted in its place; but has not yet become universally established, and according to present appearances it is not probable that it will. English is destined to be, in the next and succeeding centuries, more generally the language of the world than Latin was in the last or French is in the present age. The reason of this is obvious, because the increasing population in America and their universal connection and correspondence with all nations will, aided by the influence of England in the world, whether great or small, force their language into general use, in spite of all the obstacles that may be thrown in their way, if any such there should be.

It is not necessary to enlarge further to show the motives which the people of America have to turn their thoughts early to this subject; they will naturally turn to Congress in a much greater detail than I have time to hint at. I would therefore submit to the consideration of Congress the expediency and policy of erecting by their authority a society under the name of "The American Academy for refining, improving, and ascertaining the English language." The authority of Congress is necessary to give such a society reputation, influence, and authority through all the States and with other nations.

Adams's French–Dutch dictionary

The number of members of which it shall consist, the manner of appointing those members, whether each State shall have a certain number of members, and the power of appointing them, or whether Congress shall appoint them, whether after the first appointment the society itself shall fill up vacancies—these and other questions will easily be determined by Congress.

It will be necessary that the society should have a library, consisting of a complete collection of all writings concerning languages of every sort, ancient and modern. They must have some officers and some other expenses, which will make some small funds indispensably necessary. Upon a recommendation from Congress there is no doubt but the legislature of every State in the Confederation would readily pass a law making such a society a body-politic, enable it to sue and be sued, and to hold an estate, real or personal, of a limited value in that State.

I have the honor to submit these hints to the consideration of Congress.

ADAMS PAPERS

Site of the first American foreign legation building at The Hague

Although it was common knowledge that John Adams was in Amsterdam as agent of his government, he did not choose to adopt a public character. His friendship with Alexander Gillon, Commodore of the South Carolina Navy, enabled him to find modest lodgings in the Agterburgwal by de Hoogstraat, where he lived until he removed to Leyden for a few months. When he received his appointment as Minister Plenipotentiary to the Dutch Republic, he moved in February, 1781, to more suitable quarters in Amsterdam on the Keizersgracht; and as soon as he knew that the United States would be recognized, he bought a house in The Hague, which became the first building abroad to be acquired by the United States as a foreign legation. Adams later recalled how he came to settle in his first quarters in Amsterdam.

Boston Patriot, 1809

On my journey from Paris to Nantz, in order to embark for America in the frigate alliance, in the spring of 1779, I met upon the road a gentleman in a post chaise, whose dress, air and countenance indicated an American: He stopped his own postillion and mine, and stepping out of his carriage, asked me, very politely apologizing for his freedom, whether my name was Adams? Upon my answer in the affirmative, he said he was very glad to see me, though he was very sorry I was leaving Paris, for he had letters for me, and had depended very much

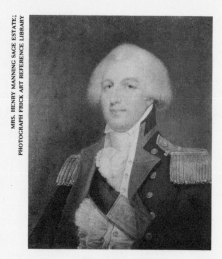

Alexander Gillon

upon me for assistance in his enterprise. He produced me several letters, particularily one from Mr. Edward Rutledge, and another from Mr. Arthur Middleton, of South Carolina. I had served in congress, for years, with both these gentlemen: the former had been with Dr. Franklin and me, to meet lord Howe, in 1776, on Staten Island, and was afterwards governor of South Carolina: the latter was the son of Mr. Middleton, whom we chose for president of congress, in 1774, after president Randolph retired to his chair of speaker of the house of burgesses in Virginia. Both these gentlemen were among the most respectable characters in the state of South Carolina, and both in their letters recommended commodore Gillon to me, in the warmest terms, as a gentleman of talents and address, in whom they had the most perfect confidence, and requesting me to assist him with my advice and countenance in his business, which they explained to me to be to purchase and equip a fleet of frigates for the state of South Carolina. When I returned to Paris, in 1780, the commodore came often to visit me, but returned to Holland some months before I made my journey to that country. When I arrived at Amsterdam, I went to the hotel de Ville, the city tavern, and there resided some time; but finding it the resort of all nations and languages, and among the rest, of many Englishmen, I wrote to commodore Gillon, who knew the city, to procure me convenient apartments in some respectable private house, where I might be more removed from the observation of spies. Gillon consulted his friends, and particularly burgomaster Hooft, the most respectable friend of America in the city, who advised him to the house of Madame Schorn, a relation of the burgomaster, represented as a worthy but unfortunate woman, of sixty or seventy years of age. Gillon was pleased with this, because the house was next door to his own lodgings, and he wished to have me near him as much as I wished to have him near me, that I might avail myself of his society, which was very agreeable, and especially of his knowledge of the language, the people, the city, and the country. I found my apartments decent and convenient for my little family, which consisted of myself, my two little sons, and a single servant. My accommodations were very good, my table well served, and we were treated by all the family with great respect and attention. I was visited there by burgomaster Hooft, Mr. Van Berckel, Mr. Visher, another pensionary, the Messrs. Crommelines, the Van Stapherts, Mr. De Neufville, Mr. Bicker, Mr. Hodgshon, and many others of the wealthiest and most respectable people of the place. I understood the lady to be a widow, and it was a long time before I learned that she had a husband, who had been a merchant in good business and credit, but had failed, and became intemperate. He had, however, some employment which kept him from home, except in the night, so that I never saw him. He fell sick, was brought home, and died in a few days, and was buried, without my ever seeing him. It was but a very little time before I left these lodgings that I ever heard a lisp of any objection to them. Then I was told that there were some remarks among the Dutch, and some whisperings among the Americans in town, that Mr. Adams was in too obscure lodgings. As I had reason to believe that this notion had been put into circulation by the English spies, I cared not for their nonsensical tittle tattle, and would not quit my quarters till some time afterwards, I removed to Leyden for the sake of the education of my children.

Shortly after his arrival in Amsterdam, John Adams received his commission from Congress authorizing him to negotiate a loan. He remembered the circumstances surrounding the reception of this new charge years later in a letter to the *Boston Patriot.*

Quincy, June 23, 1809

In August [1780], after taking a view of Brussells, Antwerp, Rotterdam, Delft, the Hague, Leyden, and Harlem, I arrived at Amsterdam, and there endeavored to form acquaintances and connections among such respectable people as were not entirely devoted to the English, Sir Joseph York [British Ambassador], and the Stadtholder [William V, Prince of Orange].

I had not been long in Holland before I received from Congress another commission. . . .

By this commission, business enough was devolved upon me, and that of a nature very difficult to execute among capitalists, brokers and Hebrews, many of whom could speak or understand as little of the French or English languages as I could of Dutch. A very humerous history might be made of it.

John Adams carefully studied the niceties of diplomatic procedure, learned the history of the nation in which he was stationed, and studied its government. His comments upon the constitution of the Dutch Republic, both at that time and later, show a penetrating understanding of a complicated republican system paralyzed by the absence of a responsible and powerful executive. It was this particular insight that enabled him at a critical moment to take, entirely on his own initiative, appropriate diplomatic action that achieved resounding success. Reporting to the president of Congress early in 1782, he included his comments on the Dutch system of government.

> Amsterdam, 14 January, 1782
>
> Every city is considered as an independent republic. The burgomasters have the administration of the executive, like little kings. There is in the great council, consisting of the burgomasters and counsellors, a limited legislative authority. The schepens are the judges. The deputies are appointed by the regency, which consists of the burgomasters, counsellors, and schepens; and in the large cities, the deputies consist of two burgomasters, two schepens or counsellors, and one pensionary. The pensionary is the secretary of state, or the minister of the city. The pensionaries are generally the speakers upon all occasions, even in the assembly of the States of the Province....
>
> The constitution of government is so complicated and whimsical a thing, and the temper and character of the nation so peculiar, that this is considered every where as the most difficult embassy in Europe.

Years later, in the *Boston Patriot,* John Adams described the historical relationship between the executive branch and the common people in the Dutch Republic from the time they won their freedom under William the Silent.

> Quincy, Sept. 5, 1809
>
> The sovereignty, by the constitution, is a pure aristocracy, residing in the regencies, which consist of about four thousand persons. The common sense, or rather the common feelings, of human nature, had instituted, or rather forced up by violence, an hereditary stadtholder, to protect the common people, or democracy, against the regencies, or aristocracy. But as the stadtholdership was always odious to the aristocracy, there had been frequent disputes between them which must have termi-

nated in the expulsion of the house of Orange, and the abolition of the stadtholdership, if it had not been for the interposition of the commons, the common people. These having no house of commons, no house of representatives to protect them, or even to petition, had no mode of interposing but by mobs and insurrections. This kind of democracy has always been dreadful, in all ages and countries. Accordingly Barneveldt had been sacrificed at one time, the De Witts at another, and in 1748, more sacrifices would have been made, if the aristocracy had not learned some wisdom by tragical experience, and given way in some degree to the popular enthusiasm. If there is any credit to be given to history or tradition, there has never existed on this globe a character more pure, virtuous, patriotic or wise, than John De Witt, or a greater hero than Cornelius. Yet these two citizens were murdered by their fellow citizens at the Hague, with circumstances of cruelty and brutality too shocking to describe. Yet the most savage of these assassins is universally believed in Holland, to have received a pension for life, from our great deliverer King William [Stadtholder and King William III of England]. . . .

There is nothing so instructive to aristocracy and democracy, as the history of Holland, unless we except that of France for the last five and twenty years: nothing which ought so forcibly to admonish them to shake hands, and mutually agree to choose an arbitrator between. Let me not be misunderstood; I have been too often misunderstood already, sometimes ignorantly, and sometimes wilfully. I mean not an hereditary arbitrator. An hereditary executive power can be limited by nothing less than an hereditary aristocracy. When one is admitted, the other must be, as the only antidote to the poison. A proper equilibrium may be formed between elective branches, as well, and perhaps better, than between hereditary ones. And our American balance has succeeded hitherto, as well as that in England, and much better than that in Holland. May it long endure. But to that end, in my humble opinion, the president's office must be less shackled than it has been.

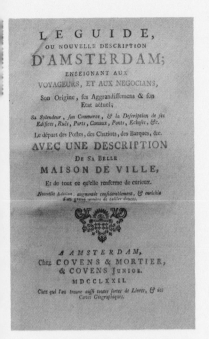

Adams's guidebook to Amsterdam

Once settled in Amsterdam, Adams proceeded to write articles in the newspapers, cultivate friends of the United States, and investigate the possibilities for a loan. Suddenly the country was precipitated into an explosive war crisis. On November 10, 1780, the British Ambassador, Sir Joseph Yorke, unexpectedly delivered an ultimatum tantamount to a declaration of war to the States General in The Hague. In retaliation the Dutch joined the League of Armed Neutrality, a coalition of northern maritime states under the leadership of Russia. But though the move isolated Great Britain politically from the rest of Europe, the League of Armed Neutrality had little if any effect upon military operations. The English simply ignored the league, attacking with impunity and great success Dutch shipping on the high seas and Dutch colonies in the East and West Indies. The enthusiasm of Holland's pro-American Patriot Party, which controlled the government and finances of Amsterdam, was visibly dampened by these reversals, and Adams's prospects for an early American loan were blasted. Adams later chronicled this series of events in his letters to the *Boston Patriot.*

Quincy, August 16, 1809

November 16, 1780.... The thunder of sir Joseph Yorke, when it had time to reach the ears of the whole [Dutch] nation, excited shudderings and amazement, like that of Mount Sinai, among the camp of the Hebrews. The nation had scarcely known a war for three quarters of a century, and a near prospect of it, though only probable, was very terrible to them all.

December 18, 1780, wrote to congress. "War is, to a Dutchman, the greatest of evils. Sir Joseph Yorke is so sensible of this, that he keeps alive a continual fear of it, by memorials after memorials, each more affronting than the former, to any sovereignty of delicate notions of dignity. By these means he keeps up the panic, and while this panic continues, I shall certainly have no success at all. No man dares to engage for me. Very few dare see me....

The Dutch nation had still flattered itself with a hope that the British government would not proceed to the last extremity; but this manifesto [Sir Joseph Yorke's declaration of December 20, 1780, announcing the British government's decision to issue letters of marque and reprisal against Dutch shipping], if it did not extinguish all hopes of avoiding a war, struck the whole republic with such a violent shock as produced an universal and solemn gloom. No man dared to speak, or to think what would be the consequence of it. Every man seemed to be afraid of his neighbor and his best friend.

Such was the terror of the vengeance of the republic against Amsterdam, and of the populace against Mr. Van Berckel [pensionary of Amsterdam, friend of America, and sponsor of a proposed treaty with the United States, which the British had seized upon as a *casus belli*], and even the American minister was not thought to be safe. I was avoided like a pestilence. I might have returned to Paris, or removed to Antwerp or Brussels, out of all danger; but I determined to abide at my post, and share the fate of my friends.

December 25, 1780, wrote to congress. "The public papers inform us, this morning, that sir Joseph Yorke left the Hague on the morning of the 24th, without taking leave of any body, and bent his course to London, by way of Antwerp and Ostend....

"A certain British ambassador, who has an inclination to taste the pleasures of Paris, in his way to Germany, conversing on the subject of American connections in Holland, said, "To be sure, the Americans will carry their point, and establish their independence; but, (with a curse that might have been expected from a British sailor sooner than a British ambassador) why should they wish to rip open our belley? The belly of their mother?" When this anecdote was related to me, I answered, the child would never have thought of hurting the mother, if she had not plucked her nipple from the boneless gums, and attempted to dash the brains out.... The ambassador added, "There will infallibly be a war between England and Holland before Christmas." If the war is considered to commence from the departure of the ambassador, sir Joseph went off exactly in time to accomplish the prophecy.

"It is very difficult to discover, with certainty, the secret springs which actuate the courts of Europe; but whatever I can find with any degree of probability, I shall transmit to congress, at one time or another. The prince of Orange himself, is of the royal family of England, his mother having been a daughter of King George the second; this relation is one among the several motives which attach the stadtholder to England. His princess is a niece of the King of Prussia (Frederick the Great, as they call him, who, not content with the character of a wit, a poet, an historian, a statesman, and

Engraving of Sir Joseph Yorke, made in 1780, with a view of Amsterdam

277

a warrior, must needs be a foolish philosopher) and it is believed, is not perfectly agreed with his most serene highness, in his enthusiasm for the English court. Frederick is supposed to have a great esteem and affection for his niece, to correspond with her frequently, and in some of his letters to have expressed his sentiments freely, upon the prince's conduct, intimating that his highness would take too much upon him, and make himself too responsible, if he persevered in a resolute opposition to the armed neutrality. The empress of Russia [Catherine the Great], who is possessed of a masculine understanding, and it is said, a decided inclination to America, is thought to have expressed some unersiness at the prince's political system. The king of Sweeden, who was lately at the Hague, is reported to have had free conversation with the prince, on the same subject. All these things together, are supposed to have made his highness hesitate, and consider whether he was not acting too dangerous a part, in exerting all his influence in the republic, in opposition to the general inclination of the people, and all the maritime powers of the world. The English court must undoubtedly be informed of all this. They dread the accession of the Dutch to the armed neutrality, more than all the other parties to that confederation, because of the rivalry in commerce, and because the Dutch will assist the marines of France and Spain more than all the others. The present conduct of the English indicates a design to go to war with the Dutch, on pretence of an insult to their crown, committed two years ago, by a treaty with America, in hopes that the Dutch will not be supported in this quarrell by the confederated powers. But they will be mistaken. The artifice is too gross. The neutral powers will easily see that the real cause of offence is the accession to the armed neutrality, and the conduct of Amsterdam only a pretext."

BOTH: BRITISH MUSEUM

William V, Prince of Orange

On February 25, 1781, John Adams received new commissions from Congress designating him Minister Plenipotentiary to the Dutch Republic with instructions to conclude treaties of alliance and commerce with the Dutch and also to accede to the League of Armed Neutrality. Believing that a formal recognition of the independence of the United States would greatly assist in achieving these goals as well as in obtaining a loan, he now resolved upon the bold step of presenting his credentials to the States General and insisting upon a decision by the regencies for or against the formal recognition of the United States. On April 19, 1781, the sixth anniversary of the Battle of Lexington and Concord, Adams launched his diplomatic offensive, as he later recorded in one of his letters to the *Boston Patriot.*

Quincy, November 3, 1809

The black cloud that hung over the whole of the seven provinces; the solemn gloom that pervaded the whole nation; the universal uncertainty and timidity that had seized upon all minds, determined me to bring my own mission to trial. If I should be rejected and ordered out of the country, our situation would not be worse. If I should be received, my object would be gained: but if I should neither be received nor rejected, but taken *ad referendum,* as the most intelligent men assured me I should be, I should then stand in a fair diplomatic character, waiting the result of the national deliberations, under the protection of the government, the public faith, and the national honor. Both myself and my friends would be in a situation of more safety and security. I determined therefore, to communicate my commission and credentials to the government: both to their high mightinesses and to the stadtholder. I wrote my memorials and signed them on the nineteenth of April, 1781: one to the states general, the other to the prince of Orange....

Wilhelmina, Princess of Orange

Considering the connection between the United States and France, it was very obvious that prudence required I should communicate my design to the French ambassador. I was not, however, without apprehensions of the consequence of it, for I could not doubt that the count de Vergennes had information of my appointment sooner than I had, and I had a thousand reasons to believe that my whole system in Holland, and even my residence in it was disagreeable to him. I might presume, as I did presume, that the duke [de La Vauguyon, French Ambassador at The Hague] had instructions from the count to counteract me. But the inconveniences that would arise from concealing my design from the French ambassador, appearing to overbalance those in the other scale, I wrote to his excellency information that I had received from congress full powers and credentials as a minister plenipotentiary to the states general and the prince of Orange. I received a reply from the duke immediately, "that he

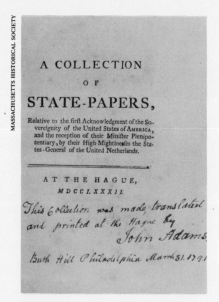

A COLLECTION
OF
STATE-PAPERS,

Relative to the first Acknowledgment of the Sovereignty of the United States of America, and the reception of their Minister Plenipotentiary, by their High Mightinesses the States-General of the United Netherlands.

AT THE HAGUE,
MDCCLXXXII.

This Collection was made translated and printed at the Hague by
John Adams.

Buch Hill Philadelphia March 31. 1791

Printed documents that led to the Dutch recognition of United States

Duc de La Vauguyon, the French Ambassador at The Hague in 1781

had received my letter, but that I had not informed him whether it was my design to present my full powers to their high mightinesses: if such was my intention, he desired a previous conference with me." I went immediately to the Hague, and made my visit to the hotel de France. The duke entered at once into conversation with me to dissuade me from presenting my credentials. He detained me two hours. I answered all his questions, and replied to all his arguments. But as is usual, neither was convinced, and I took my leave with as full a determination as ever to pursue my plan.

The next morning at eight o'clock, the duke appeared at my lodgings, at the principal inn of the city, at the sign of the parliament of England, and renewed his efforts to divert me from my purpose. He went over all the ground we had trod the day before, and ran about all Europe, especially the northern maritime confederation, to find arguments against the step I proposed to take. Although his topics appeared to me extremely frivolous, I listened to them with all the respect which was due to the ambassador of France, and to the personal character of the duke which I sincerely esteemed. It is but justice to say, that in all my intercourse with the duke de la Vaguion, I was uniformly treated by him, his duchess, their children and domestics, with the utmost politeness, and indeed with the freedom and familiarity of friendship....

The duke detained me between four and five hours at this second interview, urging all the time his objections and reasons against my going to the states. There was no solidity in them; I knew them to be mere pretexts.

At last, when he found I was not convinced, he desired me to postpone my visit to the president of their high mightinesses, until he could write to the count de Vergennes and have his opinion. I answered, by no means: Why? Because I know beforehand the count's opinion will be point blank against me; and I had rather proceed against his judgment without officially knowing his opinion, than with it, as I am determined in all events to go. The duke had one resource still left. It was to persuade me to join him or let him alone, in writing a request to the king of France, that he would order his ambassador to unite with me, in my endeavors to obtain an acknowledgment of my public character. I answered again, by no means: Why? Because monsieur le duke, if I must speak out in plain English, or in plain French, I know the decision of the king's council will be directly and decidedly against me; and I am decidedly determined to go to the president, though I had a resolution of the king in council against me, and before my eyes. Besides, the moments are critical, and there is no time to be lost—whereas, the correspondence and negociations you propose may be spun out for years. Moreover, I think that neither the king nor his ministers ought to commit themselves in this business. What! said the duke? Will you take the responsibility of it upon yourself? Indeed, monsieur le duke, I will; and I think I alone ought to be responsible; and that no other ambassador, minister, council or court, ought to be answerable for anything concerning it. "Are you willing to be responsible then?" Indeed I am, and upon my head may all the consequences of it rest. "Are you then determined?" Determined, and unalterably determined I am.

The garden front of the Prince of Orange's House in the Woods

The duke upon hearing this, changed his countenance and the tone of his voice, and said very pleasantly—well I can say no more. If you are determined, and actually go to the states general, though it will be against my opinion and advice, and although I can give you no assistance in my official capacity, yet as a man and an individual, I will give you all the countenance in my power. I thanked his excellency for his declaration, which I received in the most friendly manner; and assured him it was all the aid I expected or desired, as I fully agreed with him that neither his public character or the conduct of his court ought in any manner or degree to be compromised in the affair.

Notwithstanding all this, after our treaty was made with Holland, the count de Vergennes ordered the French minister to announce formally to congress, in the name of the king, that his majesty had assisted the United States in forming the connection between them and the states general of the United Provinces; and his majesty received a formal vote of thanks from congress, for that favor.

John Quincy, now thirteen years old, was matriculated into the University of Leyden on January 11, 1781, together with, by special permission of the Rector Magnificus, his eleven-year-old brother Charles. The boys were watched over by Dr. Benjamin Waterhouse, who was at that time a medical student at the University of Leyden and who was later to become the first professor of the theory and practice of "physic" in the Harvard Medical School as well as being one of John Adams's oldest and best friends. Abigail sent the following piece of motherly advice to John Quincy from Braintree.

May 26, 1781

My dear John,

I hope this Letter will be more Fortunate than yours have been of late. I know you must have written many times since I had the pleasure of receiving a Line from you, for this month completes a Year since the date of your last letter.

Not a line from you or my dear Charles since you arrived in Holland, where I suppose you still are. I never was more anxious to hear yet not a single Vessel arrives from that Port, tho several are looked for.

I hope my dear Boy that the universal Neatness and Cleanliness, of the people where you reside, will cure you of all your slovenly Tricks, and that you will learn from them Industery, Economy and Frugality.

I would recommend it to you to become acquainted with the History of their Country; in many respects it is similar to the Revolution of your own. Tyranny and Oppression were the original causes of the revolt of both Countries. It is from a wide and extensive view of Mankind that a just and true Estimate can be formed of the powers of humane Nature. She appears enobled or deformed, as Religion, Government, Laws, and custom Guide or direct her. Firce, rude, and savage in the uncultivated Desert, gloomy, bigoted and superstitious where Truth is veiled in obscurity and mistery. ductile, pliant, elegant and refined—you have seen her in that dress, as well as the active, bold, hardy and intrepid garb of your own Country.

Inquire of the historick Page and let your own Observations second the inquiry, whence arrises the difference? And when compared, learn to cultivate those Dispositions and to practise those Virtues which tend most to the Benifit and Happiness of Mankind.

The Great Author of our Religion frequently inculcates universal Benevolence and taught us both by precept and example when he promulgated peace and good

Eighteenth-century view of the cathedral at Leyden University, which was founded in 1575.

will to Man, a doctrine very different from that which actuates the hostile Invaders, and the cruel ravagers of mighty Kingdoms and Nations.

I hope you will be very particular when you write, and let me know how you have past your time in the course of the Year past.

Your favourable account of your Brother gave me great pleasure—not only as it convinced me that he continues to cultivate that agreable disposition of Mind and Heart, which so greatly endeared him to his Friends here, but as it was a proof of the brotherly Love and Affection of a son, not less dear to his Parents.

Your Brother Tommy has been very sicke with the Rheumatism, taken by going too early into Water, by which means he lost the use of his Limbs and a Fever ensued. He has however happily recoverd, and learnt Wisdom I hope by his sufferings. He hopes soon to write you a Letter. He has a good school and is attentive to his Books. I shall write to your Brother, so shall only add the sincere wishes for your Improvement and Happiness. Your ever affectionate Mother.

A A

On June 1, 1781, John Adams strengthened his position with the Dutch government by communicating the ratification of the Articles of Confederation to the States General. Long afterwards, writing in the *Boston Patriot*, Adams recorded his activities during this most uncertain period, when his routine duties often took the form of turning down importunate requests for money and doing what he could for American prisoners of war.

Quincy, October 14, 1809

Leyden, March 10, 1781, wrote to Commodore Gillon. "I have received the letter you did me the honor to write me on the 8th of this month, requesting me to furnish you with fifty obligations of the United States, to enable you to discharge the debts of the ships, of which you have the command, in the service of the state of South Carolina.

I have considered your letter, sir, and all the arguments contained in it, with all the attention and respect which is due to your character, and to the state in whose service you are; but the more I have reflected upon them, the more clearly I have been convinced of the impropriety of my consenting to what you request. It would be an illegal and unconstitutional step; without the color of authority. It would be a precedent that would not only be pernicious, but ruinous to the United States. In short, it would be no better than an embezzlement of the public money; to say this, is quite sufficient to justify my final refusal.

I might add to this, considerations of various other kinds; but they are unnecessary, and it would be improper for me to mention in this letter, things which ought to be kept secret, I am myself in a situation much more deplorable than yours; because the danger to the public credit of the thirteen United States, is certainly of more consequence, and more melancholy, than the danger or loss of a single ship, whether she belongs to the United States or any one of them. If this whole matter were to be laid before congress, the delegates from South Carolina themselves, would be the first to justify me. I feel for you and your disappointment. I know your exertions. But this can be no excuse for me, to do a wrong thing, knowing it to be so."

Amsterdam, June 7, 1781, wrote to Monsieur Berenger, secretary of the French embassy at the Hague. "Captain Isaac Cazneau, of Boston, lately arrived here from Norway, in his passage on board a Danish vessel, unfortunately fell in with an English privateer belonging to Hull, called the *Flying Fish*, who took away his mate, who was his brother, and a negro boy of about fifteen years of age named Pompey. The *Flying Fish* left the mate in prison in Hull, but kept the boy on board. The privateer is lately taken by a French privateer, the *Sans Peur*, and carried into Helvoetsuis with the negro on board who is a native of North America and a freeman. Captain Cazneau is very anxious to obtain for him his liberty. I have the honor to beg your interposition in this business, in the absence of the duke de la Vauguion, that if it can be done with propriety the boy may be discharged. It is the constant practice in France to set Americans at liberty, who have been captured in like manner. Captain Cazneau is a gentleman of good character and well known; so that his testimony I suppose would be sufficient to prove the facts; but other witnesses are here if they were necessary."

View of Amsterdam in 1781

In July, 1781, French Foreign Minister Vergennes summoned John Adams to Paris for consultation regarding the mediation undertaken by Russia and Austria to end the war. Adams later told the story of these abortive negotiations in the *Boston Patriot*.

Quincy, June 23, 1809

I was minister plenipotentiary for making peace: minister plenipotentiary for making a treaty of commerce with Great Britain: minister plenipotentiary to their High Mightinesses the States general: minister plenipotentiary to his serene highness the Prince of Orange and Stadtholder: minister plenipotentiary for pledging the faith of the United States to the Armed Neutrality: and what perhaps at that critical moment was of as much importance to the United States as any of those powers, I was commissioner for negociating a loan of money to the amount of ten millions of dollars, and upon this depended the support of our army at home and our ambassadors abroad.

While I was ardently engaged and indefatigably occupied in studies and efforts to discharge all these duties, I was suddenly summoned to Versailles, to consult with the Comte de Vergennes, upon something relative to peace. What should I do? My country and the world would consider my commission for peace as the most important of all my employments, and the first to be attended. I hesitated not a moment, left all other business in as good a train as I could, and set off for Paris. . . .

Though I thought I was *negotiating for peace,* to better purpose in Holland than I could in France, yet as I could not be responsible for that, I was obliged to depart. The adventures of a journey, which, in the hands of Sterne, would make a sentimental romance, are of no importance here.

On Wednesday [July 11, 1781] I went to Versailles, and met the Count at his office, with Mr. Rayneval, at nine o'clock. They communicated to me the . . . articles, proposed by the two Imperial Courts—That Spain had prepared her answer: that of France was near ready: did not know that England had yet answered.

These articles were given me in French, and they graciously condescended to let me see the original communication from the two Imperial Courts as far and no farther than these articles extended. All the rest was

Engraving of Adams drawn from life in 1782 by an Amsterdam engraver

carefully covered up with a book. I desired to see and have a copy of the whole; but no, that could not be permitted.

The articles that Adams was permitted to see allowed for a direct negotiation between Great Britain and the "American Colonies" and called for a general armistice on the basis of the existing military situation. No recognition was allowed of the independence of the United States. Never did John Adams act with more alacrity or sureness than when, that very same day, he wrote the president of Congress the following letter designed to destroy what he correctly judged, even on the incomplete evidence allowed to him, as "that sublime machine for demolishing our independence."

Paris, July 11, 1781.

I have only time, by Major Jackson, to inform Congress, that upon information from the Comte de Vergennes, that questions concerning peace, under the mediation of the two Imperial Courts, were in agitation, that required my presence here, I undertook the journey, and arrived last Friday night, the sixth of the month, and have twice waited on the Comte De Vergennes, at Versailles, who this day communicated to me the enclosed propositions.

These propositions are made to all the belligerent powers by the courts of Petersburg and Vienna, in consequence of some wild propositions made to them by the court of London, that they would undertake the office of mediators, upon condition, that the *league*, as they call it, between France and their *rebel subjects* in America, should be dissolved, and these left to make their terms with Great Britain, after having returned to their allegiance and obedience.

France and Spain have prepared their answers to these propositions of the Empress and Emperor, and I am desired to give my answer to the articles enclosed. It is not in my power, at this time, to enclose to Congress my answer, because I have not made it, nor written it; but Congress must see that nothing can come of this manoeuvre, at least for a long time. Thus much I may say, that I have no objection to the proposition of treating with the English separately, in the manner proposed, upon a peace with them, and a treaty of commerce, consistent with our engagements with France and Spain —

but that the armistice never can be agreed to by me. The objections to it are as numerous as they are momentous and decisive. I may say farther, that as there is no judge upon earth of a sovereign power but the nation that composes it, I can never agree to the mediation of any powers however respectable, until they have acknowledged our sovereignty, so far at least, as to admit a Minister Plenipotentiary from the United States as the representative of a free and independent power. After this we might discuss questions of peace or truce with Great Britain, without her acknowledging our sovereignty, but not before.

I fancy, however, that Congress will be applied to, for their sentiments, and I shall be ever ready and happy to obey their instructions, because I have a full confidence that nothing will be decided by them but what will be consistent with their character and dignity.

Peace will only be retarded by relaxations and concessions, whereas firmness, patience and perseverance will insure us a good and lasting one in the end.

The English are obliged to keep up *the talk* of peace, to lull their enemies and sustain their credit. But I hope the people of America will not be deceived. Nothing will obtain them real peace but skillful and successful war.

Francis Dana

HARPER'S MONTHLY MAGAZINE, VOL. CIV

Before returning to Holland, Adams communicated his objections to the proposals to Vergennes in language that the Foreign Minister was later to use himself in bringing the mediation efforts to an end. On his arrival back in Amsterdam at the end of July, 1781, Adams found that all his friends and family were soon to leave him, with the exception of his private secretary, John Thaxter. He recalled these events later in one of his letters to the *Boston Patriot.*

Quincy, February 8, 1810

Upon my return to Amsterdam from Paris, I found my friend Mr. Dana, in great anxiety and perplexity. Congress had ordered him to go to St. Petersburg, and had sent him a commission as their minister, with instructions to conclude a treaty of friendship and commerce with the empress of Russia; but they had given him no secretary of legation, nor made any provision for a private secretary, or even a copying clerk. They had, moreover from the unfavourable influence of a party at home, or from some suggestions from abroad, a combina-

John Quincy Adams, at age sixteen, an engraving by Sidney L. Smith

tion that had injured many other honest men, such as Mr. Arthur Lee, Mr. Izzard, Mr. William Lee and Mr. Jay, reduced Mr. Dana's compensation below that of the other ministers. Mr. Dana had taken pains to persuade some gentlemen to accompany him, but could find none who would consent to go. He had before him the dreary prospect of an immense journey by land, through Holland, Germany, Denmark, and he knew not how many other nations, of whose languages he understood not one word; and in the French, which was the travelling language of Europe, he was yet but a student. In this situation, he requested me to let him have my oldest son, John Quincy Adams, for a companion and a private secretary or clerk. The youth was, in conversation, a ready interpreter of French for an American, and of English for a Frenchman; he could easily translate in writing, as Mr. Dana had seen, any state paper. He wrote a fair hand, and could copy letters, or any other papers as well as any man; and he had the necessary patience of application to any of these services. I was at first very averse to the proposition, but from regard to Mr. Dana, at last consented. I would not however, consent to burthen Mr. Dana with his expenses, but advanced him money for that purpose, and desired Mr. Dana to draw upon me for more when that should be expended, which he did. He returned from Russia before Mr. Dana was recalled, and in this interval, Mr. Dana must have been put to other expenses for clerkship. Mr. Dana agreed with me in opinion that congress would finally make him a grant for a private secretary at least, and in that case he was to pay me the money I had advanced, or should advance for expenses, and nothing more. All this I presume was known to congress, when they made the grant to Mr. Dana, not for the form but the substance, for it was Mr. Dana's right. When Mr. Dana received the grant from Congress he returned me the sums I had advanced for expenses and no more. Neither the father nor the son ever received anything for services. And what did the son lose by this excursion? He lost the honor of a degree in the University of Leyden, and he lost what was more precious, the benefit of four or five years studies in Greek and Roman literature under Luzac and others, and in civil Law under Professor Pestell, unquestionably among the greatest masters in

Europe, I should be quite unable to estimate these losses in money. . . .

My second son, after the departure of his brother, found himself so much alone, that he grew uneasy, and importuned me so tenderly to let him return to America to his mother, that I consented to that, and thus deprived myself of the greatest pleasure I had in life, the society of my children. We lost, at the same time, almost all our American acquaintance in Holland. On or about the 10th of August, 1781, the *South Carolina*, commodore Gillon, put to sea from the Texel, with Mr. Searle, Colonel Trumbull, Major Jackson, Mr. Bromfield, Dr. Waterhouse and Charles Adams on board as passengers. These had for some time composed a very pleasant American society; but now I was left alone with Mr. Thaxter.

The surrender of Cornwallis at Yorktown on October 19, 1781, not only started a train of events leading to peace, but also added an immediate impetus to all John Adams's diplomatic and financial efforts among the Dutch. On April 19, 1782, precisely one year after presenting his memorial on the subject, the States General officially recognized Adams's role as representative of the independent United States. Events now followed in quick succession. On June 11, 1782, Adams signed a contract for the first of four Dutch loans to the United States, which were to yield three and a half million dollars and provide credit needed to support the government after the peace. On October 8, 1782, Adams signed the Treaty of Amity and Commerce, the second treaty with a European state made by the United States. On the conclusion of this treaty, he sent an account of what he had done to Robert R. Livingston, recently appointed Secretary of Foreign Affairs of the United States.

The Hague, *October* 8, 1782

At twelve o'clock to-day I proceeded, according to appointment, to the State House, where I was received with the usual formalities at the head of the stairs by M. Van Santheuvel, a deputy from the province of Holland, and M. Van Lynden, the first noble of Zealand, and a deputy from that province, and by them conducted into the chamber of business (chambre de besogne), an apartment belonging to the truce chamber (chambre de trêve) where were executed the treaty of commerce and the convention concerning recaptures, after an exchange of full powers. . . .

The proviso of conforming to the laws of the country

respecting the external show of public worship, I wished to have excluded; because I am an enemy to every appearance of restraint in a matter so delicate and sacred as the liberty of conscience; but the laws here do not permit Roman Catholics to have steeples to their churches, and these laws could not be altered. I shall be impatient to receive the ratification of Congress, which I hope may be transmitted within the time limited.

John Adams's diplomatic triumphs were matched on a smaller scale by more personal but no less satisfying accomplishments. As he recorded in his *Diary,* he was now quite adept at the Dutch language; and in a letter to his friend James Warren, he fairly crowed with pride at being able to display the flag of the United States from the American Legation at The Hague.

[The Hague] Oct. 3. Thursday [1782]. Madame Boreel next to whom I sat at Table asked me if I understood the Dutch. I answered, very little, but that I began to learn it. That I had with me two ingenious young Gentlemen with whom at Breakfast, I every Morning attempted with the Aid of a Dictionary to read the Dutch Gazettes, and that We began to comprehend some Paragraphs.

The Hague, 6 September, 1782. One thing, thank God, is certain. I have planted the American standard at the Hague. There let it wave and fly in triumph over Sir Joseph Yorke and British pride. I shall look down upon the flagstaff with pleasure from the other world.

Not the declaration of American independence, not the Massachusetts Constitution, not the alliance with France, ever gave me more satisfaction or more pleasing prospects for our country than this event. It is a pledge against friends and enemies. It is an eternal barrier against all dangers from the house of Bourbon as well as a present security against England. Perhaps every imagination does not rove into futurity as much as mine, nor care so much about it.

Truce chamber in the State House at The Hague, where treaty was signed

Chapter 9

Seasons of Triumph

After the surrender at Yorktown, when England came to realize that she had lost her American Colonies, the cornerstone of her empire, her wisest leaders began to see the necessity for cutting Britain's losses while preserving a base in India on which to construct a second and even greater empire. Just as one must admire the American commissioners' abilities at the Paris peace negotiations in securing their country's independence and a continental domain, so one must recognize the perspicacity of the British who, under the capable leadership of their twenty-six-year-old Prime Minister, William Pitt, were soon to rise phoenixlike from the ashes of defeat. The British clearly concluded with their former colonies a wise and generous peace, even if events were to prove it was not a perfect one in every respect.

By 1782 Adams was no longer sole commissioner empowered to negotiate peace with Great Britain, nor was he any longer empowered to sign a commercial treaty with the English. His loss of status was largely the work of his old antagonist Vergennes, whose deputy in Philadelphia, the Chevalier Anne César de la Luzerne, had maneuvered Congress into subduing the volatile Adams by appointing him to a joint peace commission with Benjamin Franklin, John Jay, Henry Laurens, and Thomas Jefferson. La Luzerne was also instrumental in limiting the effectiveness of the commission by having the following humiliating restrictions included in the official instructions of June 15, 1781: "...you are to make the most candid and confidential communications upon all subjects to the ministers of our generous ally, the King of France; to undertake nothing in the negotiations for peace or truce without their knowledge and concurrence; and ultimately to govern yourselves by their advice and opinion."

Jefferson never accepted his appointment to the peace commission. Laurens, captured by the British on the high seas in September, 1780, was clapped into the Tower of London, where he languished until 1782; he only attended the peace conference the very last day of the negotiations, and in failing health. The first of the commissioners to launch the negotiations was Franklin, who was also the first to violate the instructions of Congress by sending a secret paper to an old friend Lord Shelburne, who was soon to become Britain's prime minister. In his letter he pointed out that many problems might be solved, including that of compensation to the Loyalists, if Great Britain would cede Canada to the United States. When John Jay arrived in Paris from Spain on June 22, 1782, he immediately took the initiative in the negotiations by successfully requiring the British to grant prior recognition of the independence of the United States. Richard Oswald, the British negotiator, was accordingly issued credentials by his government empowering him to deal with "any Commissioners or Person vested with equal Powers, by and on the part of the Thirteen United States."

Adams, who had sabotaged efforts to partition America in the summer of 1781, remained skeptical about the way the British chose to open the talks. It was not until John Jay wrote to him in September, 1782, that he was persuaded to travel from The Hague to Paris to join Franklin and Jay for the final negotiations that were to end the war with Great Britain. The very day that he was hurrying to Paris, Abigail was writing him a pensive letter from Braintree. As she tenderly reminded him, the day was that of their wedding anniversary.

October 25 1782

My Dearest Friend

The family are all retired to rest, the Busy Scenes of the day are over, a day which I wished to have devoted in a particular manner to my dearest Friend, but company falling in prevented nor could I claim a moment untill this Silent Watch of the Night.

Look—(is there a dearer Name than Friend; think of it for me;) Look to the date of this Letter—and tell me, What are the thoughts which arise in your mind? Do you not recollect that Eighteen years have run their anual Circuit, since we pledged our mutual Faith to each other, and the Hymeneal torch was Lighted at the Alter of Love. Yet, Yet it Burns with unabating fervour, old ocean has not Quenched it, nor old Time Smootherd it, in the Bosom of Portia. It cheers her in the Lonely Hour, it comforts her even in the Gloom which sometimes possesses her mind.

It is my Friend from the Remembrance of the joys I have lost that the arrow of affliction is pointed. I recollect the untitled Man to whom I gave my Heart, and in the agony of recollection when time and dis-

Abigail Adams by Mather Brown

Henry Laurens, one of five joint peace commissioners in Paris

tance present themselves together, wish he had never been any other. Who shall give me back Time? Who shall compensate to me those *years* I cannot recall? How dearly have I paid for a titled Husband; should I wish you less wise, that I might enjoy more happiness? I cannot find that in my Heart—yet providence has wisely placed the real Blessings of Life within the reach of moderate abilities, and he who is wiser than his Neighbour sees so much more to pitty and lament, that I doubt whether the balance of happiness is in his Scale.

I feel a disposition to Quarrel with a race of Beings who have cut me of, in the midst of my days, from the only Society I delighted in. Yet No Man liveth for himself, says an authority I will not dispute. Let me draw Satisfaction from this Source and instead of murmuring and repineing at my Lot consider it in a more pleasing view. Let me suppose that the same Gracious Being who first smiled upon our union and Blessed us in each other, endowed my Friend with powers and talents for the Benifit of Mankind and gave him a willing mind, to improve them for the Service of his Country.

You have obtaind honour and Reputation at Home and abroad. O may not an inglorious Peace wither the Laurels you have won. —I wrote you per Capt. Grinnel. The Fire Brand is in great haste to return, and I fear will not give me time to say half I wish. I want you to say many more things to me than you do, but you write so wise so like a minister of State. I know your Embarrassments—thus again I pay for titles. Life takes its complexion from inferiour things; it is little attentions and assiduities that sweeten the Bitter draught and smooth the Rugged Road.

I have repeatedly expresst my desire to make a part of your Family. "But will you come and see me" cannot be taken in that serious Light I should chuse to consider an invitation from those I love. I do not doubt but that you would be glad to see me; but I know you are apprehensive of dangers and fatigues. I know your Situation may be unsetled, and it may be more permanant than I wish it. Only think how the word 3 and 4 and 5 years absence sounds!! It sinks into my Heart with a Weight I cannot express.

Do you look like the Miniature you sent? I cannot

think so. But you have a better likeness I am told. Is that designd for me? Gracious Heaven restore to me the original and I care not who has the shadow....

Adieu my dear Friend. Ever Ever Yours,

PORTIA

As John Adams approached Paris, his spirits rose joyfully in his breast like those of a sportsman finishing a long chase. He found time to record in his *Diary* some impressions of activities and places that still engage the attention of the traveler approaching Paris across the romantic Île-de-France.

Oct. 25. Fryday [1782].
Dined at Gourney. Carriage broke again. Arrived at Night, at Pont-Sainte-Maxence, two Posts from Chantilly and one and an half from Senlis.

The Ecchoing horn
The ecchoing horn calls the Sportsmen abroad
To horse, my brave Boys, and away
The morning is up and the Cry of the hounds
Upbraids our too tedious Delay.

1782 October 26. Saturday.
Parted from Pont Sainte Maxence, for Chantilly. The distance is two Postes, and We found the Road very good. We went to see the Stables, and Horses. I had on my travelling Gloves, and one of the Grooms run up to Us, with 3 Whip Sticks, and presented them to Us. This is an Air which the Grooms give themselves, in order to get Something to drink. They do the same to the Prince of Condé himself, if he enters the Stables with Gloves on his hands. I gave them six Livres, but if I had been in a private Character, I should have thought 24s. or even half of it, enough.

We went round the Castle, and took a Look at the Statue of the grand Condé, in marble, half Way up the great Stair Case, and saw the Statue on Horseback in Bronze, of the grand Constable Montmorency. Walked round the Gardens, Fish Ponds, Grottoes and Waterspouts. And looked at the Carps and Swan that came up to Us for Bread. Nothing is more curious than this. Whistle or throw a Bit of Bread into the Water and hundreds of Carps large and fat as butter will be seen swimming near the Top of the Water towards you, and

The town of Cambrai through which Adams passed on his way to Paris

294

will assemble all in a huddle, before you. Some of them will thrust up their Mouths to the Surface, and gape at you like young Birds in a Nest to their Parents for Food.

While We were viewing the Statue of Montmorency Mademoiselle de Bourbon came out into the Round house at the Corner of the Castle dressed in beautifull White, her Hair uncombed hanging and flowing about her Showlders, with a Book in her Hand, and leaned over the Bar of Iron, but soon perceiving that she had caught my Eye, and that I viewed her more attentively than she fancied, she rose up with that Majesty and Grace, which Persons of her Birth affect, if they are not taught, turned her Hair off of both her Showlders, with her Hands, in a manner that I could not comprehend, and decently stepped back into the Chamber and was seen no more. The Book in her hand is consistent, with what I heard 4 Years ago at the Palais de Bourbon in Paris, that she was fond of Reading. . . .

The Managery, where they exercise the Horses is near the end of the Stables and is a magnificent Piece of Architecture. The orangery appears large, but We did not look into it.

The Village of Chantilly, appears a small Thing. In the Forest or Park We saw Bucks, Hares, Pheasants, Partridges &c. but not in such Plenty as one would expect.

We took a Cutlet and glass of Wine, at ten at Chantilly, that We might not be tempted to stop again, accordingly We arrived, in very good Season at the Hotel de Valois, Rue de Richelieu, where the House however was so full that We found but bad Accommodations.

Now the Hill Tops are burnished, with Azure and Gold
And the Prospect around Us most bright to behold
The hounds are all trying the Mazes to trace
The Steeds are all neighing and pant for the Chase
Then rouse each true Sportsman, and join at the Dawn
The Song of the Huntsman, and Sound of the Horn.
　The Horn, The Horn, the Song of the Huntsman
　　and Sound of the Horn. . . .

Château de Chantilly, where John Adams caught a view of Mlle. de Bourbon as he was sight-seeing

The negotiations in Paris started almost immediately. Adams was suspicious of Franklin and his grandson, William Temple Franklin, who was the natural son of Franklin's natural son, William Franklin, the Royal Governor of New Jersey. The governor was an active Loyalist then in England and a cause of some embarrassment to his father. William Temple Franklin in turn had been appointed secretary of the American peace commission without Adams's prior knowledge or approval. Matthew Ridley, an American patriot living in Paris, passed on news of the latest developments to Adams, who kept a record in his *Diary*.

1782 October 26. Saturday. Arrived, at night at the Hotel de Valois, Rue de Richelieu, after a Journey of ten Days from the Hague, from whence We, Mr. John Thaxter, Mr. Charles Storer and I parted last Thursday was a Week.

The first Thing to be done, in Paris, is always to send for a Taylor, Peruke maker and Shoemaker, for this nation has established such a domination over the Fashion, that neither Cloaths, Wigs nor Shoes made in any other Place will do in Paris. This is one of the Ways, in which France taxes all Europe, and will tax America. It is a great Branch of the Policy of the Court, to preserve and increase this national Influence over the Mode, because it occasions an immense Commerce between France and all the other Parts of Europe. Paris furnishes the Materials and the manner, both to Men and Women, every where else.

Mr. Ridley lodges in the Ruë de Clairi [Cléry], No. 60. Mr. Jay. Rue des petits Augustins, Hotel D'Orleans.

1782 Oct. 27. Sunday. Went into the Bath, upon the Seine, not far from the Pont Royal, opposite the Tuilleries. You are shewn into a little Room, which has a large Window looking over the River into the Tuilleries. There is a Table, a Glass and two Chairs, and you are furnished with hot linnen, Towels &c. There is a Bell which you ring when you want any Thing.

Went in search of Ridley and found him. He says F[ranklin] has broke up the Practice of inviting every Body to dine with him on Sundays at Passy. That he is getting better. The Gout left him weak. But he begins to sit, at Table.

That J[ay] insists on having an exchange of full Powers, before he enters on Conference or Treaty. . . . Refused to treat with Oswald, untill he had a Commission to treat with the Commissioners of the United States of America. —F. was afraid to insist upon it. Was afraid We should

Benjamin Franklin in the marten fur hat he liked to wear in France

be obliged to treat without. Differed with J. Refused to sign a Letter &c. . . .

F. wrote to Madrid, at the Time when he wrote his pretended Request to resign, and supposed that J. would succeed him at this Court and obtained a Promise that W[illiam Temple Franklin] should be Sec[retary]. Jay did not know but he was well qualified for the Place.

Went to the Hotel D'orleans, Rue des petites Augustins, to see my Colleage in the Commission for Peace, Mr. Jay, but he and his Lady were gone out.

Mr. R. dined with me, and after dinner We went to view the Appartements in the Hotel du Roi, and then to Mr. J. and Mrs. Iz[ard], but none at home. R. returned, drank Tea and spent the Evening with me. Mr. Jeremiah Allen, our Fellow Passenger in the leaky Sensible . . . came in and spent the Evening. . . .

R. is still full of Js. Firmness and Independance. He has taken upon himself, to act without asking Advice or even communicating with the C[omte] de V[ergennes]— and this even in opposition to an Instruction. This Instruction, which is alluded to in a Letter I received at the Hague a few days before I left it, has never yet been communicated to me. It seems to have been concealed, designedly from me. The Commission to W. was urged to be filled up, as soon as the Commission came to O[swald] to treat with the Min[ister]s of the united States, and it is filled up and signed. W. has lately been very frequently with J. at his house, and has been very desirous of perswading F. to live in the same house with J. —Between two as subtle Spirits, as any in this World, the one malicious, the other I think honest, I shall have a delicate, a nice, a critical Part to Act. F.s cunning will be to divide Us. To this End he will provoke, he will insinuate, he will intrigue, he will maneuvre. My Curiosity will at least be employed, in observing his Invention and his Artifice. J. declares roundly, that he will never set his hand to a bad Peace. Congress may appoint another, but he will make a good Peace or none.

In a later *Diary* entry, John Adams described how Franklin rallied behind Jay and himself early in the negotiations. He also cited his own vexation at being put in the position of violating the instructions of Congress, even though the French Foreign Minister Vergennes was in-

John Trumbull's portrait of William Temple Franklin, grandson of and secretary to his famous relative

formed that the negotiations were taking place, was apprised of their progress from time to time, and never formally objected to the procedure adopted by the Americans.

Pictorial Field-Book of the War of 1812 (EXTRA-ILLUSTRATED) BY BENSON J. LOSSING, 1868

John Jay

November 30. Saturday.
St. Andrews Day [1782].

As soon as I arrived in Paris I waited on Mr. Jay and learned from him, the rise and Progress of the Negotiation. Nothing that has happened since the Beginning of the Controversy in 1761 has ever struck me more forcibly or affected me more intimately, than that entire Coincidence of Principles and Opinions, between him and me. In about 3 days I went out to Passy, and spent the Evening with Dr. Franklin, and entered largely into Conversation with him upon the Course and present State of our foreign affairs. I told him without Reserve my Opinion of the Policy of this Court, and of the Principles, Wisdom and Firmness with which Mr. Jay had conducted the Negotiation in his Sickness and my Absence, and that I was determined to support Mr. Jay to the Utmost of my Power in the pursuit of the same System. The Dr. heard me patiently but said nothing.

The first Conference We had afterwards with Mr. Oswald, in considering one Point and another, Dr. Franklin turned to Mr. Jay and said, I am of your Opinion and will go on with these Gentlemen in the Business without consulting this Court. He has accordingly met Us in most of our Conferences and has gone on with Us, in entire Harmony and Unanimity, throughout, and has been able and usefull, both by his Sagacity and his Reputation in the whole Negotiation.

1783 Tuesday. Feb. 18.

I have omitted my Journal, and several Things of some Consequence, but I am weary, disgusted, affronted and disappointed. This State of Mind I must alter—and work while the day lasts.

I have been injured, and my Country has joined in the Injury. It has basely prostituted its own honour by sacrificing mine. But the Sacrifice of me for my Virtues, was not so servile, and intollerable as putting Us all under Guardianship. Congress surrendered their own Sovereignty into the Hands of a French Minister. Blush blush! Ye guilty Records! blush and perish! It is Glory, to have broken such infamous orders. Infamous I say, for so they will be to all Posterity. How can such a Stain be washed out? Can We cast a veil over it, and forget it?

The payment of debts contracted before the war and compensation to the Loyalists who had lost property during the war were among the first matters on the agenda for negotiation.

1782. November 3. Sunday.
In my first Conversation with Franklin on Tuesday Evening last, he told me of Mr. Oswalds Demand of the Payment of Debts and Compensation to the Tories. He said their Answer had been, that we had not Power, nor had Congress. I told him I had no Notion of cheating any Body. The Question of paying Debts, and that of compensating Tories were two. —I had made the same Observation, that forenoon to Mr. Oswald and Mr. Stretchy [Strachey], in Company with Mr. Jay at his House. . . . I saw it struck Mr. Stretchy with peculiar Pleasure, I saw it instantly smiling in every Line of his Face. Mr. O. was apparently pleased with it too.

In a subsequent Conversation with my Colleagues, I proposed to them that We should agree that Congress should recommend it to the States to open their Courts of Justice for the Recovery of all just Debts. They gradually fell in to this Opinion, and We all expressed these Sentiments to the English Gentlemen, who were much pleased with it, and with Reason, because it silences the Clamours of all the British Creditors, against the Peace, and prevents them from making common Cause with the Refugees. . . .

The present Conduct of England and America resembles that of the Eagle and Cat. An Eagle scaling over a Farmers Yard espied a Creature, that he thought an Hair. He pounced upon him and took him up. In the Air the Cat seized him by the Neck with her Teeth and round the Body with her fore and hind Claws. The Eagle finding Herself scratched and pressed, bids the Cat let go and fall down. —No says the Cat: I wont let go and fall, you shall stoop and set me down.

British caricature on the resolution of the war: "Brother, Brother We Are Both In The Wrong."

The boundaries of the United States, the right to navigation on the Mississippi, and rights to the North Atlantic fisheries were all fundamental questions to be dealt with. These vital matters were eventually decided to the satisfaction of the Americans, but Jay was not convinced that either the French or the Spanish had been entirely straightforward with him.

> November 5. Tuesday [1782].
> Mr. Jay likes Frenchmen as little as Mr. Lee and Mr. Izard did. He says they are not a Moral People. They know not what it is. He dont like any Frenchman. — The Marquis de la Fayette is clever, but he is a Frenchman. — Our Allies dont play fair, he told me. They were endeavouring to deprive Us of the Fishery, the Western Lands, and the Navigation of the Mississippi. They would even bargain with the English to deprive us of them. They want to play the Western Lands, Mississippi and whole Gulph of Mexico into the Hands of Spain.

John Adams consulted with Vergennes at Versailles on the progress of the negotiations. As he noted in his *Diary*, he found that his diplomatic success in Holland had not passed unnoticed at the French Court and that there was no longer any mistaking him for his cousin Samuel.

> November 10. Sunday [1782].
> At 8 this Morning I went and waited on the Comte. He asked me, how We went on with the English? I told him We divided upon two Points the Tories and Penobscot, two ostensible Points, for it was impossible to believe that My Lord Shelburne [now Britain's prime minister] or the Nation cared much about such Points. I took out of my Pocket and shewed him the Record of Governour Pownals solemn Act of burying a Leaden Plate with this Inscription, May 23. 1759. Province of Massachusetts Bay. Penobscot. Dominions of Great Britain. Possession confirmed by Thomas Pownal Governor.
> This was planted on the East Side of the River of Penobscot, 3 miles above Marine Navigation. I shew him also all the other Records — the Laying out of Mount Desert, Machias and all the other Towns to the East of the River Penobscot, and told him that the Grant of Nova Scotia by James the first to Sir William Alexander, bounded it on the River St. Croix. And that I was possessed of the Authorities of four of the greatest Governors the King of England ever had, Shirley, Pownal, Bernard and Hutchinson, in favour of our Claim and of Learned Writings of Shirley and Hutchinson in support of it. — The Comte said that Mr. Fitzherbert

told him they wanted it for the Masts: but the C. said that Canada had an immense quantity. I told him I thought there were few Masts there, but that I fancied it was not Masts but Tories that again made the Difficulty. Some of them claimed Lands in that Territory and others hoped for Grants there.

The Comte said it was not astonishing that the British Ministry should insist upon Compensation to them, For that all the Precedents were in favour of it. That there had been no Example of an Affair like this terminated by a Treaty, without reestablishing those who had adhered to the old Government in all their Possessions. I begged his Pardon in this, and said that in Ireland at least their had been a Multitude of Confiscations without Restitution. — Here We ran into some Conversation concerning Ireland, &c. Mr. Rayneval [secretary in the French foreign office], who was present talked about the national honour and the obligation they were under to support their Adherents. — Here I thought I might indulge a little more Latitude of Expression, than I had done with Oswald and Stratchey, and I answered, if the Nation thought itself bound in honour to compensate those People it might easily do it, for it cost the Nation more Money to carry on this War, one Month, than it would cost it to compensate them all. But I could not comprehend this Doctrine of national honour. Those People by their Misrepresentations, had deceived the Nation, who had followed the Impulsion of their devouring Ambition, untill it had brought an indelible Stain on the British Name, and almost irretrievable Ruin on the Nation, and now that very Nation was thought to be bound in honour to compensate its Dishonourers and Destroyers. Rayneval said it was very true.

The Comte invited me to dine. I accepted. When I came I found the M[arquis] de la Fayette in Conference with him. When they came out the M. took me aside and told me he had been talking with the C. upon the Affair of Money. He had represented to him, Mr. Morris's Arguments and the Things I had said to him, as from himself &c. That he feared the Arts of the English, that our Army would disbande, and our Governments relax &c. That the C. feared many difficulties. That France had expended two

The Marquis de Lafayette

hundred and fifty Millions in this War &c. That he talked of allowing six millions and my going to Holland with the Scheme I had projected, and having the Kings Warranty &c. to get the rest. That he had already spoken to some of Mr. De Fleury's Friends and intended to speak to him &c.

We went up to Dinner. I went up with the C. alone. He shewed me into the Room where were the Ladies and the Company. I singled out the Comtesse and went up to her, to make her my Compliment. The Comtess and all the Ladies rose up, I made my Respects to them all and turned round and bowed to the reste of the Company. The Comte who came in after me, made his Bows to the Ladies and to the Comtesse last. When he came to her, he turned round and called out Monsieur Adams venez ici. Voila la Comtesse de Vergennes. A Nobleman in Company said Mr. Adams has already made his Court to Madame la Comtess. I went up again however and spoke again to the Comtess and she to me. — When Dinner was served, the Comte led Madame de Montmorin, and left me to conduct the Comtesse who gave me her hand with extraordinary Condescention, and I conducted her to Table. She made me sit next her on her right hand and was remarkably attentive to me the whole Time. The Comte who sat opposite was constantly calling out to me, to know what I would eat and to offer me petits Gateaux, Claret and Madeira &c. &c. — In short I was never treated with half the Respect at Versailles in my Life.

In the Antichamber before Dinner some French Gentlemen came to me, and said they had seen me two Years ago. Said that I had shewn in Holland that the Americans understand Negotiation, as well as War.

The Compliments that have been made me since my Arrival in France upon my Success in Holland, would be considered as a Curiosity, if committed to Writing. Je vous felicite sur votre Success, is common to all. One adds, Monsieur, Ma Foi, vous avez reussi, bien merveilleusement. Vous avez fait reconnoitre votre Independance. Vous avez fait un Traité, et vous avez procuré de l'Argent. Voila un Succés parfait. — Another says, vous avez fait des Merveilles en Hollande. Vous avez culbuté le Stathouder, et la Partie angloise. Vous avez donné bien de Mou[ve]ment. Vous

Marie-Antoinette BY PIERRE DE NOLHAC, PARIS

A royal banquet at Versailles in 1782, the same year that Adams was invited to dine there with Vergennes

avez remué tout le Monde. — Another said Monsieur vous etes le Washington de la Negotiation. — This is the finishing Stroke. It is impossible to exceed this.

Compliments are the Study of this People and there is no other so ingenious at them.

1782 November 12. Tuesday.
Dined with the Abby Chalut and Arnoux. The Farmer General, and his Daughter, Dr. Franklin and his Grand Son, Mr. Grand and his Lady and Neice, Mr. Ridley and I with one young French Gentleman made the Company. The Farmers Daughter is about 12 Years old and is I suppose an Enfant trouvee. He made her sing at Table, and she bids fair to be an accomplished Opera Girl, though she has not a delicate Ear. . . .

Lord Shelburne, Prime Minister of Great Britain during the peace negotiations in Paris in 1782

The Compliment of "Monsieur vous etes le Washington de la Negotiation" was repeated to me, by more than one Person. I answered Monsieur vous me faites le plus grand honour et la Compliment le plus sublime possible. —Eh Monsieur, en Verite vous l'avez bien merité. — A few of these Compliments would kill Franklin if they should come to his Ears.

The American proposals having been agreed upon and forwarded to London, John Adams talked freely with the members of the British negotiating team while waiting for an answer from the British Cabinet.

November 17. Sunday [1782].
Have spent several Days in copying Mr. Jays dispatches.

On Fryday the 15, Mr. Oswald came to Visit me, and entered with some Freedom into Conversation. I said many Things to him to convince him that it was the Policy of my Lord Shelburne and the Interest of the Nation to agree with Us upon the advantageous Terms which Mr. Stratchey carried away on the 5th. Shewed him the Advantages of the Boundary, the vast Extent of Land, and the equitable Provision for the Payment of Debts and even the great Benefits stipulated for the Tories.

November 18. Monday [1782].
Returned Mr. Oswalds Visit. He says Mr. Stratchey who sat out the 5 did not reach London untill the 10. . . . Couriers are 3, 4, or 5 days in going according as the Winds are.

Richard Oswald

We went over the old ground, concerning the Tories. He began to use Arguments with me to relax. I told him he must not think of that, but must bend all his Thoughts to convince and perswade his Court to give it up. That if the Terms now before his Court, were not accepted, the whole negotiation would be broken off, and this Court would probably be so angry with Mr. Jay and me, that they would set their Engines to work upon Congress, get us recalled and some others sent, who would do exactly as this Court would have them. He said, he thought that very probable. . . .

In another Part of his Conversation He said We should all have Gold Snuff Boxes set with Diamonds. You will certainly have the Picture. I told him no. I had dealt too freely with this Court. I had not concealed from them any usefull and necessary Truth, although it was disagreable. Indeed I neither expected nor desired any favours from them nor would I accept any. I should not refuse any customary Compliment of that Sort, but it never had been nor would be offered me. . . . My fixed Principle never to be the Tool, of any Man, nor the Partisan of any Nation, would forever exclude me from the Smiles and favours of Courts.

In another Part of the Conversation, I said that when I was young and addicted to reading I had heard about dancing on the Points of metaphisical Needles. But by mixing in the World, I had found the Points of political Needles finer and sharper than the metaphisical ones. . . .

You are afraid says Mr. Oswald to day of being made the Tools of the Powers of Europe.—Indeed I am says I.—What Powers says he.—All of them says I. It is obvious that all the Powers of Europe will be continually maneuvring with Us, to work us into their real or imaginary Ballances of Power. They will all wish to make of Us a Make Weight Candle, when they are weighing out their Pounds. Indeed it is not surprizing for We shall very often if not always be able to turn the Scale. But I think it ought to be our Rule not to meddle, and that of all the Powers of Europe not to desire Us, or perhaps even to permit Us to interfere, if they can help it.

I beg of you, says he, to get out of your head the Idea that We shall disturb you.—What says I, do you yourself believe that your Ministers, Governors and even Nation will not wish to get Us of your Side in any future War?

—Damn the Governors says he. No. We will take off their Heads if they do an improper thing towards you.

Thank you for your good Will says I, which I feel to be sincere. But Nations dont feel as you and I do, and your nation when it gets a little refreshed from the fatigues of the War, when Men and Money are become plenty and Allies at hand, will not feel as it does now. —We never can be such damned Sots says he as to think of differing again with you. —Why says I, in truth I have never been able to comprehend the Reason why you ever thought of differing with Us.

The final phase of the negotiations began on November 25, 1782, when the British commissioners indicated that the only unsettled issues were the fisheries and compensation to the Loyalists. John Adams carried the argument over the fisheries, and Franklin made an eloquent counterclaim on behalf of all those who had suffered at the hands of the British, which caused the British to yield their point on compensation.

1782 November 25. Monday.
Dr. F., Mr. J. and myself at 11. met at Mr. Oswalds Lodgings.

Mr. Stratchey told Us, he had been to London and waited personally on every one of the Kings Cabinet Council, and had communicated the last Propositions to them. They every one of them, unanimously condemned that respecting the Tories, so that that unhappy Affair stuck as he foresaw and foretold that it would.

The Affair of the Fishery too was somewhat altered. They could not admit Us to dry, on the Shores of Nova Scotia, nor to fish within three Leagues of the Coast, nor within fifteen Leagues of the Coast of Cape Breton.

The Boundary they did not approve. They thought it too extended, too vast a Country, but they would not make a difficulty.

That if these Terms were not admitted, the whole Affair must be thrown into Parliament, where every Man would be for insisting on Restitution, to the Refugees.

He talked about excepting a few by Name of the most obnoxious of the Refugees.

I could not help observing that the Ideas respecting the Fishery appeared to me to come piping hot from Versailles. I quoted to them the Words of our

Treaty with France, in which the indefinite and exclusive Right, to the Fishery on the Western Side of Newfoundland, was secured against Us, According to the true Construction of the Treaties of Utrecht and Paris. I shewed them the 12 and 13 Articles of the Treaty of Utrecht, by which the French were admitted to Fish from Cape Bona Vista to Cape Rich.

I related to them the manner in which the Cod and Haddock come into the Rivers, Harbours, Creeks, and up to the very Wharfs on all the northern Coast of America, in the Spring in the month of April, so that you have nothing to do, but step into a Boat, and bring in a parcel of Fish in a few Hours. But that in May, they begin to withdraw. We have a saying at Boston that when the Blossoms fall the Haddock begin to crawl, i.e. to move out into deep Water, so that in Summer you must go out some distance to fish. At Newfoundland it was the same. The fish in March or April, were inshore, in all the Creeks, Bays, and Harbours, i.e. within 3 Leagues of the Coasts or Shores of Newfoundland and Nova Scotia. That neither French nor English could go from Europe and arrive early enough for the first Fare. That our Vessells could, being so much nearer, an Advantage which God and Nature had put into our hands. But that this Advantage of ours, had ever been an Advantage to England, because our fish had been sold in Spain and Portugal for Gold and Silver, and that Gold and Silver sent to London for Manufactures. That this would be the Course again. That France foresaw it, and wished to deprive England of it, by perswading her, to deprive Us of it. That it would be a Master Stroke of Policy, if She could succeed, but England must be compleatly the Dupe, before She could succeed....

Mr. Jay desired to know, whether Mr. Oswald had now Power to conclude and sign with us?

Stratchey said he had absolutely.

Mr. Jay desired to know if the Propositions now delivered Us were their Ultimatum. Stratchey seemed loth to answer, but at last said No. — We agreed these were good Signs of Sincerity.

1782 November 29. Fryday.

Met Mr. Fitsherbert, Mr. Oswald, Mr. Franklin, Mr. Jay, Mr. Laurens and Mr. Stratchey at Mr. Jays, Hotel D'Orleans, and spent the whole Day in Discussions about the Fishery and the Tories. I proposed a new Article concerning the Fishery. It was discussed and turned in every Light, and multitudes of Amendments proposed on each Side, and at last the Article drawn as it was finally agreed to. The other English Gentlemen being withdrawn upon some Occasion, I asked Mr. Oswald if he could consent to leave out the Limitation of 3 Leagues from all their Shores and the 15 from those of Louisbourg. He said in his own Opinion he was for it, but his Instructions were such, that he could not do it. I perceived by this, and by several Incidents and little Circumstances before, which I had remarked to my Colleagues, who were much of the same opinion, that Mr. Oswald had an Instruction, not to settle the Articles of the Fishery and Refugees, without the Concurrence of Mr. Fitsherbert and Mr. Stratchey.

Upon the Return of the other Gentlemen, Mr. Stratchey proposed to leave out the Word Right of Fishing and make it Liberty. Mr. Fitsherbert said the Word Right was an obnoxious Expression.

Upon this I rose up and said, Gentlemen, is there or can there be a clearer Right? In former Treaties, that of Utrecht and that of Paris, France and England have claimed the Right and used the Word. When God Almighty made the Banks of Newfoundland at 300 Leagues Distance from the People of America and at 600 Leagues distance from those of France and England, did he not give as good a Right to the former as to the latter. If Heaven in the Creation gave a Right, it is ours at least as much as yours. If Occupation, Use, and Possession give a Right, We have it as clearly as you. If War and Blood and Treasure give a Right, ours is as good as yours. We have been constantly fighting in Canada, Cape Breton and Nova Scotia for the Defense of this Fishery, and have expended beyond all Proportion more than you. If then the Right cannot be denied, Why should it not be acknowledged? and put out of Dispute? Why should We leave Room for illiterate Fishermen to wrangle and chicane?

Mr. Fitsherbert said, the Argument is in your Favour. I must confess your Reasons appear to be good, but Mr. Oswalds Instructions were such that he did not see how he could agree with Us. And for my Part, I have not the Honour and Felicity, to be a Man of that Weight and Authority, in my Country, that you Gentlemen are in yours (this was very genteelly said), I have the Accidental

Eighteenth-century map illustrating Adams's discussions of the problems of American rights as to fisheries

Broadside, declaring the
cessation of arms signed in Paris

Advantage of a little favour with the present Minister, but I cannot depend upon the Influence of my own Opinion to reconcile a Measure to my Countrymen. We can consider our selves as little more than Pens in the hands of Government at home, and Mr. Oswalds Instructions are so particular.

I replied to this, The Time is not so pressing upon Us, but that We can wait, till a Courier goes to London, with your Representations upon this Subject and others that remain between Us, and I think the Ministers must be convinced.

Mr. Fitsherbert said, to send again to London and have all laid loose before Parliament was so uncertain a Measure—it was going to Sea again.

Upon this Dr. Franklin said, that if another Messenger was to be sent to London, he ought to carry Something more respecting a Compensation to the Sufferers in America. He produced a Paper from his Pocket, in which he had drawn up a claim, and He said the first Principle of the Treaty was Equality and Reciprocity. Now they demanded of Us Payment of Debts and Restitution or Compensation to the Refugees. If a Draper had sold a Piece of Cloth to a Man upon Credit and then sent a servant to take it from him by Force, and after bring his Action for the Debt, would any Court of Law or Equity give him his Demand, without obliging him to restore the Cloth? Then he stated the carrying off of Goods from Boston, Philadelphia, and the Carolinas, Georgia, Virginia &c. and the burning of the Towns, &c. and desired that this might be sent with the rest.

Upon this I recounted the History of G[eneral] Gages Agreement with the Inhabitants of Boston, that they should remove with their Effects upon Condition, that they would surrender their Arms. But as soon as the Arms were secured, the Goods were forbid to be carried out and were finally carried off in large Quantities to Hallifax.

Dr. Franklin mentioned the Case of Philadelphia, and the carrying off of Effects there, even his own Library.

Mr. Jay mentioned several other Things and Mr. Laurens added the Plunders in Carolina of Negroes, Plate &c.

After hearing all this, Mr. Fitsherbert, Mr. Oswald

and Mr. Stratchey, retired for some time, and returning Mr. Fitsherbert said that upon consulting together and weighing every Thing as maturely as possible, Mr. Stratchey and himself had determined to advise Mr. Oswald, to strike with Us, according to the Terms We had proposed as our Ultimatum respecting the Fishery and the Loyalists. — Accordingly We all sat down and read over the whole Treaty and corrected it and agreed to meet tomorrow at Mr. Oswalds House, to sign and seal the Treaties which the Secretaries were to copy fair in the mean time.

The preliminary articles of the peace treaty were duly signed, sealed, and delivered the next day, and copies were forwarded to the respective governments. During this period of further negotiation and waiting in Paris, John Adams received disturbing family news from Braintree. Abigail wrote in December, 1782, that a young Harvard graduate of the class of 1776, after having "dissipated two or 3 years of his Life and too much of his fortune" in the company of "the Gay and Fair . . . in a round of pleasure and amusement," had moved to Braintree where he hoped to establish himself in the practice of the law. The observant mother reported that he had ingratiated himself with daughter Abigail, then seventeen years old, and could not help "noticing the very particular attention and regard of this young gentleman towards her, and that it daily becomes more pleasing to her." Adams's first reaction to this news was distinctly hostile. (Although he subsequently became more conciliatory and even cordial toward Royall Tyler, the departure of mother and daughter for Europe in June, 1784, led to the end of the courtship and eventually to another marriage for the young Abigail.)

Paris Jan. 22. 1783

The Preliminaries of Peace and an Armistice, were Signed at Versailles on the 20 and on the 21. We went again to pay our Respects to the King and Royal Family upon the Occasion. Mr. Jay was gone upon a little Excursion to Normandie and Mr. Laurens was gone to Bath, both for their health, so that the signature was made by Mr. Franklin and me. I want an Excursion too.

Thus drops the Curtain upon this mighty Trajedy. It has unravelled itself happily for Us, — and Heaven be praised. Some of our dearest Interests have been Saved, thro many dangers. I have no News from my son, since the 8th december, when he was at Stockholm, but hope every hour to hear of his Arrival at the Hague.

Boylston family seal used by John Adams in signing treaty of peace

I hope to receive the Acceptance of my Resignation So as to come home in the Spring Ships.

I had written thus far when yours of 23 decr. was brought in. Its Contents have awakened all my sensibility, and shew in a stronger Light than ever the Necessity of my coming home. I confess I dont like the Subject at all. My Child is too young for such Thoughts, and I dont like your Word "Dissipation" at all. I dont know what it means. It may mean every Thing. There is not Modesty and Diffidence enough in the Traits you Send me. My Child is a Model, as you represent her and as I know her, and is not to be the Prize, I hope of any, even reformed Rake. A Lawyer would be my Choice, but it must be a Lawyer who spends his Midnights as well as Evenings at his Age over his Books not at any Ladys Fire Side. I should have thought you had seen enough to be more upon your Guard than to write Billets upon such a subject to such a youth. A Youth who has been giddy enough to Spend his Fortune or half his Fortune in Gaieties, is not the Youth for me, Let his Person, Family, Connections and Taste for Poetry be what they will. I am not looking out for a Poet, nor a Professor of *belle* Letters.

In the Name of all that is tender dont criticize Your Daughter for those qualities which are her greatest Glory her Reserve, and her Prudence which I am amazed to hear you call Want of Sensibility. The more Silent She is in Company, the better for me in exact Proportion and I would have this observed as a Rule by the Mother as well as the Daughter.

You know moreover or ought to know my utter Inability to do any Thing for my Children, and you know the long dependence of young Gentlemen of the most promising Talents and obstinate Industry, at the Bar. My Children will have nothing but their Liberty and the Right to catch Fish, on the Banks of Newfoundland. This is all the Fortune that I have been able to make for myself or them.

I know not however, enough of this subject to decide any Thing. Is he a Speaker at the Bar? If not he will never be any Thing. But above all I positively forbid, any connection between my Daughter and any Youth upon Earth, who does not totally eradicate every Taste for Gaiety and Expence. I never knew one who had it and indulged it, but what was made a Rascall by it, sooner or later.

This Youth has had a Brother in Europe, and a detestible Specimen he exhibited. Their Father had not all those nice sentiments which I wish, although an Honourable Man.

I think he and you have both advanced too fast, and I should advise both to retreat. Your Family as well as mine have had too much Cause to rue, the Qualities which by your own Account have been in him. And if they were ever in him they are not yet out.

This is too Serious a Subject to equivocate about. I dont like this method of courting Mothers. There is something too fantastical and affected in all this Business for me. It is not nature, modest virtuous noble nature. The Simplicity of Nature is the best Rule with me to judge of every Thing, in Love as well as State and War.

This is all between you and me.

I would give the World to be with you Tomorrow. But there is a vast Ocean. No Ennemies. But I have not yet Leave from my Masters. I dont love to go home in a Miff, Pet or Passion, nor with an ill Grace, but I hope Soon to have leave. I can never Stay in Holland, the Air of that Country chills every drop of Blood in my Veins. If I were to stay in Europe another Year I would insist upon your coming with your daughter but this is not to be and I will come home to you.

Adieu ah ah Adieu.

Seal that Adams had engraved in 1783 to commemorate his victory in having secured rights to fisheries and the western boundary

It was to be many months, however, before the definitive peace treaty was signed in Paris on September 3, 1783. Progress was delayed not only by the distances involved but also by the resignation of Lord Shelburne as prime minister (who was censured by the House of Commons for having granted too many concessions to the Americans) and by the refusal of the Duke of Portland's new ministry to allow reciprocal trading privileges to the United States. Owing to these difficulties it was decided to ratify the preliminary articles as the definitive treaty. Shortly after the treaty was signed Adams fell sick. As he noted in his *Diary*, he was attended to by John Jay's brother James, who was a physician.

Paris Septr. 14 [–October 6,] 1783.

Mr. Thaxter took his Leave of me to return to America, with the definitive Treaty of Peace and the original Treaty with the States General.—I had been some days unwell, but soon fell down in a Fever. Sir James Jay, who was my Physician, gave me a vomit, &c. &c.

On the 22d of September, I removed from the grand Hotel du Roi, to Mr. Barclays at Auteuil, where I have continued to this Sixth day of October 1783.

Mr. Thaxter sailed in the Packet, from L'Orient, or rather from the Island of Groa [Groix], on the 26 of Septr. with a good Wind.

At first I rode twice a day in my Carriage, in the Bois de Boulogne: but afterwards I borrowed Mr. Jays Horse, and have generally ridden twice a day, untill I have made my self Master of this curious Forest.

This period had also been full of useful diplomatic experiences and developments, which helped to ripen John Adams into the man who was destined to lead the United States through difficult years. Writing to Secretary of Foreign Affairs Robert Livingston early in 1783, Adams disclosed some of what he had learned.

Paris, 23 January, 1783.

The true designs of a minister of state are not difficult to penetrate by an honest man of common sense, who is in a position to know anything of the secret of affairs, and to observe constantly the chain of public events; for whatever ostensible appearances may be put on, whatever obliquities may be imagined, however the web may be woven, or the thread double and twisted, enough will be seen to unravel the whole....

I have lived long enough, and had experience enough of the conduct of governments and people, nations and courts, to be convinced that gratitude, friendship, unsuspecting confidence, and all the most amiable passions of human nature, are the most dangerous guides in politics.

Advised by his friends in the fall of 1783 to drink the waters of Bath and to bathe in them for his health, John Adams set out to do some sight-seeing on the way, stopping in London with his son, John Quincy, who had returned from Russia during the summer. Years later he sent to the *Boston Patriot* an entertaining account of this visit to England and how it was interrupted by the imperious necessity of rescuing the credit of the United States in Amsterdam that winter.

Quincy, 17 Feb. 1812

Curiosity prompted me to trot about London as fast as

good horses in a decent carriage could carry me. [On November 15] I was introduced by Mr. Hartley, on a merely ceremonious visit, to the Duke of Portland, Mr. [Edmund] Burke, and Mr. [Charles James] Fox; but finding nothing but ceremony there, I did not ask favours or receive any thing but cold formalities from ministers of state or ambassadors. I found that our American painters had more influence at court to procure all the favors I wanted, than all of them. Mr. [Benjamin] West asked of their majesties permission to shew me and Mr. Jay, the originals of the great productions of his pencil, such as Wolf, Bayard, Epaminondas, Regulus, &c. &c. &c. which were all displayed in the Queen's Palace, called Buckingham House. The gracious answer of the king and queen was, that he might shew us "the whole house." Accordingly, in the absence of the royal family at Windsor, we had [on November 8] an opportunity at leisure, to see all the apartments, even to the queen's bedchamber, with all its furniture, even to her majesty's German bible, which attracted my attention as much as any thing else. The king's library struck me with admiration; I wished for a weeks time, but had but a few hours. The books were in perfect order, elegant in their editions, paper, binding, &c. but gaudy and extrava[ga]nt in nothing. They were chosen with perfect taste and judgment; every book that a king ought to have always at hand, and as far as I could examine, and could be supposed capable of judging, none other. Maps, charts, &c. of all his dominions in the four quarters of the world, and models of every fortress in his empire.

American painter Benjamin West got Adams permission from the king and queen to inspect Buckingham House.

In every apartment of the whole house, the same taste, the same judgment, the same elegance, the same simplicity, without the smallest affectation, ostentation, profusion or meanness. I could not but compare it, in my own mind, with Versailles, and not at all to the advantage of the latter. I could not help comparing it with many of the gentlemen's seats which I had seen in France, England, and even Holland. The interior of this palace was perfect; the exterior, both in extent, cost and appearance, was far inferior not only to Versailles, and the seats of the princes in France, but to the country houses of many of the nobility and gentry of Great Britain. The truth is, a minister can at any time obtain

313

Detail of Copley's painting of his family (Copley himself at top) and his calling card in London (below)

from parliament an hundred millions to support any war, just or unjust, in which he chooses to involve the nation, much more easily than he can procure one million for the decent accommodation of the court. We gazed at the great original paintings of our immortal countryman, West, with more delight than on the very celebrated pieces of Vandyke and Reubens; and with admiration not less than that inspired by the cartoons of Raphaeel.

Mr. Copely [John Singleton Copley], another of my countrymen, with whom I had been much longer acquainted, and who had obtained without so much royal protection, a reputation not less glorious; and that by studies and labours not less masterly in his art, procured me, and that from the great Lord Mansfield, a place in the house of lords, to hear the king's speech at the opening of parliament [on November 11], and to witness the introduction of the Prince of Wales, then arrived at the age of twenty one. One circumstance, a striking example of the vicissitudes of life, and the whimsical antithesis of politics, is too precious for its moral, to be forgotten. Standing in the lobby of the house of lords, surrounded by a hundred of the first people of the kingdom, Sir Francis Molineux, the gentlemen usher of the black rod, appeared suddenly in the room with his long staff, and roared out with a very loud voice—"*Where is Mr. Adams, Lord Mansfield's friend!*" I frankly avowed myself Lord Mansfield's friend, and was politely conducted by Sir Francis to my place. A gentleman said to me the next day, "how short a time has passed, since I heard that same Lord Mansfield say in that same house of lords, "My Lords, if you do not kill him, he will kill you." Mr. West said to me, that this was one of the finest finishings in the picture of American Independence.

Pope had given me, when a boy, an affection for Murray [Lord Mansfield's family name]. When in the study and practice of the law, my admiration of the learning, talents and eloquence of Mansfield had been constantly increasing, though some of his opinions I could not approve. His politics in American affairs I had always detested.—But now I found more politeness and good humor in him than in Richmond, Cambden, Burke or Fox.

If my business had been travels I might write a book. But I must be as brief as possible.

I visited Sir Ashton Lever's museum [on November 4], where was a wonderful collection of natural and artificial curiosities from all parts and quarters of the globe. Here I saw again that collection of American birds, insects and other rarities, which I had so often seen before at Norwalk, in Connecticut, collected and preserved by Mr. Arnold, and sold by him to Governor Tryon for Sir Ashton. Here also I saw Sir Ashton and some other knights, his friends, practising the ancient but as I thought long forgotten art of archery. In his garden, with their bows and arrows, they hit as small a mark and at as great a distance as any of our sharpshooters could have done with their rifles.

I visited also Mr. Wedgwood's manufactory, and was not less delighted with the elegance of his substitute for porcelain, than with his rich collection of utensils and furniture from the ruins of Herculaneum, bearing incontestible evidence in their forms and figures of the taste of the Greeks, a nation that seems to have existed for the purpose of teaching the arts and furnishing models to all mankind of grace and beauty, in the mechanic arts no less than in statuary, architecture, history, oratory and poetry.

The manufactory of cut glass, to which some gentlemen introduced me, did as much honor to the English as the mirrors, the seve [Sèvres] China, or the gobeline tapestry of France. It seemed to be the art of transmitting glass into diamonds.

Westminster Abbey, St. Pauls, the Exchange and other public buildings, did not escape my attention. . . .

I went to Windsor and saw the castle and its apartments, and enjoyed its vast prospect. I was anxiously shewn the boasted chambers where Count Tallard, the captive of the Duke of Marlborough, had been confined. I visited the terrace and the environs, and what is of more importance I visited the Eaton school; and if I had been prudent enough to negotiate with my friend West, I doubt not I might have obtained permission to see the queen's lodge. But as the solicitation of these little favors requires a great deal of delicacy and many prudent precautions, I did not think it proper to ask the favor of any body. I must confess that all

Josiah Wedgwood, whose "manufactory" delighted Adams during his visit in 1783

*Windsor Castle, where John Adams
"enjoyed its vast prospect"*

*View of Bath in the eighteenth
century, where Adams went for health*

the pomps and pride of Windsor did not occupy my thoughts so much as the forest, and comparing it with what I remembered of Pope's Windsor forest.

My health was very little improved by the exercise I had taken in and about London; nor did the entertainments and delights assist me much more. The change of air and of diet from which I had entertained some hopes, had produced little effect. I continued feeble, low and drooping. The waters of Bath were still represented to me as an almost certain resource. I shall take no notice of men nor things on the road. I had not been twenty minutes at the hotel in Bath [December 24] before my ancient friend and relation, Mr. John Boylston called upon me and dined with me. After dinner he was polite enough to walk with me, about the town, shewed me the crescent, the public buildings, the card rooms, the assembly rooms, the dancing rooms, &c. objects about which I had little more curiosity than about the bricks and pavements. The baths and the accommodations for using the waters were reserved for another day. But before that day arrived, I received dispatches from America, from London, and from Amsterdam, informing me that the drafts of congress by Mr. Morris, for money to be transmitted, in silver, through the house of Le Couteux, at Paris, and through the Havana to Philadelphia; together with the bills drawn in favor of individuals in France, England and Holland, had exhausted all my loan of the last summer which had cost me so much fatigue and ill health; and that an immense flock of new bills had arrived, drawn in favour of Sir George Baring, or Sir Francis Baring, I forget which, of London, and many other persons; that these bills had been already presented, and protested for non-acceptance; and that they must be protested in their time for non-payment, unless I returned immediately to Amsterdam, and could be fortunate enough to obtain a new loan, of which my bankers gave me very faint hopes. It was winter; my health was very delicate, a journey and voyage to Holland at that season would very probably put an end to my labours. I scarcely saw a possibility of surviving it. Nevertheless no man knows what he can bear till he tries. A few moments reflection determined me, for although I had little hope of getting the money, having experienced so many difficulties before, yet making the attempt and doing all in my power would discharge my own conscience, and ought to satisfy my responsibility to the public. I returned to London [December 28], and from thence repaired to Harwich [January 3, 1784]. Here we found the packet detained by contrary winds and a violent storm. For three days detained, in a very uncomfortable inn, ill accommodated and worse provided, myself and my son, without society and without books, wore away three days of ennui, not a little chagrined with the unexpected interruption of our visit to England, and the disappointment of our journey to Bath; and not less anxious on account of our gloomy prospects for the future.

On Adams's return trip to Holland, he traveled in a cart such as this.

[After an arduous journey, first on stormy seas and then overland across Holland's bleak winter countryside, John Adams, sick and weary, arrived at The Hague on January 12.]

Here I was at home in the Hotel Des Etats Unis, but could not indulge myself. My duty lay at Amsterdam among undertakers and brokers, with very faint hopes of success. I was however successful beyond my most sanguine expectations, and obtained a loan of millions, enough to prevent all the bills of congress from being protested for non-payment and to preserve our credit in Europe for two or three years longer, after which another desperate draft of bills from congress obliged me once more to go over from England to Holland to borrow money. I succeeded also in that which preserved our credit till my return to America, in 1788, and till the new government came into operation and found itself rich enough.

In May, 1784, Congress reorganized the foreign service. John Jay was appointed Secretary of Foreign Affairs to replace Robert Livingston, and Thomas Jefferson was commissioned, together with Franklin and Adams, to negotiate commercial treaties with twenty-odd European states as well as the Barbary States of North Africa. Determined to join her husband if he were to remain abroad any longer, Abigail Adams now brought her nineteen-year-old daughter Abigail to London in July, 1784, where they were joined by John Quincy, now seventeen years old. A week later John Adams, detained in Holland on business, was reunited with his family. His daughter excitedly described the meeting at the time in her own diary.

London, Aug. 7th, 1784.
At 12, returned to our own apartments; when I entered, I saw upon the table a hat with two books in it; every thing around appeared altered, without my knowing in what particular. I went into my own room, the things were moved; I looked around—"Has mamma received letters that have determined her departure?—When does she go?—Why are these things moved?" All in a breath to Esther. "No ma'm, she has received no letter, but goes tomorrow morning." "Why is all this appearance of strangeness?—Whose hat is that in the other room?—Whose trunk is this?—Whose sword and cane?—It is my father's" said I. "Where is he?" "In the room above." Up I flew, and to his chamber, where he was lying down, he raised himself upon my knocking softly at the door, and received me with all the tenderness of an affectionate parent after so long an absence. Sure I am, I never felt more agitation of spirits in my life; it will not do to describe.

John Adams's daughter Abigail, engraving after a Copley portrait

The Adams family immediately repaired to France where they lived for the next eight months in Auteuil. In the spring of 1785, John Adams learned that he had been appointed first American Minister to the Court of St. James's and that Jefferson had been commissioned to succeed Franklin at the Court of Versailles. When Adams heard that during the debate over his appointment his opponents in Congress had accused him of being vain, he wrote a remarkable discourse on vanity in a letter to his informant, Elbridge Gerry. Although the letter was probably never sent, Adams's keen analysis of the "weak Passion," to which he knew he was susceptible, shows his sensitiveness to the criticisms directed against him.

Auteuil near Paris May 2. 1785
The Imputation of a weak Passion has made so much Impression upon me, that it may not be improper to say a little more about it, even although I should convert you, more and more to the opinion of those who think the public Interest in danger from it. The Truth should come out, and if the danger is real the Remedy is easily applied.

According to all that I have read of Morals or seen of Manners, there are, in Mankind various kinds of

Vanity. And every gradation of the Passions, and every shade of their various opperations on the good or Evil of Society should be Studied by you the Statesmen who are forming a new World.

There is a Vanity whose object is Show. . . .

There is another Sort of Vanity, real Vanity, as much as . . . the other Sort, but certainly less pernicious. It is, on the contrary, although a Weakness and, if you will a Vice, a real Proof of a valuable Character. It is even a Vanity which arises from the Testimony of a good Conscience. When a Man is conscious of Services and Exertions, from the purest Principles of Virtue & Benevolence and looks back on a course of Years, Spent in the Service of other Men, without Attention to himself, when he recollects Sacrifices, Sufferings and dangers, which have fallen in his Way, and Sees himself preserved through all and his labours crown'd with transcendant Success there arises a Satisfaction, and sometimes a Transport which he must be very wise indeed, if he can at all times conceal. I say more it is Hypocricy oftener than Wisdom that pretends to conceal it. If I were to say that I have felt this Consciousness, and experienced this Joy, I should be chargeable with Vanity, although you and every Man who knows me, must know it to be true, and that it is impossible it should be otherwise. —If at Sometimes I have betrayed in Word or Writing such a Sentiment, I have only to say in excuse for it that I am not an Hypocrite, nor a cunning Man, nor at all times wise, and that altho I may be more cautious for the future, I will never be so merely to obtain the Reputation of a cunning Politician a Character I neither admire nor esteem. I have seen So much of it, between the Years 1755 and the Years 1785, as to give me a thorough disgust to it. . . . I should be more vain than I am if I pretended to be at all times destitute of Vanity. —I never yet saw nor do I expect to see a Man without it. I never knew but one Man who pretended to be wholly free from it, or whom any body thought to be so and him I know to be in his heart the vainest Man, and the falsest Character I have ever met with in life. The Pretension to have none of it is affectation and gross Hypocrisy. And depend upon it, the Man who makes so much Pretension to it and takes so much cunning Pains to conceal at all times his Feelings, has

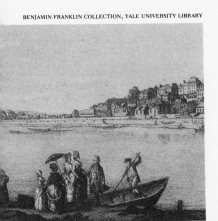

View of Auteuil (left) and Passy when Adams family lived there, 1785

319

His Excellency JOHN ADAMS.

English engraving of Adams, which appeared in European Magazine, *1783*

artful designs to carry, and infinitely more sordid Passions to gratify, Avarice Envy, Jealousy, Ambition or Revenge.

After all, with real Esteem and affection for the worthy gentlemen who were put in Competition with me, I confess to you, it would mortify me extreamly, if I thought one Member of Congress really believed, I had a larger Proportion of the weak Passion, than either of them. Surely he must be a young Member who never Satt in Congress with us.

But the Gentlemen think that a public Minister "ought never to have the weak Passion." In this I agree with them. — It is always an Imperfection, a Weakness, a Fault and if you will a vice: but do they expect to find a Minister without a fault, and is not a weak Passion universally a Smaller Fault, than a Strong one? Is not even Pride more dangerous than Vanity, as are not Avarice, & Ambition, more pernicious than both? Is not even Craft, Cunning, Intrigue, much worse than the weak Passion?

Although it is a Fault and a Scrurvy Folly which I dispize and disdain, whatever they may think of me, and even although I may have been guilty of it, We must however yeild so far to the Truth as to confess, that the greatest Men and the greatest Ministers who ever existed have sometimes been horribly infected with it. . . .

Gentlemen would do well to know a little more of the World and of the real Characters of Ministers and Negotiators, before they lay it down for a Rule that no Man is to be voted for as a Minister who has the weak Passion least they should exclude, the wisest, the most virtuous and benevolent, the ablest and most dissinterested, the most indefatigable and successfull Ministers, that nature produces for their choice. . . .

These Criticisms smell, as rank as the Ripeness of a Rabits tail, of french Politiks. . . .

When a Man is hurt he loves to talk of his Wound, and I knew of no other way to account for this very Letter, which you see is intended only for you, and as it is not worth copying cannot be made shorter.

John Quincy was packed off to Harvard College in May, 1784, on board a French packet carrying a gift sent from Lafayette to Washington of seven dogs, which the young man was charged to see were well fed. The Adams family then established their residence in London. Shortly afterward, John Adams sent an account of his reception by King George III to John Jay, the new Secretary of Foreign Affairs in Philadelphia.

Bath Hotel, Westminster, 2 June, 1785.

Dear Sir,—During my interview with the Marquis of Carmarthen [Foreign Secretary], he told me that it was customary for every foreign minister, at his first presentation to the King, to make his Majesty some compliments conformable to the spirit of his letter of credence; and when Sir Clement Cottrell Dormer, the master of the ceremonies, came to inform me that he should accompany me to the secretary of state and to Court, he said that every foreign minister whom he had attended to the Queen had always made a harangue to her Majesty, and he understood, though he had not been present, that they always harangued the King.

On Tuesday evening, the Baron de Lynden called upon me, and said he came from the Baron de Nolken, and they had been conversing upon the singular situation I was in, and they agreed in opinion that it was indispensable that I should make a speech, and that that speech should be as complimentary as possible. All this was conformable to the advice lately given by the Count de Vergennes to Mr. Jefferson; so that, finding it was a custom established at both these great Courts, and that this Court and the foreign ministers expected it, I thought I could not avoid it, although my first thought and inclination had been to deliver my credentials silently and retire.

At one, on Wednesday, the master of ceremonies called at my house, and went with me to the secretary of state's office, in Cleveland Row, where the Marquis of Carmarthen received me, and introduced me to his undersecretary, Mr. Fraser, who has been, as his Lordship told me, uninterruptedly in that office, through all the changes in administration for thirty years, having first been appointed by the Earl of Holderness. After a short conversation upon the subject of importing my effects from Holland and France free of duty, which Mr. Fraser himself introduced, Lord Carmarthen invited me to go with him in his coach to Court. When we arrived in the antechamber, the *œil de bœuf* of

View of Customs House and Tower of London from the river Thames

St. James's, the master of the ceremonies met me and attended me, while the secretary of state went to take the commands of the King. While I stood in this place, where it seems all ministers stand upon such occasions, always attended by the master of ceremonies, the room very full of ministers of state, lords, and bishops, and all sorts of courtiers, as well as the next room, which is the King's bedchamber, you may well suppose I was the focus of all eyes. I was relieved, however, from the embarrassment of it by the Swedish and Dutch ministers, who came to me, and entertained me in a very agreeable conversation during the whole time. Some other gentlemen, whom I had seen before, came to make their compliments too, until the Marquis of Carmarthen returned and desired me to go with him to his Majesty. I went with his Lordship through the levee room into the King's closet. The door was shut, and I was left with his Majesty and the secretary of state alone. I made the three reverences,—one at the door, another about half way, and a third before the presence, —according to the usage established at this and all the northern Courts of Europe, and then addressed myself to his Majesty in the following words:—

"Sir,—The United States of America have appointed me their minister plenipotentiary to your Majesty, and have directed me to deliver to your Majesty this letter which contains the evidence of it. It is in obedience to their express commands, that I have the honor to assure your Majesty of their unanimous disposition and desire to cultivate the most friendly and liberal intercourse between your Majesty's subjects and their citizens, and of their best wishes for your Majesty's health and happiness, and for that of your royal family. The appointment of a minister from the United States to your Majesty's Court will form an epoch in the history of England and of America. I think myself more fortunate than all my fellow-citizens, in having the distinguished honor to be the first to stand in your Majesty's royal presence in a diplomatic character; and I shall esteem myself the happiest of men, if I can be instrumental in recommending my country more and more to your Majesty's royal benevolence, and of restoring an entire esteem, confidence, and affection, or, in better words, the old good nature and the old

The Marquis of Carmarthen

Copies, in John Adams's writing, of his remarks to King George (top) and the monarch's reply to him

good humor between people, who, though separated by an ocean, and under different governments, have the same language, a similar religion, and kindred blood.

"I beg your Majesty's permission to add, that, although I have some time before been intrusted by my country, it was never in my whole life in a manner so agreeable to myself."

The King listened to every word I said, with dignity, but with an apparent emotion. Whether it was the nature of the interview, or whether it was my visible agitation, for I felt more than I did or could express, that touched him, I cannot say. But he was much affected, and answered me with more tremor than I had spoken with, and said:—

"Sir,—The circumstances of this audience are so extraordinary, the language you have now held is so extremely Proper, and the feelings you have discovered so justly adapted to the occasion, that I must say that I not only receive with pleasure the assurance of the friendly dispositions of the United States, but that I am very glad the choice has fallen upon you to be their minister. I wish you, sir, to believe, and that it may be understood in America, that I have done nothing in the late contest but what I thought myself indispensably bound to do, by the duty which I owed to my people. I will be very frank with you. I was the last to consent to the separation; but the separation having been made, and having become inevitable, I have always said, as I say now, that I would be the first to meet the friendship of the United States as an independent power. The moment I see such sentiments and language as yours prevail, and a disposition to give this country the preference, that moment I shall say, let the circumstances of language, religion, and blood have their natural and full effect."

I dare not say that these were the King's precise words, and it is even possible, that I may have in some particular mistaken his meaning; for, although his pronunciation is as distinct as I ever heard, he hesitated some time between his periods, and between the members of the same period. He was indeed much affected, and I confess I was not less so....

The King then asked me whether I came last from France, and upon my answering in the affirmative, he

323

put on an air of familiarity, and, smiling, or rather laughing, said, "there is an opinion among some people that you are not the most attached of all your countrymen to the manners of France." I was surprised at this, because I thought it an indiscretion and a departure from the dignity. I was a little embarrassed, but determined not to deny the truth on one hand, nor leave him to infer from it any attachment to England on the other. I threw off as much gravity as I could, and assumed an air of gayety and a tone of decision as far as was decent, and said, "that opinion, sir, is not mistaken; I must avow to your Majesty, I have no attachment but to my own country." The King replied, as quick as lightning, "an honest man will never have any other."

The King then said a word or two to the secretary of state, which, being between them, I did not hear, and then turned around and bowed to me, as is customary with all kings and princes when they give the signal to retire. I retreated, stepping backward, as is the etiquette, and making my last reverence at the door of the chamber, I went my way. The master of the ceremonies joined me the moment of my coming out of the King's closet, and accompanied me through the apartments down to my carriage, several stages of servants, gentlemen-porters and under-porters, roaring out like thunder, as I went along, "Mr. Adams's servants, Mr. Adams's carriage, &c.". . .

There are a train of other ceremonies yet to go through, in presentations to the Queen, and visits to and from ministers and ambassadors, which will take up much time, and interrupt me in my endeavors to obtain all that I have at heart,—the objects of my instructions. It is thus the essence of things is lost in ceremony in every country of Europe. We must submit to what we cannot alter. Patience is the only remedy.

St. James's Square, London

Patience was not enough to achieve the object of John Adams's instructions as American Minister in London. The resolution of such questions as the British evacuation of the western outposts and the settlement of American debts to British creditors had to wait until 1794, when John Jay successfully negotiated a separate treaty with Great Britain, settling outstanding differences that threatened a resumption of hostilities between the two countries. Nor did John Adams have conspicuous success negotiating with the piratical Barbary States, to whom the United States continued to pay tribute well into the nineteenth century. Adams reported to Jefferson on the occasion of an attempt he made to negotiate with the ambassador of one of these states.

Grosvenor Square Feb. 17. 1786.

I was sometime in doubt, whether any Notice Should be taken of the Tripoline Ambassador; but receiving Information that he made Enquiries about me, and expressed a Surprise that when the other foreign Ministers had visited him, the American had not; and finding that He was a universal and perpetual Ambassador, it was thought best to call upon him. Last Evening, in making a Tour of other Visits, I Stopped at his Door, intending only to leave a Card, but the Ambassador was announced at Home and ready to receive me. I was received in State. Two great Chairs before the Fire, one of which was destined for me, the other for his Excellency. Two Secretaries of Legation, men of no Small Consequence Standing Upright in the middle of the Room, without daring to Sitt, during the whole time I was there, and whether they are not yet upright upon their Legs I know not. Now commenced the Difficulty. His Excellency Speaks Scarcely a Word of any European Language, except Italian and Lingua Franca, in which, you know I have Small Pretensions. He began soon to ask me Questions about America and her Tobacco, and I was Surprized to find that with a pittance of Italian and a few French Words which he understands, We could so well understand each other. "We make Tobacco in Tripoli," said his Excellency "but it is too Strong. Your American Tobacco is better." By this Time, one of his secretaries or *upper servants* brought two Pipes ready filled and lighted. The longest was offered me; the other to his Excellency. It is long since I took a Pipe but as it would be unpardonable to be wanting in Politeness in so ceremonious an Interview, I took the Pipe with great Complacency, placed the Bowl upon the Carpet, for the Stem was fit for a Walking Cane, and I believe more than two Yards in length, and Smoaked in aweful Pomp, reciprocating Whiff for Whiff, with his Excellency, untill Coffee was brought in. His Excellency took a Cup, after I had taken one, and alternately Sipped at his Coffee and whiffed at

Engraving of George III from New London Magazine, *October, 1786*

Gilbert Stuart's portrait of John Adams's son-in-law, William S. Smith, married to Abigail in London in 1787

Governor John Hancock's letter to John Adams welcoming him home

his Tobacco, and I wished he would take a Pinch in turn from his Snuff box for Variety; and I followed the Example with Such Exactness and Solemnity that the two secretaries, appeared in Raptures and the superiour of them who speaks a few Words of French cryed out in Extacy, Monsieur votes [vous] etes un Turk—The necessary Civilities being thus compleated, His Excellency began upon Business; asked many Questions about America: the soil Climate Heat and Cold, etc. and said it was a very great Country. But "Tripoli is at War with it." I was "Sorry to hear that. Had not heard of any War with Tripoli. America had done no Injury to Tripoli, committed no Hostility; nor had Tripoli done America any Injury or committed any Hostility against her, that I had heard of." True said His Excellency "but there must be a Treaty of Peace. There could be no Peace without a Treaty. The Turks and Affricans were the souvereigns of the Mediterranean, and there could be no navigation there nor Peace without Treaties of Peace. America must treat as France and England did, and all other Powers. America must treat with Tripoli and then with Constantinople and then with Algiers and Morocco." Here a Secretary brought him some Papers, one of which a Full Power in French from the Pacha, Dey and Regency of Tripoli, as Ambassador, to treat with all the Powers of Europe, and to make what Treaties he pleased and to manage in short all the foreign Affairs of his Country, he delivered me to read. He was ready to treat and make Peace. If I would come tomorrow or next day, or any other day and bring an Interpreter, He would hear and propose Terms, and write to Tripoli and I might write to America, and each Party might accept or refuse them as they should think fit. How long would it be before one could write to Congress and have an Answer? Three months. This was rather too long but he should stay here sometime. When I had read his French Translation of his Full Power He Shewed me the original in his own Language. You perceive that his Excellency was more ready and eager to treat than I was as he probably expected to gain more by the Treaty. I could not see him Tomorrow or next day but would think of it.

I must now my dear sir beg of you to send me a Copy of the Project of a Treaty sent to Morocco by

Mr. Barclay and Mr. Lamb, as I had not time to take one, when it was here. You will please to write me your Thoughts and Advice upon this Occasion. This is a Sensible Man, well known to many of the foreign Ministers who have seen him before, in Sweeden, at Vienna, in Denmark etc. He has been so much in Europe that he knows as much of America, as anybody; so that nothing new will be suggested to him or his Constituents by our having Conferences with him. It seems best then to know his Demands. They will be higher I fear, than we can venture.

On June 11, 1786, the Bishop of St. Asaph married young Abigail Adams to Colonel William Stephens Smith, John Adams's Secretary of Legation, at the legation building in Grosvenor Square. In March, 1787, John Adams's first grandchild, William Steuben Smith, was born. This marriage was, unfortunately, destined to be short and less than happy. Meanwhile, John Adams, disheartened by the inability of the Congress to accomplish anything and convinced of the uselessness of his continued presence in London, wrote home for his recall in January, 1788. Still Minister to Holland and feeling obliged to take his formal leave, he traveled to The Hague in February where, as he wrote to Abigail, he found unexpected business waiting for him.

[March 6?, 1788]

[I] should have been in London at this hour if you had not...laid a Plott, which has brought me to this Town. —Mr. Jefferson at the Receipt of your Letter [of February 26, mentioning Adams's forthcoming trip to The Hague] come post to meet me, and he cutts out so much Business for me, to put the Money Matters of the United States upon a sure footing, that I certainly shall not be able to get into the Packet at Helvoet before Saturday....I thought myself dead, and that it was well with me, as a Public Man: but I think I shall be forced, after my decease, to open an additional Loan. At least this is Mr. Jeffersons opinion, and that of Mr. Vanstaphorst."

John and Abigail Adams, having left London for the United States on March 30, 1788, arrived in Massachusetts without incident on June 17, 1788, and were given a hearty welcome home by Governor John Hancock and the people of Boston.

Chapter 10

Heir Apparent

In 1789 the United States needed peace in order for its new constitutional government to start to function and to be accepted by the people. President George Washington's first administration — ably supported by John Adams as Vice President, Thomas Jefferson as Secretary of State, Alexander Hamilton as Secretary of the Treasury, and John Jay as Chief Justice of the Supreme Court — was remarkably successful in maintaining peace, building the new departments of government, and placing the country's finances on a sound basis. Washington's second term, from 1793 to 1797, was soon shadowed by the outbreak of general war in Europe, which menaced the country's defenses on land and sea. The Spanish, intent on keeping the Americans from expanding to the south and west, were manipulating the Indian tribes from Florida to the Mississippi. In the northwestern territories the British, who had never evacuated the western posts in accordance with the provisions of the Treaty of Paris of 1783, were stirring up the Six Nations against the settlers in those areas. France, at war with both Spain and England, attempted to use United States ports as bases for fitting out warships to fight its enemies on the high seas. Proclaiming a policy of strict neutrality, Washington managed to avoid war with both Great Britain and Spain. Jay's 1794 treaty with the British and Thomas Pinckney's 1795 treaty with the Spaniards left the increasingly dangerous French question to be dealt with by the President's successor.

Meantime, John Adams had found that his thoughts on government had changed in light of his own experience and that of his country. Late in 1786, while he was still living in London as ambassador to the Court of St. James's, he had commenced writing the most ambitious literary and political production of his life, the three-volume treatise on government called *A Defence of the Constitutions of Government of the United States of America.* The first volume of this work, published in London in January, 1787, reached Philadelphia during the Constitutional Convention. There, together with

Adams's earlier *Thoughts on Government* and his draft of the Massachusetts Constitution, the work played an important role in the framing of the new national constitution and earned Adams the right to be called the Father of American Political Science. Written with the intention of persuading Americans to guarantee their liberties by adhering to strong, clearly defined republican institutions, the treatise emphasized two fundamental principles that Adams felt must be strictly observed in all free republics if they were to endure. First, there must be a bicameral legislature incorporating checks and balances; and second, the executive, legislative, and judicial branches of government must be independent. In his preface to the first volume of the *Defence,* Adams traced the melancholy history of man's loss of liberty through his failure to ensure adequate governmental checks and balances as safeguards against the tyranny of an individual, the tyranny of the few, and the tyranny of the mob.

[January, 1787]

The arts and sciences, in general, during the three or four last centuries, have had a regular course of progressive improvement. The inventions in mechanic arts, the discoveries in natural philosophy, navigation, and commerce, and the advancement of civilization and humanity, have occasioned changes in the condition of the world, and the human character, which would have astonished the most refined nations of antiquity. A continuation of similar exertions is every day rendering Europe more and more like one community, or single family. Even in the theory and practice of government, in all the simple monarchies, considerable improvements have been made. The checks and balances of republican governments have been in some degree adopted at the courts of princes. By the erection of various tribunals, to register the laws, and exercise the judicial power—by indulging the petitions and remonstrances of subjects, until by habit they are regarded as rights—a control has been established over ministers of state, and the royal councils, which, in some degree, approaches the spirit of republics. Property is generally secure, and personal liberty seldom invaded. The press has great influence, even where it is not expressly tolerated; and the public opinion must be respected by a minister, or his place becomes insecure. Commerce begins to thrive; and if religious toleration were established, personal liberty a little more protected, by giving an absolute right to demand a public trial in a certain reasonable time, and the states were invested with a few more privileges, or rather restored to some

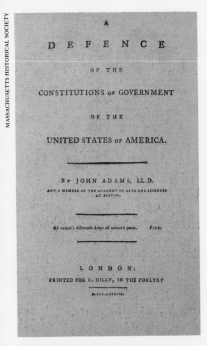

A

DEFENCE

OF THE

CONSTITUTIONS OF GOVERNMENT

OF THE

UNITED STATES OF AMERICA.

BY JOHN ADAMS, LL.D.

AND A MEMBER OF THE ACADEMY OF ARTS AND SCIENCES AT BOSTON.

All nature's difference keeps all nature's peace.   POPE

LONDON:

PRINTED FOR C. DILLY, IN THE POULTRY

M.DCC.LXXXVII.

Title page of Adams's ambitious three-volume treatise on government

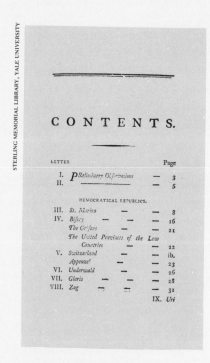

CONTENTS.

---

xxviii CONTENTS.

First two pages of the table of contents for Volume I of Adams's A Defence of the Constitutions . . .

that have been taken away, these governments would be brought to as great a degree of perfection, they would approach as near to the character of governments of laws and not of men, as their nature will probably admit of. . . .

While it would be rash to say, that nothing further can be done to bring a free government, in all its parts, still nearer to perfection, the representations of the people are most obviously susceptible of improvement. The end to be aimed at, in the formation of a representative assembly, seems to be the sense of the people, the public voice. The perfection of the portrait consists in its likeness. Numbers, or property, or both, should be the rule; and the proportions of electors and members an affair of calculation. The duration should not be so long that the deputy should have time to forget the opinions of his constituents. Corruption in elections is the great enemy of freedom. Among the provisions to prevent it, more frequent elections, and a more general privilege of voting, are not all that might be devised. Dividing the districts, diminishing the distance of travel, and confining the choice to residents, would be great advances towards the annihilation of corruption. The modern aristocracies of Holland, Venice, Bern, &c., have tempered themselves with innumerable checks, by which they have given a great degree of stability to that form of government; and though liberty and life can never be there enjoyed so well as in a free republic, none is perhaps more capable of profound sagacity. We shall learn to prize the checks and balances of a free government, and even those of the modern aristocracies, if we recollect the miseries of Greece, which arose from its ignorance of them. The only balance attempted against the ancient kings was a body of nobles; and the consequences were perpetual alternations of rebellion and tyranny, and the butchery of thousands upon every revolution from one to the other. When kings were abolished, aristocracies tyrannized; and then no balance was attempted but between aristocracy and democracy. This, in the nature of things, could be no balance at all, and therefore the pendulum was forever on the swing. . . .

Human nature is as incapable now of going through revolutions with temper and sobriety, with patience and prudence, or without fury and madness, as it was among the Greeks so long ago.... Without three orders, and an effectual balance between them, in every American constitution, it must be destined to frequent unavoidable revolutions; though they are delayed a few years, they must come in time. The United States are large and populous nations, in comparison with the Grecian commonwealths, or even the Swiss cantons; and they are growing every day more disproportionate, and therefore less capable of being held together by simple governments. Countries that increase in population so rapidly as the States of America did, even during such an impoverishing and destructive war as the last was, are not to be long bound with silken threads; lions, young or old, will not be bound by cobwebs. It would be better for America, it is nevertheless agreed, to ring all the changes with the whole set of bells, and go through all the revolutions of the Grecian states, rather than establish an absolute monarchy among them, notwithstanding all the great and real improvements which have been made in that kind of government.

The objection to it is not because it is supported by nobles, and a subordination of ranks; for all governments, even the most democratical, are supported by a subordination of offices, and of ranks too. None ever existed without it but in a state of anarchy and outrage, in a contempt of law and justice, no better than no government. But the nobles, in the European monarchies, support them more by opposing than promoting their ordinary views. The kings are supported by their armies; the nobles support the crown, as it is in full possession of the gift of all employments; but they support it still more by checking its ministers, and preventing them from running into abuses of power and wanton despotism; otherwise the people would be pushed to extremities and insurrections. It is thus that the nobles reconcile the monarchical authority to the obedience of the subjects; but take away the standing armies, and leave the nobles to themselves, and in a few years, they would overturn every monarchy in Europe, and erect aristocracies.

It is become a kind of fashion among writers, to admit, as a maxim, that if you could be always sure of a wise, active, and virtuous prince, monarchy would be the best of governments. But this is so far from being

Portrait of John Adams as Vice President by Charles Willson Peale

admissible, that it will forever remain true, that a free government has a great advantage over a simple monarchy. The best and wisest prince, by means of a freer communication with his people, and the greater opportunities to collect the best advice from the best of his subjects, would have an immense advantage in a free state over a monarchy. A senate consisting of all that is most noble, wealthy, and able in the nation, with a right to counsel the crown at all times, is a check to ministers, and a security against abuses, such as a body of nobles who never meet, and have no such right, can never supply. Another assembly, composed of representatives chosen by the people in all parts, gives free access to the whole nation, and communicates all its wants, knowledge, projects, and wishes to government; it excites emulation among all classes, removes complaints, redresses grievances, affords opportunities of exertion to genius, though in obscurity, and gives full scope to all the faculties of man; it opens a passage for every speculation to the legislature, to administration, and to the public; it gives a universal energy to the human character, in every part of the state, such as never can be obtained in a monarchy.

There is a third particular which deserves attention both from governments and people. In a simple monarchy, the ministers of state can never know their friends from their enemies; secret cabals undermine their influence, and blast their reputation. This occasions a jealousy ever anxious and irritated, which never thinks the government safe without an encouragement of informers and spies, throughout every part of the state, who interrupt the tranquillity of private life, destroy the confidence of families in their own domestics and in one another, and poison freedom in its sweetest retirements. In a free government, on the contrary, the ministers can have no enemies of consequence but among the members of the great or little council, where every man is obliged to take his side, and declare his opinion, upon every question. This circumstance alone, to every manly mind, would be sufficient to decide the preference in favor of a free government....

The people in America have now the best opportunity and the greatest trust in their hands, that Providence ever committed to so small a number, since the

Final three pages (above and at right) for table of contents of Volume I reveal the wide scope of John Adams's historical review.

transgression of the first pair; if they betray their trust, their guilt will merit even greater punishment than other nations have suffered, and the indignation of Heaven. If there is one certain truth to be collected from the history of all ages, it is this; that the people's rights and liberties, and the democratical mixture in a constitution, can never be preserved without a strong executive, or, in other words, without separating the executive from the legislative power. If the executive power, or any considerable part of it, is left in the hands either of an aristocratical or a democratical assembly, it will corrupt the legislature as necessarily as rust corrupts iron, or as arsenic poisons the human body; and when the legislature is corrupted, the people are undone.

The rich, the well-born, and the able, acquire an influence among the people that will soon be too much for simple honesty and plain sense, in a house of representatives. The most illustrious of them must, therefore, be separated from the mass, and placed by themselves in a senate; this is, to all honest and useful intents, an ostracism. A member of a senate, of immense wealth, the most respected birth, and transcendent abilities, has no influence in the nation, in comparison of what he would have in a single representative assembly. When a senate exists, the most powerful man in the state may be safely admitted into the house of representatives, because the people have it in their power to remove him into the senate as soon as his influence becomes dangerous. The senate becomes the great object of ambition; and the richest and the most sagacious wish to merit an advancement to it by services to the public in the house. When he has obtained the object of his wishes, you may still hope for the benefits of his exertions, without dreading his passions; for the executive power being in other hands, he has lost much of his influence with the people, and can govern very few votes more than his own among the senators. . . .

The United States of America have exhibited, perhaps, the first example of governments erected on the simple principles of nature; and if men are now sufficiently enlightened to disabuse themselves of artifice, imposture, hypocrisy, and superstition, they will consider this event as an era in their history. Although the detail of the formation of the American governments is at present little known or regarded either in Europe or in America, it may hereafter become an object of curiosity. It will never be pretended that any persons employed in that service had interviews with the gods, or were in any degree under the inspiration of Heaven, more than those at work upon ships or houses, or laboring in merchandise or agriculture; it will forever be acknowledged that these governments were contrived merely by the use of reason and the senses.

In the conclusion to the first volume of the *Defence*, Adams emphasized the need in a federal form of government for the independence of the three branches of government, a subject then under debate at the Constitutional Convention in Philadelphia. He pointed out that under the existing confederation the Continental Congress was not a legislative body at all, but a diplomatic assembly consisting of the representatives of sovereign states, a distinction well recognized by the law of nations.

[January, 1787]

By the authorities and examples already recited, you will be convinced that three branches of power have an unalterable foundation in nature; that they exist in every society natural and artificial; and that if all of them are not acknowledged in any constitution of government, it will be found to be imperfect, unstable, and soon enslaved; that the legislative and executive authorities are naturally distinct; and that liberty and the laws depend entirely on a separation of them in the frame of government; that the legislative power is naturally and necessarily sovereign and supreme over the executive; and, therefore, that the latter must be made an essential branch of the former, even with a negative, or it will not be able to defend itself, but will be soon invaded, undermined, attacked, or in some way or other totally ruined and annihilated by the former. This is applicable to every state in America, in its individual capacity; but is it equally applicable to the United States in their federal capacity?

The people of America and their delegates in congress were of opinion, that a single assembly was every way adequate to the management of all their federal concerns; and with very good reason, because congress is not a legislative assembly, nor a representative assembly, but only a diplomatic assembly. A single council has been found to answer the purposes of confederacies very well. But in all such cases the deputies are responsible to the states; their authority is clearly ascertained; and the states, in their separate capacities, are the checks. These are able to form an effectual balance, and at all times to control their delegates. The security against the dangers of this kind of government will depend upon the accuracy and decision with which the governments of the separate states have their own orders arranged and balanced.

The necessity we are under of submitting to a federal government, is an additional and a very powerful argument for three branches.

The conclusion to the third volume of the *Defence*, written after the publication of the report of the Constitutional Convention in Philadelphia, contained John Adams's apology for the composition of the treatise. It is indeed regrettable that the unusual form and method of writing should have contributed to the fact that this important work is little read today. Working in haste, Adams copied or translated much of his material from other authors without explaining his principles of selection or sufficiently acknowledging the origin of his sources. His comments and conclusions are sprinkled throughout the text. (About three percent of the first volume is in quotation marks, whereas it has been estimated that closer to seventy-five percent of the text could well have been so treated.) The conclusion to this curious work showed that John Adams thought the newly drafted Constitution was well suited to the needs of his country.

[1788]

It is now in our power to bring this work to a conclusion with unexpected dignity. In the course of the last summer, two authorities have appeared, greater than any that have been before quoted, in which the principles we have attempted to defend have been acknowledged.

The first is, an ORDINANCE of Congress, of the thirteenth of July, 1787, for the Government of the Territory of the United States, Northwest of the River Ohio.

The second is, the REPORT of the Convention at Philadelphia, of the seventeenth of September, 1787.

The former confederation of the United States was formed upon the model and example of all the confederacies, ancient and modern, in which the federal council was only a diplomatic body....The magnitude of territory, the population, the wealth and commerce, and especially the rapid growth of the United States, have shown such a government to be inadequate to their wants; and the new system, which seems admirably calculated to unite their interests and affections, and bring them to an uniformity of principles and sentiments, is equally well combined to unite their wills and forces as a single nation. A result of accommodation cannot be supposed to reach the ideas of perfection of any one; but the conception of such an idea, and the deliberate union of so great and various a people in such a plan, is, without all partiality or prejudice, if not the greatest exertion of human understanding, the greatest single effort of national deliberation that the world has ever seen. That it may be improved is not to be doubted, and provision is made for that purpose in the report itself. A people who could conceive, and can adopt it, we need not fear will be able to amend it, when, by experience, its inconveniences and imperfections shall be seen and felt.

In 1787 John Adams and Thomas Jefferson were still on duty in Europe, and they both followed developments at home with great interest. A fundamental difference in temperament between the two friends can be seen in their letters at this time. Adams's reaction to Shays' Rebellion, for instance, was one of deep concern, although he was able to console himself, and he thought Jefferson as well, when he wrote to his friend, "Don't be alarmed at the late Turbulence in New England... this Commotion will terminate in additional Strength to Government." Jefferson, who advocated the least amount of government possible, felt differently about New England's troubles, as he made clear when writing to Madison in late 1787: "I hold it that a little rebellion now and then is a good thing, and is as necessary in the political world as storms in the physical." Adams's remarks to Jefferson regarding the threat of monarchy in the United States, written before the ratification of the Constitution, show another aspect of this basic difference in viewpoint between the two friends, a difference that accidents and partisan politics were soon to magnify into a breach in their long-standing friendship.

London Decr. 6. 1787

The Project of a new Constitution, has Objections against it, to which I find it difficult to reconcile my self, but I am so unfortunate as to differ somewhat from you in the Articles, according to your last kind Letter.

You are afraid of the one—I, of the few. We agree perfectly that the many should have a full fair and perfect Representation.—You are Apprehensive of Monarchy; I, of Aristocracy. I would therefore have given more Power to the President and less to the Senate. The Nomination and Appointment to all offices I would have given to the President, assisted only by a Privy Council of his own Creation, but not a Vote or Voice would I have given to the Senate or any Senator, unless he were of the Privy Council. Faction and Distraction are the sure and certain Consequence of giving to a Senate a vote in the distribution of offices.

You are apprehensive the President when once chosen, will be chosen again and again as long as he lives. So much the better as it appears to me.—You are apprehensive of foreign Interference, Intrigue, Influence. So am I.—But, as often as Elections happen, the danger of foreign Influence recurs. The less frequently they happen the less danger.—And if the Same Man may be chosen again, it is probable he will be, and the danger of foreign Influence will be less. Foreigners, seeing little Prospect will have less Courage for Enterprize.

Elections, my dear sir, Elections to offices which are great objects of Ambition, I look at with terror. Experiments of this kind have been so often tryed, and so universally found productive of Horrors, that there is great Reason to dread them.

Contemporary engraving by Doolittle of Washington's inauguration at Federal Hall, New York, in 1789

In February, 1789, John Adams was elected Vice President of the United States. During his eight years in office, while carrying out his duties as presiding officer in the Senate, he was to cast his deciding vote twenty times, more than any other Vice President. His votes on important precedent-setting issues, such as the President's right to dismiss appointees without the concurrence of the Senate, were to contribute greatly to the orderly growth of good government. Meantime, leaving directions for the operation of the Braintree farm, the new Vice President and his lady traveled to New York City, where he administered the oath of office to George Washington in a simple ceremony held in Federal Hall on Wall Street on April 30, 1789. The Adamses now settled in a comfortable manor house at Richmond Hill, about a mile and a half outside of the city. The house, located on an eminence overlooking the Hudson River near what is now the corner of Varick and Charlton streets in Greenwich Village, had been used as headquarters by Washington in 1776 and was to be purchased later by Aaron Burr. Here Abigail managed the social functions appropriate to the Vice President's household, took her place in the formal receptions held by the Washingtons, and struggled with the ever-present problem of servants. In letters to her older sister, Mrs. Richard Cranch, she described some of the contrasts of her life at this time.

Richmond Hill, June 28th, 1789

I reach'd Richmond Hill on Thursday one oclock to my no small joy. I found Mr. Adams in better Health than I feard, Mr. & Mrs. Smith quite well & everything so well arranged that Beds & a few other articles seem only necessary towards keeping House with comfort, and I begin to think that my furniture will be troublesome to me, some part of it I mean, whilst Mrs. Smith remains with me. Master John was grown out of my knowledge. William is still at Jamaica. Our House has been a mere Levee ever since I arrived morning & evening. I took the earliest opportunity (the morning after my arrival) to go & pay my respects to Mrs. Washington. Mrs. Smith accompanied me. She received me with great ease & politeness. She is plain in her dress, but that plainness is the best of every article. She is in mourning. Her Hair is white, her Teeth beautifull, her person rather short than otherways, hardly so large as my Ladyship, and if I was to speak sincerly, I think she is a much better figure. Her manners are modest and unassuming, dignified and femenine, not the Tincture of ha'ture about her. *His Majesty* was ill & confined to his Room. I had not the pleasure of a presentation to him, but the satisfaction of hearing that he regreted it equally with myself. Col. Humphries, who had paid his compliments to me in the morning & Breakfasted with me, attended Mrs. Washington & Mr. Lear, the Private Secretary, was the introducter. Thus you have an account of my first appeerence. The Principal Ladies who have visited me are the Lady & daughter of the Governour, Lady Temple, the Countess de Brehim [i.e., the Marquise de Bréhan], Mrs. Knox & 25 other Ladies, many of the Senators, all their Ladies, all the Foreign ministers & some of the Rep[resentative]s.

Richmond Hill, July 12th, 1789

Our August Pressident is a singular example of modesty

and diffidence. He has a dignity which forbids Familiarity mixed with an easy affibility which creates Love and Reverence. The fever which he had terminated in an absess, so that he cannot sit up. Upon my second visit to Mrs. Washington he sent for me into his Chamber. He was laying upon a settee and half raising himself up, beggd me to excuse his receiving me in that posture, congratulated me upon my arrival in N[ew] York and asked me how I could Relish the simple manners of America after having been accustomed to those of Europe. I replied to him that where I found simple manners I esteemed them, but that I thought we approachd much nearer to the Luxury and manners of Europe according to our ability, than most persons were sensible of, and that we had our full share of taste and fondness for them. The Pressident has a Bed put into his Carriage and rides out in that way, allways with six Horses in his Carriage & four attendants. Mrs. Washington accompanies him. I requested him to make Richmond Hill his resting place, and the next day he did so, but he found walking up stairs so difficult, that he has done it but once. Mrs. Washington is one of those unassuming characters which create Love & Esteem. A most becoming pleasentness sits upon her countanance & an unaffected deportment which renders her the object of veneration and Respect. With all these feelings and Sensations I found myself much more deeply impressd than I ever did before their Majesties of Britain. ... Richmond Hill is situated upon the North River which communicates with Albany. Pauls hook as it is calld is in full sight & the Jersy shore. Vessels are constantly passing up & down. The House is situated upon a high Hill which commands a most extensive prospect. On one side we have a view of the city & of Long Island, the river in Front, Jersy and the adjasant country on the other side. You turn a little from the Road and enter a Gate. A winding Road with trees in clumps leads you to the House, and all round the House, it looks wild and Rural as uncultivated Nature. The House is convenient for one family, but much too small for more. You enter under a piazza into a Hall & turning to the right Hand ascend a stair case which lands you in an other of equal dimensions of which I make a drawing Room. It has a Glass door which opens into a gal-

When Adams was Vice President, he asked Edward Savage to paint these portraits of President and Mrs. Washington. They still hang in the Adams homestead in Quincy.

lery the whole Front of the house which is exceeding pleasant. The Chambers are on each side. The House is not in good repair, wants much done to it, and if we continue here I hope it will be done. There is upon the back of the House a Garden of much greater extent than our Braintree Garden, but it is wholy for a walk & flowers. It has a Hawthorn hedge & Rows of Trees with a Broad Gravel walk.

Richmond Hill

[Richmond Hill], Janry. 5th, 1790
The New Years day in this state, & particularly in this city is celebrated with every mark of pleasure and satisfaction. The shops and publick offices are shut. There is not any market upon this day, but every person laying aside Buisness devote[s] the day to the social purpose of visiting & receiving visits. The churches are open & divine service performed begining the year in a very proper manner by giving Thanks to the great Governour of the universe for past mercies, & imploring his future Benidictions. There is a kind of cake in fashion upon this day call'd New Years Cooky. This & Cherry Bounce as it is calld is the old Dutch custom of treating their Friends upon the return of every New Year. The common people, who are very ready to abuse Liberty, on this day are apt to take rather too freely of the good things of this Life, and finding two of my servants not all together qualified for Buisness, I remonstrated to them, but they excused it by saying it was New Year, & every body was joyous then. The V. P. visited the President & then returnd home to receive His Friends. In the Evening I attended the drawing Room, it being Mrs. W[ashington']s publick day. It was as much crowded as a Birth Night at St. James, and with company as Briliantly drest, diamonds & great hoops excepted. My station is always at the right hand of Mrs. W.; through want of knowing what is right I find it sometimes occupied, but on such an occasion the President never fails of seeing that it is relinquished for me, and having removed Ladies several times, they have now learnt to rise & give it me, but this between our selves, as *all distinction* you know is unpopular. Yet this same P[resident] has so happy a faculty of appearing to accommodate & yet carrying his point, that if he was not really one of the best intentiond men

in the world he might be a very dangerous one. He is polite with dignity, affable without familiarity, distant without Haughtyness, Grave without Austerity, Modest, wise & Good. These are traits in his Character which peculiarly fit him for the exalted station he holds, and God Grant that he may Hold it with the same applause & universal satisfaction for many many years, as it is my firm opinion that no other man could rule over this great peopl & consolidate them into one mighty Empire but He who is set over us.

Richmond Hill, Janry 24, [1790]
I could give an account of visiting and receiving visits, but in that there is so little variety that one Letter only might contain the whole History. For Instance on Monday Evenings Mrs. Adams Receives company. That is her Rooms are lighted & put in order. Servants & Gentlemen and Ladies, as many as inclination, curiosity or Fashion tempts, come out to make their Bow & Curtzy, take coffe & Tea, chat an half hour, or longer, and then return to Town again. On Tuesday the same Ceremony is performed at Lady Temple's, on Wednesday at Mrs. Knox's, on Thursdays at Mrs. Jays and on Fryday at Mrs. Washingtons, so that if any person has so little to employ themselves in as to want an amusement five Evenings in a week, they may find it at one or other of these places. To Mrs. Washingtons I usually go as often as once a fortnight, and to the others occasionally.

Vice President John Adams appears second from left in this detail from a nineteenth-century picture called Lady Washington's Reception.

John Adams never owned slaves as a matter of principle, and Abigail's letters are full of complaints about the difficulties she had in running her household in New York and later in Philadelphia. She seemed to do best with the help of local New Englanders, as she made clear in another letter to her sister.

Richmond Hill, April 28, 1790
It is next to imposible here to get a servant from the highest to the lowest grade that does not drink, male or Female. I have at last found a footman who appears sober, but he was Born in Boston, has lived a very short time in the city & has very few acquaintance there. You would be surprizd if I was to tell you that tho I have been long trying to get a Boy here I cannot find

one that any Body will Recommend, and I should be very glad to get one from Boston, I mean Peters son. My Housekeeper who on many accounts has been the most Respectable Female I have had in the Family, is so sick and infirm that she is obliged to leave me, partly I know because she will not live with Polly. If I could find any middle aged woman of a Reputable Character who understands Pastry &c in Boston I would send for her. I give 5 dollars a month to my Housekeeper. My kitchen and offices are all below stairs, and where there are a Number of servants there must be one respectable Head amongst them to oversee & take care that they do not run headlong as well as to overlook the cooking & to make Tea for me upon my publick Evenings, to make my pastry to assist in the Ironing &c. This is the Buisness which falls to her share. Ruthe I want for a house maid. She will have no concern with cooking at all, as I keep a woman solely for that purpose. I wish you would be upon the inquiry for me. If I had not Brisler with me I should be tempted to give up publick Life. The chief of the servants here who are good for any thing are Negroes who are slaves. The white ones are all Foreigners & chiefly vagabonds. I really know now more than ever how to Prize my English servants.

Map of Philadelphia in Adams's day

In 1790 the seat of the Federal government was moved from New York to Philadelphia, where it remained for the next ten years until a new capital was built along the Potomac River. John Adams moved to Philadelphia in September of 1790, where he had rented a suitable house called Bush Hill, two miles outside the city. Abigail described the house in letters to her sisters in New England, not omitting details of the continuing problem of obtaining domestic help.

Philadelphia, Janry. 9th, 1791
You inquire how I like my situation. I answer you the one I removed from, was in Burk[e]s stile, the sublime. This is the Beautifull. The House is better; that is the work within is superiour. The Architecture of the other House was Grand and the Avenue to it perfectly Romantick. The British Troops rob'd this place of its principal Glory by cutting down all the Trees in front of the House and leaving it wholly Naked. Behind the House is a fine Grove; through which is a gravell walk; which must in

A view near Philadelphia (above) and the house that John and Abigail occupied during the Vice Presidency (above right), from a contemporary journal New-York Magazine

summer add greatly to the delight of the place....

When we have been well ourselves, our servants have been laid up. When I come to this place again I am determined to bring a *decent woman* who understands plain cooking with me. Such a vile low tribe you never was tormented with & I hope never will be. I brought all my servants from N[ew] York, cook excepted, and thought I could not be worse of than I had been. I have had in the course of 18 months seven, and I firmly believe in the whole Number, not a virtuous woman amongst them all: the most of them drunkards. I recruited with a new one last Monday, who brought written recommendations with her, and who to all appearence is very capable of her buisness, but on thursday got so drunk that she was carried to Bed, and so indecent, that footman, Coachman & all were driven out of the House. Consequently she has turnd herself out of doors. We know little of vileness in our state when compared to those cities who have such Numbers of Foreigners as N[ew] York and Philadelphia.

Bush Hill, (near Philadelphia,)
20 March, 1791

The house is spacious. The views from it are rather beautiful than sublime; the country round has too much of the level to be in my style. The appearance of uniformity wearies the eye, and confines the imagination. We have a fine view of the whole city from our windows; a beautiful grove behind the house, through which there is a spacious gravel walk, guarded by a number of marble statues, whose genealogy I have not yet studied, as the last week is the first time I have visited them. A variety of fine fields of wheat and grass are in front of the house, and, on the right hand, a pretty view of the Schuylkill presents itself. But now for the reverse of

343

*Original pen-and-wash sketch of
"The State House at Philadelphia,"
published by J. Easton in 1796*

the picture. We are only two miles from town, yet have I been more of a prisoner this winter than I ever was in my life. The road from hence to the pavement is one mile and a half, the soil a brick clay, so that, when there has been heavy rain, or a thaw, you must wallow to the city through a bed of mortar without a bottom, the horses sinking to their knees. If it becomes cold, then the holes and roughness are intolerable. From the inhabitants of this place I have received every mark of politeness and civility. The ladies here are well-educated, well-bred, and well-dressed. There is much more society than in New York, and I am much better pleased and satisfied than I expected to be when I was destined to remove here.

John Adams now presided over the Senate in Independence Hall. Although convinced that he should remain impartial as the Senate's presiding officer, Adams nevertheless chafed in the role of a neutral arbiter. "My country has in its wisdom contrived for me the most insignificant office that ever the invention of man contrived or his imagination conceived." Irked by the duties of his office and dismayed by the progress of the French Revolution, he now turned to writing—with unfortunate results. The "Discourses on Davila," published as a series in the *Gazette of the United States* in 1790 and 1791, reflected Adams's conviction that the French were sliding rapidly into despotism because they refused to set up a bicameral legislature with checks and balances and did not respect the independence of the three branches of government. The "Discourses," a heated extension of Adams's *Defence of the Constitutions,* summarized the views of an Italian historian and participant in the eight wars of religion fought in France in the sixteenth century. As the essays were published hastily, without proper editing, their unguarded language exposed them to torrents of criticism from Adams's political opponents. Adams's belief, for instance, that the history of Europe showed that men had turned invariably to monarchy to avoid the horrors of anarchy was interpreted as proof that he was at heart a monarchist. As Adams later wrote, "the Rage and Fury of the Jacobinical journals vs. the discourses increased as they proceeded, intimidated the Printer John [Fenno] and convinced me that to proceed would do more harm than good." An exchange with Jefferson arising out of the "Discourses" resulted in a cooling of relations between the two. In 1805 the "Discourses" were published in book form, and Adams, looking back in retirement to write a new preface, commented on his controversial work.

Discourses on Davila, 1805

This dull, heavy volume, still excites the wonder of its author,—first, that he could find, amidst the constant scenes of business and dissipation in which he was enveloped, time to write it; secondly, that he had the courage to oppose and publish his own opinions to the universal opinion of America, and, indeed, of all mankind. Not one man in America then believed him. He knew not one and has not heard of one since who then believed him. The work, however, powerfully operated to destroy his popularity. It was urged as full proof, that he was an advocate for monarchy, and laboring to introduce a hereditary president in America.

About the time Adams was first starting to publish the "Discourses," he chided his Republican friend Dr. Benjamin Rush for misinterpreting his views on monarchy.

Title page of Discourses on Davila

New York, 18 April, 1790.

My friend Dr. Rush will excuse me, if I caution him against a fraudulent use of the words *monarchy* and *republic.* I am a mortal and irreconcilable enemy to monarchy. I am no friend to *hereditary limited* monarchy in America. This I know can never be admitted without an hereditary Senate to control it, and a hereditary nobility or Senate in America I know to be unattainable and impracticable. I should scarcely be for it, if it were. Do not, therefore, my friend, misunderstand me and misrepresent me to posterity. I am for a balance between the legislative and executive powers, and I am for enabling the executive to be at all times capable of maintaining the balance between the Senate and House, or in other words, between the aristocratical and democratical interests. Yet I am for having all three branches elected at stated periods, and these elections, I hope, will continue until the people shall be convinced that fortune, providence, or chance, call it which you will, is better than election. If the time should come when corruption shall be added to intrigue and manoeuvre in elections, and produce civil war, then, in my opinion, chance will be better than choice for all but the House of Representatives.

The year 1796 was a presidential election year. John Adams recorded his innermost thoughts and feelings on this subject in the following series of letters to Abigail.

345

Portrait of John Quincy Adams done by John Singleton Copley in 1795

Philadelphia, 7 January, 1796.
I must tell you that I now believe the President will retire. The consequence to me is very serious, and I am not able, as yet, to see what my duty will demand of me. I shall take my resolutions with cool deliberation. I shall watch the course of events with more critical attention than I have done for some time, and what Providence shall point out to be my duty, I shall pursue with patience and decision. It is no light thing to resolve upon retirement. My country has claims, my children have claims, and my own character has claims upon me; but all these claims forbid me to serve the public in disgrace. Whatever any one may think, I love my country too well to shrink from danger in her service, provided I have a reasonable prospect of being able to serve her to her honor and advantage. But if I have reason to think that I have either a want of abilities or of public confidence to such a degree as to be unable to support the government in a higher station, I ought to decline it. But in that case, I ought not to serve in my present place under another, especially if that other should entertain sentiments so opposite to mine as to endanger the peace of the nation. It will be a dangerous crisis in public affairs if the President and Vice President should be in opposite boxes.

Philadelphia, 20 January, 1796.
I am, as you say, quite a favorite. I am to dine to-day again. I am heir apparent, you know, and a succession is soon to take place. But, whatever may be the wish or the judgment of the present occupant, the French and the demagogues intend, I presume, to set aside the descent. All these hints must be secrets. It is not a subject of conversation as yet. I have a pious and a philosophical resignation to the voice of the people in this case, which is the voice of God. I have no very ardent desire to be the butt of party malevolence. Having tasted of that cup, I find it bitter, nauseous, and unwholesome.

Philadelphia, 15 February, 1796.
If Jay or even Jefferson (and one or the other it certainly will be) if the succession should be passed over, should be the man, the government will go on as well as ever. Jefferson could not stir a step in any other system than

that which is begun. Jay would not wish it. The votes will run for three persons. Two, I have mentioned; the third, being the heir apparent, will not probably be wholly overlooked. If Jefferson and Jay are President and Vice-President, as is not improbable, the other retires without noise, or cries, or tears to his farm. If either of these two is President and the other Vice-President, he retires without murmur or complaint to his farm forever. If this other should be President and Jefferson or Jay Vice-President, four years more, if life last, of residence in Philadelphia will be his and your portion, after which we shall probably be desirous of imitating the example of the present pair; or if, by reason of strength and fortitude, eight years should be accomplished, that is the utmost limit of time, that I will ever continue in public life at any rate.

Philadelphia, 25 March, 1796.
Yesterday I dined at the President's, with ministers of state and their ladies, foreign and domestic. After dinner the gentlemen drew off after the ladies, and left me alone with the President in close conversation. He detained me there till nine o'clock, and was never more frank and open upon politics. I find his opinions and sentiments are more exactly like mine than I ever knew before, respecting England, France, and our American parties. He gave me intimations enough that his reign would be very short. He repeated it three times at least, that this and that was of no consequence to him personally, as he had but a very little while to stay in his present situation. This must be a confidential secret.

Washington had established the precedent of returning to his farm in Virginia when Congress was not in session, and John Adams was glad to leave fever-ridden Philadelphia in summer for the more salubrious climate of Quincy, into which new town his Braintree homestead was incorporated in the year 1792. Life on the farm had its healthy diversions and pleasures, particularly during the period immediately after the wearisome partisan debates in Congress over Jay's Treaty and just before the election. In the summer of 1796, after many years of neglect, John Adams resumed his old practice of making daily entries in his *Diary;* following are excerpts from the months of July, August, and September.

Quincy July 12. Tuesday [1796]. Yesterday mow'd all the Grass on Stony field Hill. To day ploughing for Hilling among the Corn over against the House.

July 13. Wednesday [1796]. Billings went out to hoe this morning but soon came in. Said he had sprained his Arm and could not work.

July 14. 1796 Thursday. The Wind N. W. after a fine rain. A firing of Cannon this morning in the Harbour. I arose by four O Clock and enjoyed the Charm of earliest Birds. Their Songs were never more various, universal, animating or delightful.

July 16. 1796 Saturday. Paid off Puffer, for Eleven Days Works at a Dollar a Day. Trask and Stetson at work in the Garden. Sullivan and Bass gone for another Load of Red Cedar Posts. Billings over at Bass's in the Morning and going up in Town with Seth as usual.

July 17. 1796 Sunday. Warm but clear. Billings at home but running down Cellar for Cyder.

July 18 1796. Monday. Billings is at hoe. The Kitchen Folk say he is steady. A terrible drunken distracted Week he has made of the last. A Beast associating with the worst Beasts in the Neighborhood. Drunk with John Copeland, Seth Bass &c. Hurried as if possessed, like Robert the Coachman, or Turner the Stocking Weaver. Running to all the Shops and private Houses swilling Brandy, Wine and Cyder in quantities enough to destroy him. If the Ancients drank Wine as our People drink rum and Cyder it is no wonder We read of so many possessed with Devils.

Went up to Penns hill. Trask has the Rheumatism in his Arm and is unable to work. He told me that Rattlesnakes began to appear—two on Saturday by Porters and Prays. One kill'd. The other escaped.

July 19. 1796. Tuesday. A plentifull Shower of Rain with Thunder and Lightning this Morning. Took a Tea spoonful of Bark [quinine] in Spirit.

Billings steady: but deep in the horrors, gaping, stretching, groaning.

Early book illustration showing farmer's method of sowing the grain

July 21. Thursday [1796].
Sullivan Lathrop and Bass carting earth into the Yard from the Ground which is to be thrown into the High Way over against my House. The old Appletree, probably an hundred Years of Age is to fall.

Billings and Thomas Lathrop mowing in the Meadow.

Six hogsheads of Lime, 50 Gallons each were brought home Yesterday for Manure. I have it of Mr. Brackett, at 15s. the Hdd.

I am reading Dr. Watsons Apology for the Bible in Answer to T. Paines 2nd Part of Age of Reason.

That Appletree, over the Way, to which the Beauty and Convenience of the Road has been sacrificed for an hundred Years, has now in its turn, with Apples enough upon it to make two Barrells of Cyder, fallen a Sacrifice to the Beauty and Convenience of the Road. It has been felled this morning, never to rise again and the Road is to be widened and enlarged. The Stump and Roots are to be dug out of the Ground and the Wall to be removed Back....

Engraving of medal of Massachusetts Society for Promoting Agriculture, of which Adams was president, illustrates early method of plowing.

Billings had a mind to go on Wall. I went with him from Place to Place, and could resolve on nothing. I then set him to split and mortise some Posts for the fence vs. Mrs. Veasie. We went up, carried the Posts but when We came there We found that the Wall was too heavy and Stones too large for two hands—four at least were necessary. Billings was wild and We came to some Explanation. He must go off &c. Mrs. Adams paid him off, and then He thought he would not go. After long Conversations Billings came to a Sort of Agreement to stay a Year from this day, at £ 45. He declared he would not drink Spirit nor Cyder for the whole Year. He reserved however twelve days for himself. We shall see tomorrow Morning how he behaves.

July 22. Fryday [1796].
Billings sober and steady, persevering in his declaration that he will not drink, these 12 months. Paid Trask in full sixteen Dollars for 24 Days Works. He insisted on 4s. a Day. He has finished clearing the Swamp on Penns Hill this day.

July 23. 1796. Saturday.
Road down to the Barley and Black grass at the Beach. The Barley is better than I hoped. The Clover has taken pretty well in general. Parts where the Tide has flowed

are kill'd. Weeds very thick round the Margin of the Salt Meadow, or rather Black grass meadow. Twitch grass scattering and thin. Billings sober, composed as ever. Bass and Brisler mowing with him. James the Coachman, enjoying the Pleasures of a Sportsman, shooting marsh Birds instead of mowing....

Began the Life of Petrarch by Susanna Dobson.

July 26. 1796. Tuesday.

Cloudy and begins to rain, the Wind at N. E. The Men gone up the Hill to rake the Barley.

In conformity to the fashion I drank this Morning and Yesterday Morning, about a Jill of Cyder. It seems to do me good, by diluting and dissolving the Phlegm or the Bile in the Stomach.

The Christian Religion is, above all the Religions that ever prevailed or existed in ancient or modern Times, The Religion of Wisdom, Virtue, Equity and Humanity, let the Blackguard Paine say what he will. It is Resignation to God—it is Goodness itself to Man.

July 29. 1796. Fryday.

Hot after Thunder, Lightening and an Hours Rain. The two Lathrops threshing. Billing and Bass carting Earth. Lathrops threshing. Billing and Bass brought up a third Load of Seaweed. They go on making the Heap of Compost with Lime, Seaweed, Earth, Horse Dung, Hogs dung &c.

Still reading the Second Volume of Petrarchs Life.

July 30th. Saturday [1796].

All hands carting Earth and making Compost, i.e. 4 hands Billings, Bass and the two Lathrops. Billings is in his Element. Building Wall and making manure are his great delights, he says. He says he will cover all my Clover with green Seaweed. Drop part of a Load on the lower Part and carry the rest up the hill to the Barley Stubble. He will make a heap of Compost too upon the Top of the Hill to dung the Corn in the holes next Year upon the Piece which I propose to break up, and he will make an heap of Compost in the Spring with winter Dung to dung Corn beyond the Ditch. He will get a Scow load of Rockweed, and Scow loads of Seaweed and marsh mud. If he did not execute as well as plann, I should suppose this all Gasconade. But he is the most ingenious, the most laborious, the most resolute and the most indefatigable Man I ever employed.

Farmers cut and stack wheat in two primitive woodcut illustrations from early children's books.

August 6. 1796. Saturday.

Billings and Bass off by Day for Seaweed....

Omnium Rerum Domina, Virtus. Virtue is the Mistress of all Things. Virtue is The Master of all Things. Therefore a Nation that should never do wrong must necessarily govern the World. The Might of Virtue, The Power of Virtue is not a very common Topick, not so common as it should be.

Bass and Billings brought another Load of Seaweed in the Evening for the Swine.

August 19. 1769 [i.e., 1796]. Fryday. Ten Yoke of Oxen and twelve hands ploughing in the meadow. It is astonishing that such a Meadow should have lain so long in such a State. Brakes, Hassock Grass, Cramberry Vines, Poke or Skunk Cabbage, Button Bushes, alder Bushes, old Stumps and Roots, Rocks, Turtles, Eels, Frogs, were the Chief Things found in it. But I presume it may be made to produce Indian and English grain, and English Grass, especially Herdsgrass in Abundance. At least the Beauty of the Meadow and the Sweetness of it and the Air over it will be improved.

September 2. 1796. Fryday.

To work again on the high Ways. They have taxed me this Year between forty nine and fifty days Works on the Roads besides the other Farm in Quincy and the farm in Braintree. This is unjust, more than my Proportion, more than Mr. Black or Mr. Beale.

Stumbled over a Wheelbarrow in the dark and hurt my Shin.

Septr. 8. 1796. Thursday.

I think to christen my Place by the Name of Peace field, in commemoration of the Peace which I assisted in making in 1783, of the thirteen Years Peace and Neutrality which I have contributed to preserve, and of the constant Peace and Tranquility which I have enjoyed in this Residence.

John Adams returned to Philadelphia in November, 1796, to face the results of the election. (It was not the practice for candidates to campaign in those days.) In December Adams, as presiding officer of the Senate, counted the votes and announced the election to be in favor of himself for President and Thomas Jefferson for Vice President.

Chapter 11

Mr. President

The Adams administration was dominated by a quasi war with France, the peaceful solution of which was Adams's great accomplishment as President, and by a split within the Federalist Party that was eventually to open the way for the election of a Republican President, Thomas Jefferson, in 1801. The split and the subsequent Republican victory were brought on in part by Adams himself, who made two major tactical errors during his administration. The first was his failure immediately to appoint a new Cabinet. Instead, he tried to work with the mediocre men recruited by Washington when the ablest men, including Jay, Jefferson, Hamilton, and Henry Knox, resigned their posts. It should be pointed out that Adams felt considerable deference toward Washington, who was still alive. Moreover, there was as yet no precedent for a general resignation of top government officials with a change of administration. Calling for such a resignation might well have precipitated a crisis in the Federalist Party at a moment when Adams was concerned most of all with getting on with the business of government.

But a crisis was brewing nonetheless, as Alexander Hamilton, now the leader of the Federalists, sought to control the President by intriguing with three disloyal members of his Cabinet: James McHenry, Secretary of War; Timothy Pickering, Secretary of State; and Oliver Wolcott, Secretary of the Treasury. That Hamilton and the three Cabinet members were able for so long to undermine Adams's authority was due largely to Adams's second fatal error, which was to spend almost half his time running the government from his farm in Quincy, Massachusetts, instead of at the seat of government in Philadelphia, where he might have ferreted out the weasels before too much damage had been done.

Adams was inaugurated at Congress Hall in Philadelphia on March 4, 1797. President Washington appeared in a handsome suit of black, with a black cockade in his military hat, and with his hair fully powdered. Thomas

Jefferson, the incoming Vice President, wore a long blue frock coat that accentuated his tall frame. John Adams, in marked contrast to his usual simple mode of dress, had clothed his plump five-foot-seven-inch figure in a pearl-gray broadcloth suit, with a sword girded around his midriff and a cockade set in his hat. His inaugural speech, a strong public reaffirmation of his belief in republican institutions in general and in the Constitution in particular, calmed somewhat the agitation of the parties.

Inaugural Speech, 1797

When it was first perceived, in early times, that no middle course for America remained between unlimited submission to a foreign legislature and a total independence of its claims, men of reflection were less apprehensive of danger from the formidable power of fleets and armies they must determine to resist, than from those contests and dissensions which would certainly arise concerning the forms of government to be instituted over the whole and over the parts of this extensive country. Relying, however, on the purity of their intensions, the justice of their cause, and the integrity and intelligence of the people, under an overruling Providence, which had so signally protected this country from the first, the representatives of this nation, then consisting of little more than half its present numbers, not only broke to pieces the chains which were forging, and the rod of iron that was lifted up, but frankly cut asunder the ties which had bound them, and launched into an ocean of uncertainty.

The zeal and ardor of the people during the revolutionary war, supplying the place of government, commanded a degree of order, sufficient at least for the temporary preservation of society. The confederation, which was early felt to be necessary, was prepared from the models of the Batavian and Helvetic confederacies, the only examples which remain, with any detail and precision, in history, and certainly the only ones which the people at large had ever considered. But, reflecting on the striking difference in so many particulars between this country and those where a courier may go from the seat of government to the frontier in a single day, it was then certainly foreseen by some, who assisted in Congress at the formation of it, that it could not be durable.

Negligence of its regulations, inattention to its recommendations, if not disobedience to its authority, not only in individuals but in States, soon appeared, with their melancholy consequences; universal languor, jealousies, rivalries of States; decline of navigation and commerce; discouragement of necessary manufactures; universal fall in the value of lands and their produce; contempt of public and private faith; loss of consideration and credit with foreign nations; and, at length, in discontents, animosities, combinations, partial conventions, and insurrections; threatening some great national calamity.

In this dangerous crisis the people of America were not abandoned by their usual good sense, presence of mind, resolution, or integrity. Measures were pursued to concert a plan to form a more perfect union, establish justice, ensure domestic tranquillity, provide for the common defence, promote the general welfare, and secure the blessings of liberty. The public disquisitions, discussions, and deliberations, issued in the present happy constitution of government.

Employed in the service of my country abroad, during the whole course of these transactions, I first saw the Constitution of the United States in a foreign country. Irritated by no literary altercation, animated by no public debate, heated by no party animosity, I read it with great satisfaction, as a result of good heads, prompted by good hearts; as an experiment better adapted to the genius, character, situation, and relations of this nation and country than any which had ever been proposed or suggested. In its general principles and great outlines, it was conformable to such a system of government as I had ever most esteemed, and in some States, my own native State in particular, had contributed to establish. Claiming a right of suffrage in common with my fellow-citizens, in the adoption or rejection of a constitution, which was to rule me and my posterity as well as them and theirs, I did not hesitate to express my approbation of it on all occasions, in public and in private. It was not then nor has been since any objection to it, in my mind, that the Executive and Senate were not more permanent. Nor have I entertained a thought of promoting any alteration in it, but such as the people themselves, in the course of their experience, should see and feel to be necessary or expedient, and by their representatives in Congress and the State legislatures, according to the Constitution itself, adopt and ordain.

Returning to the bosom of my country, after a painful

*Portrait of John Adams by William
Winstanley in the pearl-gray
broadcloth suit and sword that
he wore for his 1797 inauguration*

separation from it for ten years, I had the honor to be elected to a station under the new order of things, and I have repeatedly laid myself under the most serious obligations to support the Constitution. The operation of it has equalled the most sanguine expectations of its friends; and, from an habitual attention to it, satisfaction in its administration, and delight in its effect upon the peace, order, prosperity, and happiness of the nation, I have acquired an habitual attachment to it, and veneration for it.

What other form of government, indeed, can so well deserve our esteem and love?

[After a moving tribute to Washington, Adams closed his speech—in a sentence of nearly a thousand words—with a summary of his republican principles that moved the assembly to tears.]

On this subject it might become me better to be silent, or to speak with diffidence; but, as something may be expected, the occasion, I hope, will be admitted as an apology if I venture to say that, if a preference upon principle of a free republican government, formed upon long and serious reflection, after a diligent and impartial inquiry after truth; if an attachment to the Constitution of the United States, and a conscientious determination to support it, until it shall be altered by the judgments and the wishes of the people, expressed in the mode prescribed in it; if a respectful attention to the constitutions of the individual States, and a constant caution and delicacy towards the State governments; if an equal and impartial regard to the rights, interests, honor, and happiness of all the States in the Union, without preference or regard to a northern or southern, eastern or western position, their various political opinions on essential points, or their personal attachments; if a love of virtuous men of all parties and denominations; if a love of science and letters, and a wish to patronize every rational effort to encourage schools, colleges, universities, academies, and every institution for propagating knowledge, virtue, and religion among all classes of the

First page of inaugural address

people, not only for their benign influence on the happiness of life in all its stages and classes and of society in all its forms, but as the only means of preserving our constitution from its natural enemies, the spirit of sophistry, the spirit of party, the spirit of intrigue, profligacy, and corruption, and the pestilence of foreign influence, which is the angel of destruction to elective governments; if a love of equal laws, of justice and humanity, in the interior administration; if an inclination to improve agriculture, commerce, and manufactures for necessity, convenience, and defence; if a spirit of equity and humanity towards the aboriginal nations of America, and a disposition to meliorate their condition by inclining them to be more friendly to us, and our citizens to be more friendly to them; if an inflexible determination to maintain peace and inviolable faith with all nations, and that system of neutrality and impartiality among the belligerent powers of Europe which has been adopted by the government, and so solemnly sanctioned by both Houses of Congress, and applauded by the legislatures of the States and the public opinion, until it shall be otherwise ordained by Congress; if a personal esteem for the French nation, formed in a residence of seven years chiefly among them, and a sincere desire to preserve the friendship which has been so much for the honor and interest of both nations; if, while the conscious honor and integrity of the people of America, and the internal sentiment of their own power and energies must be preserved, an earnest endeavor to investigate every just cause, and remove every colorable pretence of complaint; if an intention to pursue, by amicable negotiation, a reparation for the injuries that have been committed on the commerce of our fellow-citizens by whatever nation, and (if success cannot be obtained) to lay the facts before the legislature, that they may consider what further measures the honor and interest of the government and its constituents demand; if a resolution to do justice, as far as may depend upon me, at all times, and to all nations, and maintain peace, friendship, and benevolence with all the world; if an unshaken confidence in the honor, spirit, and resources of the American people, on which I have so often hazarded my all, and never been deceived; if elevated ideas of the high destinies of this country, and of my own duties towards it, founded on a knowledge of the moral principles and intellectual improvements of the people, deeply engraven on my mind in early life, and not obscured, but exalted by experience and age; and with humble reverence I feel it my duty to add, if a veneration for the religion of a people, who profess and call themselves Christians, and a fixed resolution to consider a decent respect for Christianity among the best recommendations for the public service;—can enable me in any degree to comply with your wishes, it shall be my strenuous endeavor that this sagacious injunction of the two Houses shall not be without effect.

With this great example before me, with the sense and spirit, the faith and honor, the duty and interest of the same American people, pledged to support the Constitution of the United States, I entertain no doubt of its continuance in all its energy; and my mind is prepared without hesitation to lay myself under the most solemn obligations to support it to the utmost of my power.

And may that Being who is supreme over all, the patron of order, the fountain of justice, and the protector, in all ages of the world, of virtuous liberty, continue his blessing upon this nation and its government, and give it all possible success and duration, consistent with the ends of his providence!

Trade card of Adams's stationer while he lived in Philadelphia

In the course of the next few days, Adams described the inauguration to his wife and speculated gloomily on the future.

Philadelphia, 5 March, 1797.
Your dearest friend never had a more trying day than yesterday. A solemn scene it was indeed, and it was made more affecting to me by the presence of the General, whose countenance was as serene and unclouded as the day. He seemed to me to enjoy a triumph over me. Methought I heard him say, "Ay! I am fairly out and you fairly in! See which of us will be happiest." When the ceremony was over, he came and made me a visit, and cordially congratulated me, and wished my administration might be happy, successful, and honorable.

It is now settled that I am to go into his house. It is whispered that he intends to take French leave tomorrow. I shall write you as fast as we proceed. My chariot is finished, and I made my first appearance in it yesterday. It is simple but elegant enough. My horses are young, but clever.

In the chamber of the House of Representatives was a multitude as great as the space could contain, and I believe scarcely a dry eye but Washington's. The sight of the sun setting full orbed, and another rising, though less splendid, was a novelty. Chief Justice Ellsworth administered the oath, and with great energy. Judges Cushing, Wilson, and Iredell, were present. Many ladies.

Philadelphia, March 17, 1797.
It would have given me great pleasure to have had some of my family present at my inauguration, which was the most affecting and overpowering scene I ever acted in. I was very unwell, had no sleep the night before, and really did not know but I should have fainted in presence of all the world. I was in great doubt whether to say anything or not besides repeating the oath. And now, the world is as silent as the grave. All the federalists seem to be afraid to approve any body but Washington. The Jacobin papers damn with faint praise, and undermine with misrepresentation and insinuation. If the federalists go to playing pranks, I will resign the office, and let Jefferson lead them to peace, wealth, and power if he will.

From the situation where I now am, I see a scene of ambition beyond all my former suspicions or imaginations; an emulation which will turn our government topsy-turvy. Jealousies and rivalries have been my theme, and checks and balances as their antidotes till I am ashamed to repeat the words; but they never stared me in the face in such horrid forms as at present. I see how the thing is going. At the next election England will set up Jay or Hamilton, and France, Jefferson, and all the corruption of Poland will be introduced; unless the American spirit should rise and say, we will have neither John Bull nor Louis Baboon.

Chief Justice Oliver Ellsworth, who administered the oath to John Adams

The French question was the most immediate problem facing the new President. France had refused to accept President Washington's envoy, Charles Cotesworth Pinckney, and had passed a decree authorizing the capture of all American commercial shipping on the high seas and the treatment as pirates of all American seamen found on board British ships. President Adams called a special session of Congress for April 14, 1797, during which he rallied public opinion behind a dual policy of negotiation for peace and preparation for war. He then dispatched John Marshall and Elbridge Gerry to join Pinckney in Paris. A year later, when the commissioners' reports revealed the sordid attempt by Talleyrand's agents—code named X, Y, and Z—to extract a bribe from the Americans, the United States was swept by a wave of war frenzy led by the Hamiltonian faction of the Federalists. Toasts were drunk to the words: "Millions for defense, but not one cent for tribute!" Republicans, meanwhile, expressed their opposition to anti-French opinion by wearing tricolor cockades and singing the first popular song of the French Revolution, "Ça ira." Abigail Adams's letters to her sister Mary Cranch capture well the mood of violent party spirit that dominated the capital.

[Philadelphia,] April 26, 1798

I inclose to you a National Song ["Hail, Columbia"] composed by this same Mr. Hopkinson. French Tunes have for a long time usurped an uncontrould sway. Since the Change in the publick opinion respecting France, the people began to lose the relish for them, and what had been harmony, now becomes discord. Accordingly their had been for several Evenings at the Theatre something like disorder, one party crying out for the Presidents March and Yankee Doodle, whilst Ciera ["Ça ira"] was vociferated from the other. It was hisst off repeatedly. The Managers were blamed. Their excuse was that they had not any words to the Presidents March—Mr. Hopkinson accordingly composed these to the tune. Last Eve'ng they were sung for the first time. I had a Great curiosity to see for myself the Effect. I got Mr. Otis to take a Box, and silently went off with Mr. and Mrs. Otis, Mr. & Mrs. Buck to the play, where I had only once been this winter. I meant now to be perfectly in cogg, so did not sit in what is called the Presidents Box. After the Principle Peice was performd, Mr. Fox came upon the stage, to sing the song. He was welcomed by applause. The House was very full, and at every Choruss, the most unbounded applause ensued. In short it was enough to stund one. They had the song repeated— After this Rossina was acted. When Fox came upon the stage after the Curtain dropt, to announce the Peice for fryday, they calld again for the song, and made him repeat it to the fourth time. And the last time, the whole Audience broke forth in the Chorus whilst the

Contemporary cartoon of the XYZ Affair showing hydra-headed French government trying to extract a bribe from America at dagger point

thunder from their Hands was incessant, and at the close they rose, gave 3 Huzzas, that you might have heard a mile—My head aches in concequence of it. The Managers have requested the President to attend the Theater, and twesday next he goes. A number of the inhabitants have made the same request, and now is the proper time to gratify them. Their have been six differents addresses presented from this city alone; all expressive of the Approbation of the measures of the Executive.

First page of "Hail, Columbia" with portrait of Adams looking very much like his predecessor, Washington

Philadelphia, May 10th, 1798

The Young Men of the city as I wrote you on Monday to the amount of near Eleven Hundred came at 12 oclock in procession two and two. There were assembled upon the occasion it is said ten thousand Persons. This street as wide or wider than State Street in Boston, was full as far as we could see up & down. One might have walkd upon their Heads, besides the houses window & even tops of Houses. In great order & decorum the Young Men with each a black cockade marchd through the Multitude and all of them enterd the House preceeded by their committe. When a Young Gentleman by the Name of Hare, a Nephew of Mrs. Binghams, read the address, the President received them in his Levee Room drest in his uniform, and as usual upon such occasions, read his answer to them, after which they all retired. The Multitude gave three Cheers, & followd them to the State House Yard, where the answer to the address was again read by the Chairman of the committe, with acclamations. They then closed the scene by singing the new song ["Hail, Columbia"], which at 12 oclock at night was sung by them under our windows, they having dinned together or rather a part of them. This scene burnt in the Hearts of some Jacobins and they determined eitheir, to terrify, or Bully the young men out of their Patriotism. Baches [Benjamin Bache, publisher of a Jeffersonian newspaper] publishd some saussy peices, the young men resented and he would have felt the effects of their resentment if some cooler Heads had not interposed. Yesterday was observed with much solemnity. The meeting Houses & churches were fill'd. About 4 oclock as is usual the State House Yard, which is used for a walk, was very full of the inhabitants, when about

The yard in back of the State House,
where young men of city assembled

30 fellows, some with snow Balls in their Hats, & some with tri-coulourd cockades enterd and attempted to seize upon the Hats of the Young Men to tear out their cockades. A scuffel ensued when the Young Men became conquerors, and some of these tri-coulourd cockades were trampled in the dust. One fellow was taken, and committed to Jail, but this was sufficient to allarm the inhabitants, and there were every where large collections of people. The light Horse were calld out & patrold the streets all Night. A gaurd was placed before this House, tho through the whole of the Proceedings, and amidst all the collection, the Presidents name was not once mentiond, nor any one grievance complaind of, but a foreign attempt to try their strength & to Awe the inhabitants if possible was no doubt at the bottom. Congress are upon an Allien Bill.

It was left to the President to direct the extreme chauvinism of the Federalists into positive channels while preserving his dual policy of maintaining the peace and preparing for war. On June 21, 1798, Adams sent to Congress a short message announcing the end of the attempt to negotiate with France. The last sentence of the message was to prove a difficult hurdle for the administration when Talleyrand decided to change his tune.

21 June, 1798.

Gentlemen of the Senate, and Gentlemen of the House of Representatives,

Cartoon of 1798 showing the fight
in Congress that erupted after the
passage of the Alien and Sedition
Acts at height of the quasi war

While I congratulate you on the arrival of General [John] Marshall, one of our late envoys extraordinary to the French republic, at a place of safety, where he is justly held in honor, I think it my duty to communicate to you a letter received by him from Mr. Gerry, the only one of the three who has not received his *congé*. This letter, together with another from the minister of foreign relations to him, of the third of April, and his answer of the fourth, will show the situation in which he remains, his intentions, and prospects.

I presume that before this time he has received fresh instructions (a copy of which accompanies this message) to consent to no loans; and therefore the negotiation may be considered at an end.

I will never send another minister to France, without assurances that he will be received, respected, and honored as the representative of a great, free, powerful, and independent nation.

Meanwhile the Federalists pushed through Congress the Alien and Sedition Acts, instituting stricter measures of control over aliens and authorizing the prosecution of people defaming the person of the President. Adams was held responsible in the public mind for these unpopular measures, which he neither recommended nor took steps to enforce, but which he felt obliged to sign into law. Years later during another war, Adams commented upon this legislation in a letter to Jefferson.

Quincy June 14, 1813

In your Letter to Dr. Priestley of March 21. 1801, you "...disclaim the legitimacy of that Libel on legislation...." This Law, I presume was, the Alien Law....

As your name is subscribed to that law, as Vice President, and mine as President, I know not why you are not as responsible for it as I am. Neither of Us were concerned in the formation of it. We were then at War with France: French Spies then swarmed in our Cities and in the Country. Some of them were, intollerably, turbulent, impudent and seditious. To check these was the design of this law. Was there ever a Government, which had not Authority to defend itself against Spies in its own Bosom? Spies of an Ennemy at War? This Law was never executed by me, in any Instance.

But what is the conduct of our Government now? Aliens are ordered to report their names and obtain Certificates once a month: and an industrious Scotchman, at this moment industriously labouring in my Garden is obliged to walk once a month to Boston, eight miles at least, to renew his Certificate from the Marshall. And a fat organist is ordered into the Country. etc. etc. etc. All this is right. Every Government has by the Law of Nations a right to make prisoners of War, of every Subject of an Enemy. But a War with England differs not from a War with France. The Law of Nations is the same in both.

The commission signed by President Adams appointing George Washington Commander in Chief again in 1798

In the summer of 1798, the President took steps to prepare the country for war by creating the Department of the Navy under Benjamin Stoddert and by appointing George Washington Commander in Chief of the provisional army of ten thousand men. He also reluctantly appointed Alexander Hamilton Inspector General of the Army, after Hamilton had intrigued for the position through Secretary of War McHenry. While he was taking these steps, however, Adams received news of Talleyrand's reversal of policy toward America. The French minister, becoming convinced that the United States could not be conquered even by Napoleon, decided instead to play the Americans against the British. He accordingly let it be known that he wished to reestablish friendly relations with the United States and would accept an emissary under the conditions specified by the President. Adams responded in February, 1799. Without notifying his Cabinet members, whom he had begun to distrust, he announced the appointment of a second mission to France—to the overwhelming consternation of the prowar faction of the Federalists. The martial Hamilton, who had visions of commanding a fifty-thousand-man army against the French, was outraged, and through his confidants in the Cabinet, he did his best to undermine the President's initiative. By the summer of 1799, the peace mission still had not left for France, while Adams, living at Quincy, could do little but wonder at the cause of the delay. It was October before he discovered the connivance between Hamilton and his Cabinet and, over their protests, peremptorily ordered the departure of the mission. But not until a meeting with Secretary of War McHenry in early May, 1800, did Adams begin to perceive the extent of Hamilton's sinister influence over his closest advisers and decided to dismiss them. McHenry's report of the President's animated conversation at this meeting is recorded in a letter he wrote to Adams confirming his resignation as Secretary of War.

War Department 31 May 1800

I respectfully take the Liberty to state to you my recollection of the substance and incidents of the conversation which passed between us on the evening (the 5th instant) preceding my Resignation of the Office of Secretary for the Department of War. . . .

P[resident]: "Hamilton is an intriguant—the greatest intriguant in the world—a man devoid of every moral principle—a Bastard, and as much a foreigner as Gallatin. Mr. Jefferson is an infinitely better man; a wiser one I am sure, and, if President, will act wisely. I know it, and would rather be vice president under him, or even minister resident at the Hague, than indebted to such a being as Hamilton for the Presidency. But I can retire to Quincy, and like Washington write Letters, and leave them behind me. You are subservient to Hamilton, who ruled Washington, and would still rule if he could. Washington saddled me with three Secretaries who would controul me; but I shall take care of that. Wolcott is a good Secretary of the Treasury, but what do any of you know

Engraving of The Boston Troops on Boston Common, *as formed for review on John Adams's birthday*

of the diplomatic interests of Europe? You are all mere children who can give no assistance in such matters."

S[ecretary]: "I am very ready to acknowledge your superior opportunities and experience in affairs of Diplomacy, and, if you please, my own comparative ignorance."

P[resident]: "How could such men presume to advise in such matters or dare to recommend a suspension of the Mission to France? . . .

"You cannot, Sir, remain longer in office."

Unfortunately for Adams, Oliver Wolcott, the most treacherous of his advisers, remained in the Cabinet carrying on a duplicitous correspondence with Hamilton until his resignation at the end of 1800. But with the departure of McHenry and Pickering, and the appointment of John Marshall as Secretary of State and Samuel Dexter as Secretary of War, there was a distinct improvement in the operation of the government. One of the issues faced by Adams and his new Cabinet at this time involved the aftermath of Fries's Rebellion. In 1798 angry farmers in northeastern Pennsylvania, led by a popular and vocal auctioneer named John Fries, had risen against Federal tax officials collecting revenue for the provisional army. Fries had been taken into custody and tried for treason, and he and two others had been sentenced to be hanged. In considering whether or not to pardon the three, Adams raised a number of questions in a memorandum to his Cabinet.

Philadelphia 20 May, 1800.

1. Among the three criminals under sentence of death, is there any discrimination in the essential circumstances of their cases, which would justify a determination to pardon or reprieve one or two, and execute the other?
2. Is the execution of one or more so indispensably demanded by public justice and by the security of the public peace, that mercy cannot be extended to all three, or any two, or one?
3. Will the national Constitution acquire more confidence in the minds of the American people by the execution than by the pardon of one or more of the offenders?
4. Is it clear beyond all reasonable doubt that the crime of which they stand convicted, amounts to a levying of war against the United States, or, in other words, to treason?
5. Is there any evidence of a secret correspondence or combination with other anti-federalists of any denomination in other States in the Union, or in other parts of this

Mrs. John Fries begging President Adams to pardon her husband, which he did despite advice to contrary

365

*By intriguing for the position
through Secretary of War McHenry
(above), Alexander Hamilton (below)
was appointed Inspector General of
the Army by Adams even though
the President considered him
his "Arch Ennemy."*

State, to rise in force against the execution of the law for taxing houses, &c., or for opposing the commissioners in general in the execution of their offices?

6. *Quo animo* [In what spirit] was this insurrection? Was it a design of general resistance to all law, or any particular law? Or was it particular to the place and persons?

7. Was it any thing more than a riot, high-handed, aggravated, daring, and dangerous indeed, for the purpose of a rescue? This is a high crime, but can it strictly amount to treason?

8. Is there not great danger in establishing such a construction of treason, as may be applied to every sudden, ignorant, inconsiderate heat, among a part of the people, wrought up by political disputes, and personal or party animosities?

9. Will not a career of capital executions for treason, once opened, without actual bloodshed or hostility against any military force of government, inflict a deep wound in the minds of the people, inflame their animosities, and make them more desperate in sudden heats, and thoughtless riots in elections, and on other occasions where political disputes run high, and introduce a more sanguinary disposition among them?

10. Is not the tranquillity in the western counties, since the insurrection there, and the subsequent submission to law, a precedent in favor of clemency?

11. Is there any probability that a capital execution will have any tendency to change the political sentiments of the people?

12. Will not clemency have a greater tendency to correct their errors?

13. Are not the fines and imprisonments, imposed and suffered, a sufficient discouragement, for the present, of such crimes?...

May not the long imprisonment of Fries, the two solemn, awful trials, his acknowledgment of the justice of his sentence, his professions of deep repentance, and promises of obedience, be accepted, and turned more to the advantage of government and the public peace, than his execution?

In their reply to the President, the members of the Cabinet were almost unanimously opposed to a pardon, as were most Federalists.

Philadelphia, 20 May, 1800.

Having considered the questions proposed by the President for our consideration, we respectfully submit the following opinions.

That the intent of the insurgents in Pennsylvania, in 1798, was to prevent the execution of the law, directing the valuation of houses and lands, and the enumeration of slaves, in the particular district of country where they resided. That we know of no combination in other States, and presume that no combination, pervading the whole State of Pennsylvania, was actually formed. We believe, however, that if the government had not adopted prompt measures, the spirit of insurrection would have rapidly extended.

We are of opinion that the crime committed by Fries, Heyney, and Getman, amounted to treason, and that no danger can arise to the community from the precedents already established by the judges upon this subject. We cannot form a certain judgment of the effect upon public opinion, of suffering the law to have its course, but we think it must be beneficial, by inspiring the well disposed with confidence in the government, and the malevolent and factious with terror.

The Attorney-General and the Secretary of the Navy, however, believe that the execution of one will be enough for example, the great end of punishment, and that Fries deserves most to suffer; because, though all are guilty, and all have forfeited their lives to the justice of their country, he was the most distinguished in the commission of the crime. The Secretary of the Treasury perceives no good ground for any distinction in the three cases, and he believes that a discrimination, instead of being viewed as an act of mercy, would too much resemble a sentence against an unfortunate individual. He also believes that the mercy of government has been sufficiently manifested by the proceedings of the Attorney of the United States, and that the cause of humanity will be most effectually promoted by impressing an opinion that those who are brought to trial, and convicted of treason, will not be pardoned....

The Attorney-General and Secretary of the Navy beg leave to add, as their opinion, that it will be more just and more wise that all should suffer the sentence of the law, than that all should be pardoned.

In 1798 President Adams created the Department of the Navy, appointing Benjamin Stoddert (above) its head.

John Adams was always proud of having exercised his independent judgment in pardoning Fries and the others. He gave his reasons in a letter to his Attorney General and acting Secretary of State Charles Lee.

Philadelphia, 21 May, 1800.

Sir,—I received yesterday the opinion of yourself, the Secretary of the Treasury, and the Secretary of the Navy, on the case of the prisoners under sentence of death for treason, formed, as I doubt not, under the full exercise of integrity and humanity. Nevertheless, as I differ in opinion, I must take on myself alone the responsibility of one more appeal to the humane and generous natures of the American people.

I pray you, therefore, to prepare for my signature, this morning, a pardon for each of the criminals, John Fries, Frederic Heyney, and John Getman.

I pray you, also, to prepare the form of a proclamation of a general pardon of all treasons, and conspiracies to commit treasons, heretofore committed in the three offending counties, in opposition to the law laying taxes on houses, &c., that tranquillity may be restored to the minds of those people, if possible.

I have one request more; that you would consult the judge, and the late and present attorneys of this district, concerning the circumstances of guilt and punishment of those now under sentence for fines and imprisonment, and report to me a list of the names of such, if there are any, as may be proper objects of the clemency of government.

In late May and early June, 1800, John Adams traveled to Washington to inspect the new seat of government. A letter to his wife at this time shows that he was pleased with what he saw.

Washington June 13. 1800

I have seen many Cities and fine Places since you left me and particularly Mount Vernon. Mrs. Washington and her whole Family very kindly enquired after your health and all your Children and Louisa; and send many friendly Greetings.

I like the Seat of Government very well and shall Sleep, or lie awake next Winter in the Presidents house. I have Slept very well on my Journey and been pretty well. An Abundance of Company and many tokens of respect have attended my Journey, and my Visit is well received. Mr. Marshall and Mr. Dexter lodge with me at Tunnicliffs City Hotel, very near the Capitol. The Establishment of the public officers in this place has given it the Air of the seat of Government and all Things seem to go on well.

I am particularly pleased with Alexandria. Mr. [Henry] Lee lives very elegantly neatly and agreably there among his sisters and friends and among his fine Lotts of Clover and Timothy. I scarcely know a more eligible situation. Oh! that I could have a home! But this felicity has never been permitted me. Rolling rolling rolling, till I am very near rolling into the bosom of mother Earth.

In November, 1800, Abigail traveled from Quincy to join her husband in Washington where the President's House (not to be known as the White House until many years later) was nearing completion. She wrote her sister Mrs. Cranch an account of the end of her journey and a not uncritical account of the condition of her new home.

Washington, Nov'br 21, 1800

I arrived in this city on Sunday the 16th ult. Having lost my way in the woods on Saturday in going from Baltimore, we took the road to Frederick and got nine miles out of our road. You find nothing but a Forest & woods on the way, for 16 and 18 miles not a village. Here and there a thatchd cottage without a single pane of glass, inhabited by Blacks. My intention was to have reachd Washington on Saturday. Last winter there was a Gentleman and Lady in Philadelphia by the Name of Snowden whose hospitality I heard much of. They visited me and were invited to dine with us, but did not, as they left the city before the day for dinner. They belong to Maryland, and live on the road to this place 21 miles distant. I was advised at Baltimore to make their House my stage for the night, the only Inn at which I could put up being 36 miles ride from Baltimore. Judge [Samuel] Chase who visited me, at Baltimore, gave Mr. T[homas Boylston] Adams a Letter to Major Snowden, but I who have never been accustomed to quarter myself and servants upon private houses, could not think of it, particularly as I expected the chariot & 5 more Horses with two servants to meet

BOSTON ATHENAEUM

The original plan of the city of Washington called for Pennsylvania Avenue to connect the Capitol (center) with the President's House. Georgetown is at top left.

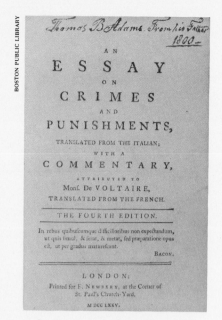

A book on crime that Adams gave to his son Thomas in 1800

Although Georgetown looks idyllic in this early view, Abigail called it "the very dirtyest Hole."

me. I sit out early, intending to make my 36 miles if possible: no travelling however but by day light; We took a direction as we supposed right, but in the first turn, went wrong, and were wandering more than two hours in the woods in different paths, holding down & breaking bows of trees which we could not pass, untill we met a solitary black fellow with a horse and cart. We inquired of him our way, and he kindly offerd to conduct us, which he did two miles, and then gave us such a clue as led us out to the post road and the Inn, where we got some dinner. Soon after we left it, we met the chariot then 30 miles from Washington, and 20 from our destination. We road as fast as the roads would allow of, but the sun was near set when we came in sight of the Majors. I halted but could not get courage to go to his House with ten Horses and nine persons. I therefore ordered the coach man to proceed, and we drove rapidly on. We had got about a mile when we were stoped by the Major in full speed, who had learnt that I was comeing on; & had kept watch for me, with his Horse at the door; as he was at a distance from the road. In the kindest, and politest manner he urged my return to his House, represented the danger of the road, and the impossibility of my being accomodated at any Inn I could reach: A mere hovel was all I should find. I plead my numbers. That was no objection. He could accomodate double the number. There was no saying nay and I returnd to a large, Handsome, Elegant House, where I was received with my Family, with what we might term true English Hospitality, Friendship without ostentation, and kindness without painfull ceremony. Mrs. Snowden is a charming woman of about 45. She has a lovely daughter of 16 & one of 6, a son whom I had seen often in Philadelphia and who had several times dinned with us. I need not add that they are all true federal Characters. Every attention possible was shown me and the next morning I took my departure, having share in the common bounty of Major Snowdens hospitality, for which he is universally celebrated—I arrived about one oclock at this place known by the *name* of *the city*, and the Name is all that you can call so. As I expected to find it a new country, with Houses scatterd over a space of ten miles, and trees & stumps in plenty with, a castle of a House—so

I found it—The Presidents House is in a beautifull situation in front of which is the Potomac with a view of Alexandr[i]a. The country around is romantic but a wild, a wilderness at present.

I have been to George Town and felt all that Mrs. [William] Cranch described when she was a resident there. It is the very dirtyest Hole I ever saw for a place of any trade, or respectability of inhabitants. It is only one mile from me but a quagmire after every rain. Here we are obliged to send daily for marketting; The capital is near two miles from us. As to roads we shall make them by the frequent passing before winter, but I am determined to be satisfied and content, to say nothing of inconvenience &c. That must be a worse place than even George Town, that I would not reside in for three Months.

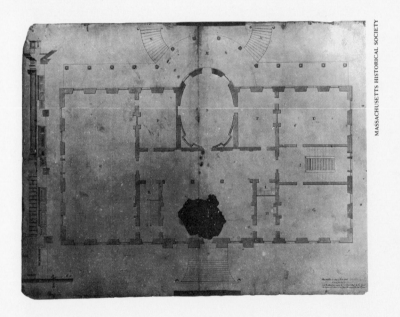

This floor plan by James Hoban, whose design for the President's House won the prize, outlines a colonnaded portico never built.

MASSACHUSETTS HISTORICAL SOCIETY

There was no little irony in Abigail's account to her daughter of the expenses and inconveniences of living in a large and uncompleted "castle."

Washington, 21 November, 1800.
The house is upon a grand and superb scale, requiring about thirty servants to attend and keep the apartments in proper order, and perform the ordinary business of the house and stables; an establishment very ill proportioned to the President's salary. The lighting the apartments, from the kitchen to parlors and cham-

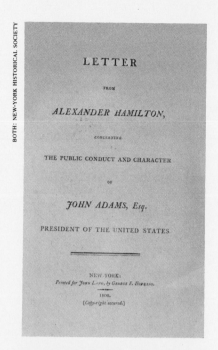

LETTER

FROM

ALEXANDER HAMILTON,

CONCERNING

THE PUBLIC CONDUCT AND CHARACTER

OF

JOHN ADAMS, Esq.

PRESIDENT OF THE UNITED STATES.

NEW-YORK:
Printed for *John Lang,* by George F. Hopkins.
1800.
[Copy-right secured.]

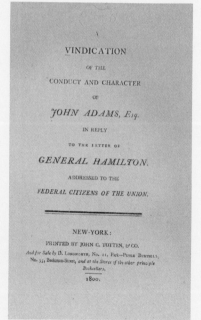

A

VINDICATION

OF THE

CONDUCT AND CHARACTER

OF

JOHN ADAMS, Esq.

IN REPLY

TO THE LETTER OF

GENERAL HAMILTON.

ADDRESSED TO THE

FEDERAL CITIZENS OF THE UNION.

NEW-YORK:
PRINTED BY JOHN C. TOTTEN, &CO.
And for Sale by B. Longworth, *No.* 11, *Park—*Peter Burtsell,
No. 35, *Beekman-Street, and at the Stores of the other principle
Booksellers.*
1800.

*Title page of Hamilton's scathing
pamphlet about Adams (top) and
one published in his defense (below)*

bers, is a tax indeed; and the fires we are obliged to keep to secure us from daily agues is another very cheering comfort. To assist us in this great castle, and render less attendance necessary, bells are wholly wanting, not one single one being hung through the whole house, and promises are all you can obtain. This is so great an inconvenience, that I know not what to do, or how to do.... If they will put me up some bells, and let me have wood enough to keep fires, I design to be pleased. I could content myself almost anywhere three months; but, surrounded with forests, can you believe that wood is not to be had, because people cannot be found to cut and cart it! [John] Briesler [an old family retainer brought from Quincy] entered into a contract with a man to supply him with wood. A small part, a few cords only, has he been able to get. Most of that was expended to dry the walls of the house before we came in, and yesterday the man told him it was impossible for him to procure it to be cut and carted. He has had recourse to coals; but we cannot get grates made and set. We have, indeed, come into *a new country.*

You must keep all this to yourself, and, when asked how I like it, say that I write you the situation is beautiful, which is true. The house is made habitable, but there is not a single apartment finished, and all withinside, except the plastering, has been done since Briesler came. We have not the least fence, yard, or other convenience, without, and the great unfinished audience-room I make a drying-room of, to hang up the clothes in. The principal stairs are not up, and will not be this winter. Six chambers are made comfortable; two are occupied by the President and Mr. [William Smith] Shaw [Adams's nephew and private secretary]; two lower rooms, one for a common parlor, and one for a levee-room. Up stairs there is the oval room, which is designed for the drawingroom, and has the crimson furniture in it. It is a very handsome room now; but, when completed, it will be beautiful. If the twelve years, in which this place has been considered as the future seat of government, had been improved, as they would have been if in New England, very many of the present inconveniences would have been removed. It is a beautiful spot, capable of every improvement, and, the more I view it, the more I am delighted with it.

The death of Charles Adams in New York was a grievous blow to his parents, who were already weighted down with cares. John Adams left a record of his feelings on this mournful occasion in a letter to his friend François Adriaan Van der Kemp.

Charles Adams who died in 1800

Washington, 28 December, 1800.

I had last night your letter of the 12th, the friendly sentiments of which have tenderly affected me. The affliction in my family from the melancholy death of a once beloved son, has been very great, and has required the consolation of religion, as well as philosophy, to enable us to support it. The prospects of that unfortunate youth were very pleasing and promising, but have been cut off, and a wife and two very young children are left with their grandparents to bewail a fate, which neither could avert, and to which all ought in patience to submit. I have two sons left, whose conduct is worthy of their education and connections. I pray that their lives may be spared and their characters respected.

The growing schism among Federalists boded ill for the party in the presidential elections of 1800. In May the Republicans won a majority in the New York legislature, where votes would soon be cast for presidential electors. Had New York remained in the Federalist camp, Adams would have received sixteen more votes that either Jefferson or Burr. The Republican victory in New York threw the Federalists into disarray, made worse by the publication in September of Alexander Hamilton's *Letter... Concerning the Public Conduct and Character of John Adams, Esq.* Originally intended as private advice to Federalists, the pamphlet was an attempt to divide the vote of New England Federalists equally between Adams and vice presidential candidate Charles Cotesworth Pinckney, leaving southern Federalists to cast the deciding votes for Pinckney. Hamilton charged that Adams "does not possess the talents adapted to the administration of government, and that there are great and intrinsic defects in his character, which unfit him for the office of Chief Magistrate." Disclosure of these attacks delighted Republicans. Though Hamilton soon urged all-out support for Adams in an effort to avoid a complete Federalist defeat, the damage had been done. The Republicans won the election, Jefferson became President, and Aaron Burr became Vice President. Several years later, after Hamilton was killed in a duel with Burr, Adams summed up his opinion of his great opponent, whom he had once referred to as the "bastard brat of a Scottish peddlar."

Autobiography, 1802–7

Although I have long since forgiven this Arch Ennemy,

John Marshall, appointed by John Adams in 1801 to be Chief Justice

yet Vice, Folly and Villany are not to be forgotten, because the guilty Wretch repented, in his dying Moments. Although David repented, We are no where commanded to forget the Affair of Uriah: though the Magdelene reformed, We are not obliged to forget her former *Vocation:* though the Thief on the cross was converted, his Felony is still upon Record. The Prodigal Son repented and was forgiven, yet his Harlots and riotous living, and even the Swine and the husks that brought him to consideration, cannot be forgotten. Nor am I obliged by any Principles of Morality or Religion to suffer my Character to lie under infamous Calumnies, because the Author of them, with a Pistol Bullet through his Spinal Marrow, died a Penitent. Charity requires that We should hope and believe that his humiliation was sincere, and I [sincerely] hope that he was forgiven: but I will not conceal his former Character at the Expense of so much injustice to my own, as this Scottish Creolian Bolingbroke in the days of his disappointed Ambition and unbridled Malice and revenge was pleased falsely to attempt against it. Born on a Speck more obscure than Corsica, from an original not only contemptible but infamous, with infinitely less courage and Capacity than Bonaparte, he would in my Opinion, if I had not controuled the fury of his Vanity, instead of relieving this country from Confusion as Bonaparte did France, he would have involved it in all the Bloodshed and distractions of foreign and civil War at once.

News of the Adams administration's success in negotiating the Convention of Mortefontaine ending the quasi war with France did not arrive until after Adams's defeat at the polls. Even if the news had come earlier, it would not have been sufficient to turn the tide. Nevertheless, the settlement was a great personal triumph for the President. This victory was soon followed by an act which has rightly been considered one of Adams's greatest contributions to strong, national government in the United States: his appointment of John Marshall to be Chief Justice of the Supreme Court. The appointment of the so-called "midnight judges" in the final hours of his administration was John Adams's last official act as President. Before dawn on March 4, 1801, he left Washington in his coach for Quincy, without attending the inauguration of his successor. There is no evidence that he had been invited.

A Picture Portfolio

Service to the New Nation

ADAMS PAPERS

IN AT THE BEGINNING

In June, 1774, John Adams was elected a delegate to the First Continental Congress. His reaction was one of "Unutterable Anxiety," for he felt: "We have not Men, fit for the Times. We are deficient in Genius, in Education, in Travel, in Fortune—in every Thing." Despite this, he entered the political arena with dedication. As a member of the committee that drafted the Declaration of Independence, he stands at far left—along with Roger Sherman, Robert R. Livingston, Thomas Jefferson, and Benjamin Franklin—in the detail opposite from Trumbull's painting. A copy of the Declaration in his own handwriting appears above. His writings later played an important role in the framing of the Constitution and earned Adams the title Father of American Political Science.

378

"THE MOST INSIGNIFICANT OFFICE"

After the Constitution was ratified and the new nation went to the polls for the very first time in 1789, George Washington (left, above) became its first President and John Adams its first Vice President. As presiding officer of the Senate, he cast his deciding vote more times than any other Vice President to date; yet he complained that "My country in its wisdom contrived for me the most insignificant office that ever the invention of man contrived or his imagination conceived." Despite his frustration at the lack of political challenge, the ceremonial side was brisk. In New York the Adamses occupied a comfortable house (left), in front of which "the noble Hudson rolls his majestic waves," and where Abigail discovered "I have never before been in a situation in which morning, noon, and afternoon I have been half as much exposed to company . . . at Richmond Hill it is expected that I am at Home to Gentlemen and Ladies whenever they come out, which is almost every-day." Within a year the seat of government was moved to Philadelphia and again the Adamses found an attractive home, Bush Hill (above). Abigail found "the ladies here . . . well-educated, well-bred, and well-dressed. There is much more society than in New York." Adams had said "I am possessed of two separate powers: the one in *esse* and the other in *posse*. I am Vice President. In this I am nothing, but I may be everything." His turn did not come until after eight years of being in second place, but then, indeed, he did become "everything."

379

A New DISPLAY of the UNITED STATES

CHIEF EXECUTIVE

The election that brought John Adams to the Presidency was close—a majority of only three electoral votes over Thomas Jefferson—and was the only time a President and his Vice President belonged to bitterly opposed factions. The great seals of sixteen states ring Adams's portrait in the 1799 broadside at left, the year before he and Abigail became the first presidential family to preside in Washington. Due to endless construction delays, the Capitol (above) boasted only its north wing. Abigail found the White House (below)—or the President's House as it was then called—"upon a grand and superb scale." With a fitting sense of history, John offered a prayer to Heaven "to bestow the best of Blessings on this House and all that shall hereafter inhabit it. May none but honest and wise Men ever rule under this roof."

FIAT JUSTITIA

382

CHALLENGES AND ACHIEVEMENTS

Adams's administration was threatened at home by the unceasing hostility of
Alexander Hamilton (left, above), and abroad by a quasi war with France. Adams
was successful in restoring good relations with the French, culminating in the signing of the Convention of Mortefontaine in 1800 (above). So pleased was he that
soon after he composed his own epitaph: "Here lies John Adams, who took upon
himself the responsibility of the peace with France in the year 1800." With Hamilton, however, he had no such success. "Hamilton is an intriguant — the greatest
intriguant in the world — a man devoid of every moral principle," he wrote, as
Hamilton worked to undermine the loyalty of his Cabinet and sought ways to turn
the Federalists against him. One of Adams's last official acts was the superb appointment of John Marshall (left) to be Chief Justice of the Supreme Court. It had
been a turbulent four years. "Had I been chosen President again," he acknowledged, "I am certain I could not have lived another year."

"PEACE AND TRANQUILITY"

Just before John and Abigail left public life in 1801, Gilbert Stuart started their portraits. Of Abigail's (left), a friend wrote: "Stewart says, he wishes to god, he could have taken Mrs. Adams when she was young, he believes he should have a perfect Venus." Her devoted husband of thirty-seven years agreed emphatically. They returned home to Quincy to the house (below) they had bought in 1788 and which John had christened "Peace field, in commemoration of the Peace which I assisted in making in 1783 . . . and of the constant Peace and Tranquility which I have enjoyed in this Residence." Peace came to him in another guise. At the urging of a mutual friend, he opened a correspondence with Thomas Jefferson, from whom he had been estranged so long. Their renewed friendship was to afford him tremendous pleasure throughout his remaining years. A memorial plaque (right), with their portraits and their Declaration, still hangs in "Peace field."

Chapter 12

Sage of Quincy

John Adams's retirement from public life was followed by a quarter of a century of growth in wisdom as well as age. As the harvest moon sheds its mellow luster on the passing summer scene, so the mind of John Adams illuminated in old age some of man's most persistent questions with insights distilled from years of experience and reflection.

The first years of his retirement found the vigorous gentleman farmer of Quincy setting straight the facts of earlier controversies in fragmentary writings for his family, friends, and posterity. The inevitable resentments felt by a sensitive man after a long and active life of public service gradually gave way to more positive feelings of satisfaction. Always a voracious reader and keen observer of contemporary affairs, Adams led an active intellectual life as president of various learned societies and correspondent of scholarly friends. But it was as the "farmer of Stony field" that he wrote to the Marquis de Lafayette to congratulate him on his release by Napoleon from the fortress at Olmutz, where he had been imprisoned for five years.

Quincy, 6 April, 1801.

"I live" also "with my family in a rural, solitary place of retirement," after an uninterrupted toil of six-and-twenty years in the service of the public. Like you, also, "I preserve the love, the doctrines, and the independence of true liberty." It is a lamentable truth, that mankind has always been ill treated by government, and a most unfortunate circumstance, which renders the evil totally desperate, is, that they are never so ill used as when they take the government into their own hands. . . .

Your country by adoption has grown and prospered since you saw it. You would scarcely know it, if you should make it a visit. It would be a great pleasure to the farmer of Stony field to take you by the hand in his little *chaumière*.

During the early years of his retirement, John Adams found it helpful "to throw off that intolerable burden of obloquy and insolence" that had been heaped upon him by indulging himself in several different kinds of writing. From 1802 to 1807 he worked on his *Autobiography*, first published by his grandson, Charles Francis Adams, in 1850. This work had only reached the year 1780 when Adams turned angrily in July, 1807, to the task of refuting Mrs. Mercy Otis Warren. This lady had dared to quote in her *History . . . of the American Revolution* (1805) her husband's charge that Adams's years in Europe had corrupted him. "Corrupted! Madam, what provocation, what evidence, what misrepresentation could he have received that could prompt him to utter this execrable calumny? Corruption is a charge that I cannot and will not bear. I challenge the whole human race, and angels and devils too, to produce an instance of it from my cradle to this hour." After carefully putting the record straight in a series of ten crushing letters, he felt impelled to write a longer series that was published in the *Boston Patriot* between 1809 and 1812, in which he explained in great detail his actions as negotiator in Europe. Meantime, in many of his private writings, Adams pondered the great writers and issues of his time. He realized, for instance, that Thomas Paine had had a great influence in forming public opinion; but he denied to Dr. Benjamin Waterhouse that Paine's propaganda had much to do with honest thought.

Quincy, October 29, 1805.

Adams's granddaughter, Abigail Smith Adams, sketched Peacefield around 1820, when she was living there with the former President.

I am willing you should call this the Age of Frivolity as you do: and would not object if you had named it the Age of Folly, Vice, Frenzy, Fury, Brutality, Daemons, Buonaparte, Tom Paine, or the Age of the burning Brand from the bottomless Pitt: or any thing but the Age of Reason. I know not whether any Man in the World has had more influence on its inhabitants or affairs for the last thirty years than Tom Paine. There can be no severer Satyr on the Age. For such a mongrel between Pigg and Puppy, begotten by a wild Boar on a Bitch Wolf, never before in any Age of the World was suffered by the Poltroonery of mankind, to run through such a Career of Mischief. Call it then the Age of Paine. He deserves it much more, than the Courtezan who was consecrated to represent the Goddess [of Reason] in the Temple at Paris, and whose name, Tom has given to the Age. The real intellectual faculty has nothing to do with the Age, the Strumpet or Tom.

387

Disillusioned with the prophets of progress, Adams nevertheless respected the quality of thought of the great French *philosophes,* whom he considered worthy antagonists. Dr. Benjamin Rush, Adams's most faithful correspondent at this time, received the following discourse on the perfectibility of man. Written in Adams's best Rabelaisian manner, the "artillery of language" as Rush once called it, the letter reveals an earthy, robust, humorous side of Adams.

Quincy Novr. 11. 1806.

Dear Sir,—When I recd. your favour of the 24 Oct. I soberly expected a grave dissertation on the Perfectibility of Man. Although I thank you for the political information you give me, which is amusing,...I was disappointed in finding nothing upon the great subject of the Perfectibility of human Nature, which I suppose is to be ranged under the head of Ethicks. I really wish you would tell me what you understand by this mighty discovery of [Richard] Price, [Joseph] Priestly or [Marquis de] Condorcet. Perfectibility, I should suppose to mean, capability of Perfection; or susceptibility of perfection. But what is Perfection? It is self evident, there cannot be more than one perfect Being in the Universe.... These great Phylosophers then cannot be supposed to mean that every Man, Woman and Child is capable of becoming a Supream and all perfect Being. What then do they mean? Do they mean perfection in this world or in a future state? Do they mean perfection of Mind or Body or both? Condorcet and Priestly believed in no soul, spirit or Mind distinct from the Body: they must therefore have meant that the Perfectibility resided in the Body or matter. Do they mean that in a future state, the Body may be purified from all causes of disease and death, liberated from all Pain, Grief, Sorrow and Uneasiness and that forever. If this is all their meaning, it is no more than the Christian Doctrine.... The greatest part however of the modern Philosophers, who have written and discoursed upon this Mysterious doctrine, have confined their Ideas to this terrestrial existence and have believed in no other. If they mean that Man is capable, by abstract meditation, and habitual practice of acquiring that self possession and command which can bear pain and think it no more intollerable than Pleasure, the *Felicis Animi immota tranquilitis* [undisturbed tranquility of a happy mind], this is no more than the Perfectibility of the Stoick Philosophy. If they

Portrait of Mrs. Mercy Otis Warren, by John Singleton Copley in 1763, when she was a much younger woman

Disagreeing violently with D'Alembert, Adams called him a "Louse, Flea, Tick... or whatever Vermin thou art" in the margin of a book containing the French philosophe's letters to Frederick the Great.

mean that by banishing all Ideas of God or Gods, of future Rewards and Punishments and of moral Government or Providence in the Universe, every Man may get into an habit of taking pleasure in every Thing, this is no more than the Perfectibility of Epicurus or Lucretius.... What then do they mean?... The greater part of Politicians and Phylosophers who prated about the Perfectibility of Man, mean nothing but to seize, occupy and confound the attention of the Public, while they were amusing and cheating the Populace with principles of equality and Levellism, which they knew impracticable and never intended to promote any further than for the purposes of present plunder. It is really humiliating to the pride of human nature that so frivolous a piece of Pedantry should have made so much noise in the world and been productive of such melancholly and tragical effects; especially as another discovery had been made long before, of much more importance, by which this and most of the other Theories and events of the last twenty years might have been more justly estimated.

The discovery I mean is this. If we take a survey of the greatest actions which have been performed in the world, which are the establishment of new empires by Conquest and the advance and progress of new schemes in Phylosophy, we shall find the authors of them all to have been persons whose Brains had been shaken out of their natural position. For the upper region of Man is furnished like the middle region of the air. Mists arise from the earth, steams from dunghills, exhalations from the sea and smoke from fire; yet all Clouds are the same in composition as well as consequences; and fumes issuing from a Jakes will furnish as comely and usefull a vapour as incense from an altar. As the face of nature never produces rain, but when it is overcast and disturbed; so human understanding seated in the brain, must be troubled and overspread by vapours, ascending from the lower faculties to water the invention and render it fruitful. Two instances may be produced to prove and explain this Theory. The first is that of Henry the fourth of France, whose whole project of universal empire, as well as that of subduing the Turk and recovering Palestine, arose from an absent female, whose eyes had raised a protuberancy, and

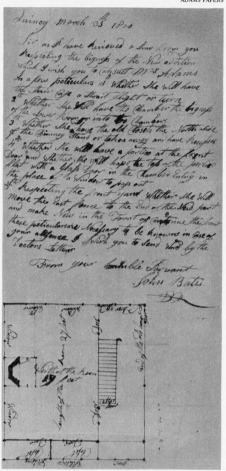

*Letter from John Bates to Adams,
who was in Washington, discussing
new additions to the Quincy house*

before emission she was sent into an ennemy's country. The collected part of the semen, raised and inflamed became a Lust converted to choler turned head upon the spinal duct, and ascended to the brain. The very same principle that influences a bully to break the windows of a whore that has jilted him, naturally stirrs up a great Prince to raise mighty armies, and dream of nothing but sieges, battles and victories. In this place I cannot avoid introducing a reflection by way of digression. What a pity it is that our Congress had not known this discovery, and that Alexander Hamiltons projects of raising an army of fifty thousand Men, ten thousand of them to be Cavalry and his projects of sedition Laws and Alien Laws and of new taxes to support his army, all arose from a superabundance of secretions which he could not find whores enough to draw off! and that the same vapours produced his Lyes and Slanders by which he totally destroyed his party forever and finally lost his Life in the field of Honor. But to return from this digression.

The second instance is that of Louis 14th. who for the space of above thirty years amused himself to take and lose Towns; beat armies and be beaten; drive Princes out of their dominions; fright children from their bread and butter; burn, lay waste, plunder, dragoon, massacre subject and stranger, friend and foe, male and female: it is recorded that the Phylosophers of each Country, were in grave dispute upon causes natural, moral and political, to find out where they should assign an original solution of this Phenomenon. At last the vapour or spirit, which animated the Hero's brain being in perpetual circulation, seized upon that region of the human Body so renowned for furnishing the *Zibeta occidentalis* [western civet], and gathering there into a tumour, left the rest of the world for that time in Peace. Of such mighty consequences it is, where these exhalations fix; and of so little whence they proceed. The same spirits which in their superiour progress, would conquer a Kingdom, descending upon the Anus conclude in a fistula.

And here again I feel an irresistable inclination, to introduce a Reflection by way of digression. How very desirable it is that all the vapours in the heads of our modern Philosophers, should take a turn downwards, and relieve the world from their silly and mischievous speculations. And above all how devoutly it is to be wished that Napoleon may have a Fistula large enough to carry off all his vapours and set the world at peace.

The Phylosopher from whom I have borrowed this ingenious Theory is Dr. Swift, who in that great Phylosophical effort the Tale of a Tub, has in the ninth section given the world a profound discourse on the original use and improvement of madness in a Commonwealth, which whole section I earnestly recommend to your serious meditation, as one of the profoundest and most important systems of Phylosophy which the last Century produced, and by which I have been convinced that all modern Ideas of the Perfectibility of Man will be drawn from the Brains of every Philosopher upon earth, as soon as a fistula shall be formed in its proper place, and either break or be skillfully cutt, so as to occasion a plentiful discharge.

Promissory note dated March 29, 1802, from John Adams to his brother-in-law Richard Cranch

Adams needed no stimulus to defend his actions and views, but when Rush urged him to leave behind "a posthumous address to the citizens of the United States, in which shall be inculcated all those great social, domestic, and religious virtues which alone can make a people free, great, and happy," Adams's refusal to comply suggests he was still smarting from the stings of public life.

Quincy, August 28, 1811

Your letter of the 20th...has filled my eyes with tears and, indurate stoic as I am, my heart with sensations unutterable by my tongue or pen. Not the feelings of vanity, but the overwhelming sense of my own unworthiness of such a panegyric from such a friend. Like Louis the 16, I said to myself, *"Qu'est ce que J'ai fait pour le meriter?"* [What have I done to merit this?] Have I not been employed in mischief all my days? Did not the American Revolution produce the French Revolution? And did not the French Revolution produce all the calamities and desolations to the human race and the whole globe ever since? I meant well, however. My conscience was clear as a crystal glass without a scruple or a doubt. I was borne along by an irresistible sense of duty. God prospered our labors; and awful, dreadful, and deplorable as the consequences have been, I cannot but hope that the ultimate good of the world, of the human race, and of our beloved country is intended and will be accomplished by it. . . .

If, by dedicating all the rest of my days to the composition of such an address as you propose, I could have any rational assurance of doing any real good to my fellow citizens of United America, I would cheerfully lay aside all other occupations and amusements and devote myself to it. But there are difficulties and embarrassments in the way which to me, at present, appear insuperable.

1. "The sensibility of the public mind," which you anticipate at my decease, will not be so favorable to my memory as you seem to foresee. By the treatment I have received and continue to receive I should expect that a large majority of all parties would cordially rejoice to hear that my head was laid low.

2. I am surprised to read your opinion that "my integrity has never been called in question" and that "friends and enemies agree in believing me to be an honest man." If I am to judge by the newspapers and pamphlets that have been printed in America for twenty years past, I should think that both parties believed me the meanest villain in the world.

3. If they should not "suspect me of sinning in the grave," they will charge me with selfishness and hypocrisy before my death, in preparing an address to move the passions of the people and excite them to promote my children and perhaps to make my son a king. Washington and Franklin could never do anything but what was imputed to pure disinterested patriotism. I never could do anything but what was ascribed to sinister motives.

At the age of seventy-seven, John Adams took an active interest in the progress of the War of 1812; and he was more than willing to voice his opinions about it, as he reported to Dr. Rush.

Quincy, December 29, 1812

You must know that I have the honor to be president of the American Academy of Arts and Sciences, of the Massachusetts Society for Promoting Agriculture, and of the Board of Trustees of this Society and of the Board of Visitors of the Professorship of Natural History at the University. There are twelve of us of these boards. We meet once a month, on the last Saturday, at each other's houses at our own expense. Every one but myself is a staunch Anti-Jeffersonian and Anti-Madisonian. ...These are all real gentlemen; all but me, very rich; have their city palaces and country seats, their fine gardens and greenhouses and hot houses, &c., &c., &c., &c. Men of science, letters, and urbanity, even *Spartacus* [John Lowell, Jr?] *out of a newspaper or a pamphlet* is all this.

On the last Saturday of October at Mr. Pomroy's of Brighton, the gentlemen were in good spirits and indulged in a little political conversation, the detail of which would be too long. I had not agreed to the selection of Mr. [De Witt] Clinton, though I should acquiesce if he were chosen.

Spartacus the Slave! Spartacus the Rebel! Spartacus the Rebel Slave! Spartacus the Rebel Leader of Rebel Slaves! asked me with an air of candor what course I would have pursued had I been continued President to this time? I said that must have depended upon Congress. The gentlemen expressed a wish to know my single opinion of the best plan. I said time would fail me to give details, but I could give in short hand a sketch of a few principal strokes....I said I would not have repealed the taxes; no, not a shilling of them. With that revenue I would have fortified the frontiers on the lakes and rivers as well as on the ocean. I would have gradually increased the navy by additional ships every year that we might be in a condition to meet the mighty mistress of the ocean on her own element and convince her that she is not all powerful there. I would have declared war against Great Britain five or six years ago when the King issued that most atrocious of all violations of the law of nations, his proclamation for impressing seamen from our ships. I would not have said a word about Canada....I would not have invaded it till we had a decided supremacy of naval power upon all the lakes and waters from Michilimackinac to Montreal if not to Quebec; nor then till I had an army of 35 or 40 thousand men. With such an army in four divisions, a small one in Michilimackinac, a larger at Kennebec River, a larger at Detroit, and the largest of all at Niagara, I would have made short work with

Adams's great friend, Dr. Rush, in a portrait by C.W. Peale after Sully

Canada and incorporated it into the union. "What a satire," said Spartacus, "upon our administration!" Here I was called to my carriage to come home, having a dozen miles to ride after dark, and consequently heard no more remarks.

Adams's once friendly relations with Jefferson, which had been deteriorating for years, had declined even further during their presidencies, when they frequently found themselves in opposition on important public issues. It fell to Dr. Rush to be the instrument for effecting a lasting reconciliation between the two men, for as well as being a warm personal friend of Adams, who had appointed him Treasurer of the Mint in 1797, Dr. Rush was also one of Jefferson's most loyal political followers. His account of a dream he had had, which he sent to Adams in the fall of 1809, proved to be the first step toward a reconciliation.

[Philadelphia,] October 16, 1809

"What book is that in your hands?" said I to my son Richard a few nights ago in a DREAM. "It is the history of the United States," said he. "Shall I read a page of it to you?" "No, no," said I. "I believe in the truth of no history but in that which is contained in the Old and New Testaments." "But, sir," said my son, "this page relates to your friend Mr. Adams." "Let me see it then," said I. I read it with great pleasure and herewith send you a copy of it.

"1809

"Among the most extraordinary events of this year was the renewal of the friendship and intercourse between Mr. John Adams and Mr. Jefferson, the two ex-Presidents of the United States. They met for the first time in the Congress of 1775. Their principles of liberty, their ardent attachment to their country, and their views of the importance and probable issue of the struggle with Great Britain in which they were engaged being exactly the same, they were strongly attracted to each other and became personal as well as political friends. They met in England during the war while each of them held commissions of honor and trust at two of the first courts of Europe, and spent many happy hours together in reviewing the difficulties and success of their respective negotiations. A difference of opinion upon the objects and issue of the French Revolution separated them during the years in which that great

Thomas Jefferson by Rembrandt Peale, painted from life in 1805

BOSTON,
mouth & Sandwich
MAIL STAGE,

This coach passed through Quincy
and may have been taken by Adams.

event interested and divided the American People. The predominance of the party which favored the French cause threw Mr. Adams out of the Chair of the United States in the year 1800 and placed Mr. Jefferson there in his stead. The former retired with resignation and dignity to his seat at Quincy, where he spent the evening of his life in literary and philosophical pursuits surrounded by an amiable family and a few old and affectionate friends. The latter resigned the Chair of the United States in the year 1808, sick of the cares and disgusted with the intrigues of public life, and retired to his seat at Monticello in Virginia, where he spent the remainder of his days in the cultivation of a large farm agreeably to the new system of husbandry. In the month of November 1809, Mr. Adams addressed a short letter to his friend Mr. Jefferson in which he congratulated him upon his escape to the shades of retirement and domestic happiness, and concluded it with assurances of his regard and good wishes for his welfare. This letter did great honor to Mr. Adams. It discovered a magnanimity known only to great minds. Mr. Jefferson replied to this letter and reciprocated expressions of regard and esteem. These letters were followed by a correspondence of several years, in which they mutually reviewed the scenes of business in which they had been engaged, and candidly acknowledged to each other all the errors of opinion and conduct into which they had fallen during the time they filled the same station in the service of their country. Many precious aphorisms, the result of observation, experience, and profound reflection, it is said, are contained in these letters. It is to be hoped the world will be favored with a sight of them when they can neither injure nor displease any persons or families whose ancestors' follies or crimes were mentioned in them. These gentlemen sunk into the grave nearly at the same time, full of years and rich in the gratitude and praises of their country (for they outlived the heterogeneous parties that were opposed to them), and to their numerous merits and honors posterity has added that they were rival friends."

Adams's response to the dream of his friend was "that it is not History. It may be Prophecy"; and indeed it was. When it was reported to Jefferson late in 1811 that Adams had said to some of his Virginia neighbors visiting in New England, "I always loved Jefferson and still love him," Jefferson wrote to Dr. Rush, "This is enough for me." On January 1, 1812, Adams wrote Jefferson a friendly letter announcing that he was forwarding under separate cover two pieces of locally produced homespun. Jefferson responded enthusiastically with a loyal description of local weaving in his area. A few days later, he was surprised to receive Adams's gift in the form of two stout volumes on rhetoric and oratory spun from the agile brain of his eldest son, John Quincy Adams, who was for a time professor of rhetoric at Harvard. Adams's reply to Jefferson's slightly embarrassed acknowledgment of this New England "homespun" really begins the magnificent, discursive correspondence between the two men. One of the subjects of great interest to both was the nature of the true aristocrat, upon which Adams discoursed enthusiastically.

Quincy August [14?] 1813

Behold my translation [from Theognis].

"My Friend Curnis, When We want to purchace, Horses, Asses or Rams, We inquire for the Wellborn. And every one wishes to procure, from the good Breeds. A good Man, does not care to marry a Shrew, the Daughter of a Shrew; unless They give him, a great deal of Money with her." . . .

Theognis lived five hundred and forty four Years before Jesus Christ. Has Science or Morals, or Philosophy or Criticism or Christianity, advanced or improved, or enlightened Mankind upon this Subject, and shewn them, that the Idea of the "Well born" is a prejudice, a Phantasm, a Point no point, a Gape Fly away, a dream? I say it is the Ordonance of God Almighty, in the Constitution of human nature, and wrought into the Fabrick of the Universe. Philosophers and Politicians, may nibble and quibble, but they never will get rid of it. Their only resource is, to controul it. Wealth is another Monster to be subdued. Hercules could not subdue both or either. To subdue them by regular approaches by a regular Seige, and strong fortifications, was my Object in writing on Aristocracy, as I proposed to you in Grovenor Square.

If you deny any one of these Positions, I will prove them to demonstration by Examples drawn from your own Virginia, and from every other State in the Union, and from the History of every Nation civilized and savage, from all We know of the time of the Creation of the World.

Quincy November 15.13

We are now explicitly agreed, in one important point, vizt. That "there is a natural Aristocracy among men; the grounds of which are Virtue and Talents."

You very justly indulge a little merriment upon this solemn subject of Aristocracy. I often laugh at it too, for there is nothing in this laughable world more ridiculous than the management of it by almost all the nations of the Earth. But while We smile, Mankind have reason to say to Us, as the froggs said to the Boys, What is Sport to you is Wounds and death to Us. When I consider the weakness, the folly, the Pride, the Vanity, the Selfishness, the Artifice, the low craft and meaning cunning, the want of Principle, the Avarice the unbounded Ambition, the unfeeling Cruelty of a majority of those (in all Nations) who are allowed an aristocratical influence; and on the other hand, the Stupidity with which the more numerous multitude, not only become their Dupes, but even love to be Taken in by their Tricks: I feel a stronger disposition to weep at their destiny, than to laugh at their Folly.

But tho' We have agreed in one point, in Words, it is not yet certain that We are perfectly agreed in Sense. Fashion has introduced an indeterminate Use of the Word "Talents." Education, Wealth, Strength, Beauty, Stature, Birth, Marriage, graceful Attitudes and Motions, Gait, Air, Complexion, Physiognomy, are Talents, as well as Genius and Science and learning. Any one of these Talents, that in fact commands or influences true Votes in Society, gives to the Man who possesses it, the Character of an Aristocrat, in my Sense of the Word.

Pick up, the first 100 men you meet, and make a Republick. Every Man will have an equal Vote. But when deliberations and discussions are opened it will be found that 25, by their Talents, Virtues being equal, will be able to carry 50 Votes. Every one of these 25, is an Aristocrat, in my Sense of the Word; whether he obtains his one Vote in Addition to his own, by his Birth Fortune, Figure, Eloquence, Science, learning, Craft Cunning, or even his Character for good fellowship and a bon vivant....

Your distinction between natural and artificial Aristocracy does not appear to me well founded. Birth and Wealth are conferred on some Men, as imperiously by

John Henri Isaac Browere came to Quincy in 1825 to make this life mask of the aged ex-President.

NEW YORK STATE HISTORICAL ASSOCIATION, COOPERSTOWN

Nature, as Genius, Strength or Beauty. The Heir is honours and Riches, and power has often no more merit in procuring these Advantages, than he has in obtaining an handsome face or an elegant figure. When Aristocracies, are established by human Laws and honour Wealth and Power are made hereditary by municipal Laws and political Institutions, then I acknowledge artificial Aristocracy can never last. The everlasting Envys, Jealousies, Rivalries and quarrells among them, their cruel rapacities upon the poor ignorant People their followers, compell these to sett up Caesar, a Demagogue to be a Monarch and Master, *pour mettre chacun a sa place* [to put each one in his place]. Here you have the origin of all artificial Aristocracy, which is the origin of all Monarchy. And both artificial Aristocracy, and Monarchy, and civil, military, political and hierarchical Despotism, have all grown out of the natural Aristocracy of "Virtues and Talents." We, to be sure, are far remote from this. Many hundred years must roll away before We shall be corrupted. Our pure, virtuous, public spirited federative Republick will last for ever, govern the Globe and introduce the perfection of Man, his perfectability being already proved by Price Priestly, Condorcet Rousseau Diderot and Godwin....

No Romance would be more amusing, than the History of your Virginian and our new England Aristocratical Families. Yet even in Rhode Island, where there has been no Clergy, no Church, and I had almost said, no State, and some People say no religion, there has been a constant respect for certain old Families. 57 or 58 years ago, in company with Col. Counsellor, Judge, John Chandler, whom I have quoted before, a Newspaper was brought in. The old Sage asked me to look for the News from Rhode Island and see how the Elections had gone there. I read the List of Wantons, Watsons, Greens, Whipples, Malbones etc. "I expected as much" said the aged Gentleman, "for I have always been of Opinion, that in the most popular Governments, the Elections will generally go in favour of the most ancient families." To this day when any of these Tribes and We may Add Ellerys, Channings Champlins etc are pleased to fall in with the popular current, they are sure to carry all before them.

You suppose a difference of Opinion between You

and me, on the Subject of Aristocracy. I can find none. I dislike and detest hereditary honours, Offices Emoluments established by Law. So do you. I am for ex[c]luding legal hereditary distinctions from the U. S. as long as possible. So are you. I only say that Mankind have not yet discovered any remedy against irresistable Corruption in Elections to Offices of great Power and Profit, but making them hereditary.

John Adams's house at this period seemed always to be full of members of the family, including children and grandchildren of every age. It was the indefatigable Abigail who kept this diverse company together, saw to their meals and clothes, presided at their parties, and nursed them when they were ill. In his memoirs Josiah Quincy, a neighbor with family connections, left a charming description of what family life was like in the Adams home while Abigail was still alive.

Figures of the Past, 1883

When I was about six years old, I was put to school to the Reverend Peter Whitney; and, spending the winter in his family, was often asked to dine on Sunday with Mr. and Mrs. Adams. This was at first somewhat of an ordeal for a boy; but the genuine kindness of the President, who had not the smallest chip of an iceberg in his composition, soon made me perfectly at ease in his society. With Mrs. Adams there was a shade more formality. A consciousness of age and dignity, which was often somewhat oppressive, was customary with old people of that day in the presence of the young. Something of this Mrs. Adams certainly had, though it wore off or came to be disregarded by me, for in the end I was strongly attached to her. She always dressed handsomely, and her rich silks and laces seemed appropriate to a lady of her dignified position in the town. If there was a little savor of patronage in the generous hospitality she exercised among her simple neighbors, it was never regarded as more than a natural emphasis of her undoubted claims to precedence. The aristocratic colonial families were still recognized, for the tide of democracy had not risen high enough to cover these distinctions. The parentage and descent of Mrs. Adams were undoubtedly of weight in establishing her position; although, as we now look at things, the strong personal claims of herself and husband would

WHITE HOUSE HISTORICAL ASSOCIATION

Silhouette of Abigail Adams, which today hangs in the White House

seem to have been all sufficient.

I well remember the modest dinners at the President's, to which I brought a schoolboy's appetite. The pudding, generally composed of boiled corn meal, always constituted the first course. This was the custom of the time,—it being thought desirable to take the edge off of one's hunger before reaching the joint. Indeed, it was considered wise to stimulate the young to fill themselves with pudding, by the assurance that the boy who managed to eat the most of it should be helped most abundantly to the meat, which was to follow. It need not be said that neither the winner nor his competitors found much room for meat at the close of their contest; and so the domestic economy of the arrangement was very apparent. Miss Smith, a niece of Mrs. Adams, was an inmate of the President's family and one of these ladies always carved. Mr. Adams made his contribution to the service of the table in the form of that good-humored, easy banter, which makes a dinner of herbs more digestible than is a stalled ox without it. At a later period of our acquaintance, I find preserved in my journals frequent though too meager reports of his conversation. But of the time of which I am writing there is not a word recoverable. I can distinctly picture to myself a certain iron spoon which the old gentleman once fished up from the depths of a pudding in which it had been unwittingly cooked; but of the pleasant things he said in those easy dinner talks no trace remains.

These portraits of Mr. and Mrs. John Quincy Adams were made the year before they returned from London.

Eliza Susan Quincy, another neighbor and relative, described in her diary a reception given at the Adams home when John Quincy Adams returned from London, where he had been minister to Great Britain, to become Secretary of State under President James Monroe.

5 September 1817

Evening went to a party given by Mrs. Adams on the arrival of Mr. and Mrs. J.Q.A. About sixty of the ladies and gentlemen of the Quincy society. The Greenleafs, Marstons, Millers, Apthorps &c. &c. Mrs. Adams usually was seated in the middle of the Sofa opposite the fireplace in the long drawing room—with the principal ladies, my mother generally beside her. The rest of the company in a formal circle. The young ladies near the door, the elder gentlemen at the farther end of the room.

These parties were pretty formal and stiff as there was a great want, if not a total absence of beaux....Mr. J. Q. Adams was at the farther end of the room, with Mr. Beale, the Messrs. Greenleaf &c., who all seemed to be rather in awe of him and he sat in silence, enjoying his own reflections. But I was so desirous to hear him converse, that I arose from my place among the young ladies, crossed the formidable circle, and drew a chair beside him, and began a conversation by asking some question about Russia. He seemed rather surprised and amused, looking good naturedly down upon me as if to say "So this young lady is coming to talk to me" (I was then a young lady of nineteen years). He answered my question and we were in full talk when my father arrived and took Mr. Adams from me. I then obtained a place next Mrs. J. Q. Adams, conversed with her about the countries and courts she had visited and obtained many new ideas.

In the spring of 1818, George Bancroft, then a young graduate of Harvard College, made a trip from Cambridge with a Harvard tutor, Andrews Norton, to see the ex-President at his home in Quincy, and he long afterwards described the visit. The last year of Abigail's life must have contained other similar moments of domestic felicity.

Century Illustrated Magazine, July, 1887

We arrived early in the afternoon. The venerable ex-President received us cordially in the parlor of his homestead at Quincy; and so did the wife of his youth, the accomplished woman now known to the world by the publication of two volumes of her own letters, and two more of letters which she received from her husband. Several younger persons, seemingly their grandchildren, came in and went out as occasion served, and it was plain that the aged man was thoroughly well ministered to by youthful attendants whose whole demeanor was marked by reverence and affection. A more respectable or a more lovely family group, of which the head is an octogenarian, can hardly be conceived of.

I was presented as one who before many days was to embark for purposes of study at a German university. With a frankness which did not at all clash with the welcome of my reception, the venerable man broke out in somewhat abrupt and very decisive words against

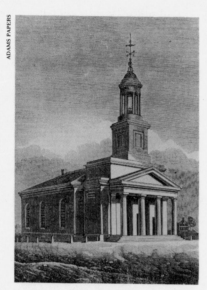

In 1822, Adams gave property to the Town of Quincy to build a church (above) and school (opposite). Adams Academy was closed in 1907, but income from the Adams Temple and School Fund still contributes to the education of local children.

educating young Americans in European schools, insisting, and from a certain point of view very correctly, that a home education is the best for an American.

Mr. Norton soon entered upon the errand on which he came, by leading conversation to the career and character of Franklin. The ex-President listened and answered; but not one single word unfavorable to Franklin fell from his lips. His visitor pushed his inquiries, striving to come nearer to details; but still Adams had not a word of evil to say of his former colleague. With no man in his life had he had so vexatious a rivalry. There at his side sat a scholar of varied culture, in the opening years of manhood, of great ability, a very skillful writer, of the highest repute for integrity of character and fidelity to his convictions, prepared to accept views unfavorable to the character and statesmanship of Franklin, and through the "North American Review" able to present them to the American public as final truth. But, to every renewed questioning, Adams in his answers steadfastly put the inquiries aside, and uttered not one word that in the least reflected on the public or private character of Franklin.

Presently the tea-table was spread in the middle of the room, and my friend and I sat down with the family. It was indeed a great privilege for one just out of college to sit at table with the venerated man under whose colossal courage and inspiring eloquence the men of the Congress of 1776, who had not the gift of speaking in public, confidently sheltered themselves. He did not look younger than the record of his birth indicated, but he was hale and vigorous; and as I sat near him I could not but notice that he carried his full cup of tea to his lips as safely as any one around him, without spilling a drop from tremor. The table was spread with the neatness and simplicity that prevailed at that day in New England homes. Could a foreigner have looked in an seen the second President of the United States at his sufficient but simple and unostentatious meal, the central figure in the group of his own family, it must have been confessed that his manner of life presented a perfect pattern for a republican chief magistrate in retirement....

The impression left upon my mind by the interview was, that while Adams at the time of active antagonism might be ready to treat an adversary roughly, there remained on his mind no enduring malice; and when those who seemed to him to have wronged him had passed away from the world, he had no ignoble desire to wreak revenge on their memory, but impartially left their controversies to the jurisdiction of history.

With more of his friends and relatives passing away every year, Adams's letters to Jefferson revealed his increasing interest in religion and the afterlife.

Quincy April 19 1817

Twenty times, in the course of my late Reading, have I been upon the point of breaking out, "This would be the best of all possible Worlds, if there were no Religion in it"!!! But in this exclamati[on] I should have been as fanatical as Bryant or Cleverly [the younger Adams's minister and tutor respectively]. Without Religion this World would be Something not fit to be mentioned in polite Company, I mean Hell. So far from believing in the total and universal depravity of human Nature; I believe there is no Individual totally depraved. The most abandoned Scoundrel that ever existed, never Yet Wholly extinguished his Conscience, and while Conscience remains there is some Religion. Popes, Jesuits and Sorbonists and Inquisitors have some Conscience and some Religion. So had Marius and Sylla, Caesar Cataline and Anthony, and Augustus had not much more, let Virgil and Horace say what they will.

What shall We think of Virgil and Horace, Sallust Quintillian, Pliny and even Tacitus? and even Cicero, Brutus and Seneca? Pompey I leave out of the question, as a mere politician and Soldier. Every One of these great Creatures has left indelible marks of Conscience and consequently of Religion, tho' every one of them has left abundant proofs of profligate violations of their Consciences by their little and great Passions and paltry Interests.

The vast prospect of Mankind, which these Books have passed in Review before me, from the most ancient records, histories, traditions and Fables that remain to Us, to the present day, has sickened my very Soul; and almost reconciled me to Swifts Travels among The Yahoo's. Yet I never can be a Misanthrope. *Homo Sum*

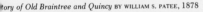

tory of Old Braintree and Quincy BY WILLIAM S. PATEE, 1878

403

[I am a man]. I must hate myself before I
Fellow Men: and that I cannot and will n
will not hate any of them, base, brutal and
some of them have been to me.

When Abigail Adams died in 1818, Eliza Susan Q
recorded the melancholy event in her journal.

Thursday, October 28, 1818.
Our excellent friend Mrs. Abigail Adams died today.
For several days we had given up all hope of her recovery
but this preparation did not render the event less affecting to us all. Her place can never be filled in society. Advanced as she was in life, that life was never more useful
and valuable to those around her than when she cheerfully resigned it. For many days she was unable to
converse with her friends. But the day before her death
she sent for Mr. Adams, and had a long conversation
with him, said she was resigned and willing to depart,
and entreated him to support their separation with firmness and evince his Faith,—by fortitude on her loss.

When our privileges are withdrawn we feel as if we
had not justly estimated their value, but I shall ever
remember with gratitude that of having enjoyed the
society and friendship of this excellent and remarkable
woman, and notwithstanding the difference in our ages,
I have in some degree appreciated the advantages to be
derived from her experienced conversation. Her place
is in History—she will never be forgotten.

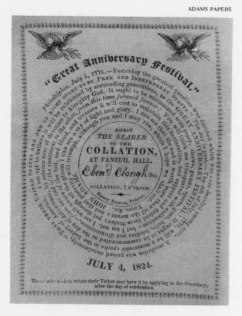

Ticket to a collation held on July 4, 1824, with quotation by John Adams

As soon as he heard the news of Abigail's death, Jefferson
sent Adams his condolences, writing that it was "of some comfort to us both
that the term is not very distant at which we are to deposit, in the same
cerement, our sorrows and suffering bodies, and to ascend in essence to an
ecstatic meeting with the friends we have loved and lost and whom we shall
still love and never lose again." Adams was greatly consoled.

Quincy Dec. 8. 18.
Your Letter of Nov. 13 gave me great delight not only
by the divine Consolation it Afforded me under my great
Affliction: but as it gave me full Proof of your restoration
to Health.

While you live, I seem to have a Bank at Montecello
on which I can draw for a Letter of Friendship and en-

404

tertainment when I please.

I know not how to prove physically that We shall meet and know each other in a future State; Nor does Revelation, as I can find give Us any possitive Assurance of such a felicity. My reasons for believing, it, as I do, most undoubtingly, are all moral and divine.

I believe in God and in his Wisdom and Benevolence: and I cannot conceive that such a Being could make such a Species as the human merely to live and die on this Earth. If I did not believe a future State I should believe in no God. This Un[i]verse; this all; this τὸπᾶν [totality]; would appear with all its swelling Pomp, a boyish Fire Work.

And if there be a future State Why should the Almighty dissolve forever all the tender Ties which Unite Us so delightfully in this World and forbid Us to see each other in the next?

Sick or Well the frien[d]ship is the same of your old Acquaintance.

JOHN ADAMS

Of the several likenesses that testify to John Adams's robust physique and sturdy appearance in old age, one of the finest is the last portrait of Adams done from life by Gilbert Stuart, which was designed to be completed in time for Adams's eighty-ninth birthday. Josiah Quincy explained in his memoirs some of the reasons for the success of the work.

Figures of the Past, 1883

COLLECTION OF MR. CHARLES FRANCIS ADAMS

Stuart's portrait of Adams at 89

During 1825 Gilbert Stuart, the famous artist, came to Quincy to paint the portrait of John Adams, then in his eighty-ninth year. And this portrait is a remarkable work; for a faithful representation of the extreme age of the subject would have been painful in inferior hands. But Stuart caught a glimpse of the living spirit shining through the feeble and decrepit body. He saw the old man at one of those happy moments when the intelligence lights up its wasted envelope, and what he saw he fixed upon his canvas. And the secret of the artist's success was revealed in a remark which Mr. Adams made to me, while the sittings were in progress. "Speaking generally," said he, "no penance is like having one's picture done. You must sit in a constrained and unnatural position, which is a trial to the temper. But I should like to sit to Stuart from the first of January to the last of December, for he lets

405

me do just what I please and keeps me co..........
by his conversation." The method of Stuart is given in
these few words. It was his habit to throw his subject off
his guard, and then, by his wonderful powers of conversation, he would call up different emotions in the face he
was studying. He chose the best or that which he thought
most characteristic, and with the skill of genius used it
to animate the picture.

When John Quincy Adams was elected President of
the United States on February 9, 1825, his father sent him this letter.

*Presidential race cartoon of 1824
campaign, with John Adams holding
his hat over son John Quincy Adams*

Quincy, 18 February, 1825.

My Dear Son,

Never did I feel so much solemnity as upon this occasion.
The multitude of my thoughts, and the intensity of my
feelings are too much for a mind like mine, in its nine-
tieth year. May the blessing of God Almighty continue
to protect you to the end of your life, as it has heretofore
protected you in so remarkable a manner from your
cradle! I offer the same prayer for your lady and your
family, and am your affectionate father.

JOHN ADAMS.

Dr. Benjamin Waterhouse sent the President the following account of his father's health that summer.

4 July 1825

Physicians do not always consider how much the powers
of the mind, and what is called good spirits can recover
the lost energies of the body. I really believe that your
Father's revival is mainly owing to the demonstration
that his Son had not served an ungrateful public. He can
raise himself up from a supine posture, in bed, relate
anecdotes, and laugh heartily, and what is more, eats
heartily, more than any other at table. We staid until he
smoked out his cigar after dinner.

As the end of life drew near, John Adams described his
innermost feelings to Thomas Jefferson.

Quincy December 1st. 1825

You say that you would like to go over life again. In this
I could not agree; I had rather go forward and meet what-

Broadside on the deaths of John Adams and Thomas Jefferson

ever is to come. I have met in this life with great trials. I have had a Father, and lost him. I have had a Mother and lost her. I have had a Wife and lost her. I have had Children and lost them. I have had honorable and worthy Friends and lost them—and instead of suffering these griefs again, I had rather go forward and meet my destiny.

Quincy 14th. January 1826

I am certainly very near the end of my life. I am far from trifling with the idea of Death which is a great and solemn event. But I contemplate it without terror or dismay, "*aut transit, aut finit* [either it is a transformation, or it is the end]," if *finit*, which I cannot believe, and do not believe, there is then an end of all but I shall never know it, and why should I dread it, which I do not; if *transit* I shall ever be under the same constitution and administration of Government in the Universe, and I am not afraid to trust and confide in it.

At the end of June, 1826, one of the leading men of Quincy called on John Adams and recorded the following account in his diary.

[June 30, 1826]

Spent a few minutes with him in conversation, and took from him a toast, to be presented on the Fourth of July as coming from him. I should have liked a longer one; but as it is, this will be acceptable. "I will give you," said he, "INDEPENDENCE FOREVER!"

He was asked if he would not add any thing to it, and he replied, "not a word."

On the afternoon of the Fourth of July, 1826, the fiftieth anniversary of the Declaration of Independence, John Adams, then in his ninety-first year, uttered his last words: "Thomas Jefferson survives." He was mistaken, as Jefferson had died a few hours earlier in his home at Monticello. About sunset that same day, Adams died peacefully in his home in Quincy. He lies buried today beside his wife in a crypt lined with Quincy granite beneath the portico of the "Stone Temple," or First Parish Church of Quincy, which his generosity helped to build. His son, John Quincy Adams, had the following words inscribed on a marble tablet placed next to his tomb.

On the Fourth of July, 1826,
He was summoned
To the Independence of Immortality
And to the JUDGMENT OF HIS GOD.

Selected Bibliography

Adams, John. *Diary and Autobiography.* Edited by L. H. Butterfield *et al.* (4 vols.) Cambridge, Mass.: The Belknap Press of Harvard University Press, 1961.

————. *The Earliest Diary of John Adams: June 1753–April 1754, September 1758–January 1759.* Edited by L. H. Butterfield *et al.* Cambridge, Mass.: The Belknap Press of Harvard University Press, 1966.

————. *Legal Papers of John Adams.* Edited by L. Kinvin Wroth and Hiller B. Zobel. Cambridge, Mass.: The Belknap Press of Harvard University Press, 1965.

————. *Letters of John Adams, Addressed to His Wife.* Edited by Charles Francis Adams. (2 vols.) Boston: Little, Brown and Co., 1841.

————. *The Works of John Adams, Second President of the United States.* Edited by Charles Francis Adams. (10 vols.) Boston: Little, Brown and Co., 1850–1856.

Allison, John M. *Adams and Jefferson: The Story of a Friendship.* Norman, Okla.: University of Oklahoma Press, 1966.

Bowen, Catherine Drinker. *John Adams and the American Revolution.* Boston: Little, Brown and Co., 1950.

Burnett, Edmund C. *The Continental Congress.* New York: Macmillan, 1941.

Butterfield, L. H. *et al.,* eds. *Adams Family Correspondence.* (4 vols to date.) Cambridge, Mass.: The Belknap Press of Harvard University Press, 1963–1973.

————, ed. *John Adams and the Beginnings of Netherlands-American Friendship, 1780–1783.* Boston: G. K. Hall, 1959.

Cappon, Lester J., ed. *The Adams-Jefferson Letters: The Complete Correspondence between Thomas Jefferson and Abigail and John Adams.* Chapel Hill: University of North Carolina Press, for the Institute of Early American History and Culture, 1959.

Chinard, Gilbert. *Honest John Adams.* Boston: Little, Brown and Co., 1933.

Dauer, Manning J. *The Adams Federalists.* Baltimore: Johns Hopkins Press, 1953.

Haraszti, Zoltán. *John Adams and the Prophets of Progress.* Cambridge, Mass.: Harvard University Press, 1952.

Hawke, David. *A Transaction of Free Men: The Birth and Course of the Declaration of Independence.* New York: Charles Scribner's Sons, 1964.

Howe, John R. *The Changing Political Thought of John Adams.* Princeton: Princeton University Press, 1966.

Kurtz, Stephen G. *The Presidency of John Adams: The Collapse of Federalism, 1795–1800.* Philadelphia: University of Pennsylvania Press, 1957.

Morris, Richard B. *The Peacemakers: The Great Powers and American Independence.* New York: Harper & Row, 1965.

Oliver, Andrew. *Portraits of John and Abigail Adams.* Cambridge, Mass.: The Belknap Press of Harvard University Press, 1967.

Smith, Page. *John Adams.* (2 vols.) Garden City: Doubleday, 1962.

Zobel, Hiller B. *The Boston Massacre.* New York: W. W. Norton, 1970.

Acknowledgments

The Editors are particularly grateful to the Massachusetts Historical Society in Boston for permission to print documents from the Adams Papers, the largest and most important collection of documents relating to John Adams and his family. Unless otherwise specifically credited below, all documents reproduced in this volume are from that collection, either directly or from The Belknap Press edition in course of publication as heretofore acknowledged. In addition, the Editors make grateful acknowledgment for the use of documents from the following institutions and published works:

Bancroft, George. Letter taken from *The Adamses at Home*. Portland, Maine: The Colonial Society of Massachusetts, Anthoensen Press, 1970. Pages 401 (bottom)–403 (top)

Butterfield, L. H., ed. *The Letters of Benjamin Rush, Vol I*. Philadelphia: The American Philosophical Society, 1951. Page 202 (center)

Cappon, Lester J., ed. *The Adams-Jefferson Letters* (2 vols.) Chapel Hill, N.C.: University of North Carolina Press, 1959. Pages 325–327 (top), 336 (bottom)–337, 363, 396–399 (top), 403–404 (top), 404 (bottom)–405 (top), 406 (bottom)–407 (top)

Ford, Worthington C., ed. *Statesman and Friend: Correspondence of John Adams with Benjamin Waterhouse*. Boston: Little, Brown, & Co., 1927. Page 387 (bottom)

————. *Warren-Adams Letters* (2 vols.) Boston: *Collection of the Massachusetts Historical Society*. Vols. 72–73 (1917–25). Pages 172 (bottom)–173 (top), 175 (center)

Howe, Mark A. DeW., ed., *The Articulate Sisters: Passages from Journals and Letters of the Daughters of President Josiah Quincy of Harvard University*. Cambridge, Mass.: Harvard University Press, 1946. Page 404 (center)

Library of Congress, *McHenry Papers*. Letter of James McHenry to John Adams Pages 364–365

Mitchell, Stewart, ed. *New Letters of Abigail Adams 1788–1801*. Boston: Houghton Mifflin Company, 1947. Pages 338–341 (center), 341 (bottom)–342 (center), 342 (bottom)–344 (top), 360–362 (top), 369–371 (center), 371 (bottom)–372

Quincy, Josiah. *Figures of the Past*. Boston: Little, Brown, and Co., 1926. Pages 61 (center), 399 (center)–400, 405 (bottom)–406 (top)

Schutz, John A., and Adair, Douglass. *The Spur of Fame: Dialogues of John Adams and Benjamin Rush, 1805–1813*. San Marino, Calif.: The Huntington Library, 1966. Pages 391 (bottom)–392 (top), 392 (bottom)–394 (top), 394 (center)–395

Vermont Historical Society. Diary of John Adams. Pages 26 (center)–28 (top), 28 (bottom)–29 (top). Published as *The Earliest Diary of John Adams*. Edited by L.H. Butterfield. Cambridge, Mass.: The Belknap Press of Harvard University Press, 1966.

The Editors also wish to express their appreciation to the many institutions and individuals who made available their pictorial materials for use in this volume. In particular the Editors are grateful to:

The Adams Papers, Boston—L. H. Butterfield, Editor in Chief; Marc Friedlaender, Editor; Kate Heath

Adams National Historic Site, Quincy, Massachusetts—Wilhelmina S. Harris

Massachusetts Historical Society, Boston—Stephen T. Riley, Director; Malcolm Freiberg; Winifred Collins

Beinecke Rare Book and Manuscript Library, Yale University, New Haven

Bibliothèque Nationale, Paris

Boston Athenaeum

Boston Public Library

Bostonian Society

British Museum, London

Connecticut Historical Society, Hartford

Harvard University Portrait Collection, Cambridge

Her Majesty Queen Juliana of the Netherlands

Independence National Historical Park Collection, Philadelphia

Lewis Walpole Library, Farmington, Connecticut

Library of Congress, Washington, D.C.

Museum of Fine Arts, Boston

New-York Historical Society

New York Public Library

Yale University Art Gallery, New Haven

Mr. Charles Francis Adams

Mr. and Mrs. George C. Homans

Mrs. Robert Homans

Finally, the Editors would like to thank Catherine Fennelly in Old Sturbridge Village; Andrew Oliver, William Osgood, Walter Muir Whitehill, George M. Cushing in Boston; and Peter Engel in the Netherlands for advice and assistance in obtaining pictorial material; Janet H. Meacham for copyediting and proofreading; and Mary-Jo Kline for compiling the chronology and bibliography.

Index

Rector of the Parish of

Chaplain to the Brig[ade]

If you present this

you, to procure the

you will find it fa[r]

the Statesman, the

torian and the Ph[ilosopher]

Something of the P[oet]

I am with much

Mr J. Q. Adams